Culture and Policy in Northern Ireland

To John Blacking (1928–90)
who believed that anthropology
is the "reformer's science",
in Ireland as elsewhere.

Culture and Policy in Northern Ireland
Anthropology in the public arena

Edited by

Hastings Donnan and Graham McFarlane

The Institute of Irish Studies
The Queen's University of Belfast

First published 1997
The Institute of Irish Studies
The Queen's University of Belfast
Belfast

This book has received support from the Cultural Traditions Programme
of the Community Relations Council, which aims to encourage acceptance and
understanding of cultural diversity.

British Library Cataloguing-in-Publication Data. A catalogue
record for this book is available from the British Library.

Cover image: *Red on Green*, etching in an edition of fifteen, 1975
by Mary Farl Powers (1948–1992) reproduced by kind permission of
the estate of the artist.

ISBN 0 8539 690 9

Cover design and typesetting by W. & G. Baird Ltd
Typeset in 10/12 Times Roman

Printed by W. & G. Baird Ltd, Antrim, Northern Ireland

Acknowledgements

Grateful acknowledgement for financial assistance is made to the Cultural Traditions programme of the Community Relations Council which aims to encourage acceptance and understanding of cultural diversity. We are grateful to J. F. Powers and Jane Powers for giving permission to reproduce the work of the late Mary Farl Powers and to the Ormeau Baths Gallery for allowing access to and the use of their illustrations archive. We also thank Michael Donnelly of University College Galway for his careful and efficient preparation of the index, as well as Elizabeth Tonkin and our colleagues in the Department of Social Anthropology at The Queen's University of Belfast for supporting a number of workshops on the themes addressed in this volume. Finally, a big thank-you to Graham Gingles for his brains, and to Margaret McNulty for her thorough professionalism.

Contents

Contributors

Dominic Bryan is a research officer at the Centre for the Study of Conflict at the University of Ulster at Coleraine and is currently carrying out research into disputed parades in Northern Ireland. He has published a number of articles on parades in Northern Ireland and has recently completed a doctoral thesis on Orange parades and anthropological theories of ritual.

Rosanne Cecil studied at the universities of London, Edinburgh and Ulster. She has worked at The Queen's University of Belfast since 1988, researching into informal care, sectarianism and various aspects of women's reproductive health. Her publications include *Informal welfare: a sociological study of care in Northern Ireland* (with John Offer and Fred St Leger) and *The anthropology of pregnancy loss: comparative studies in miscarriage, stillbirth and neonatal death.* She has also published many journal articles and chapters in books.

Andrew Dawson lectures in social anthropology at the University of Hull. He has carried out fieldwork in England and Ireland and is currently working on Eastern European issues. His research focuses on questions of cultural identity, particularly in relation to ageing, migration and the economy, and he has published extensively in these and related fields, including books with Routledge and Berg (forthcoming). While at The Queen's University of Belfast between 1990-93, he completed research on economic decision-making in farm households in Northern Ireland, the Republic of Ireland and Greece. For this research he was made European Society of Rural Sociology Young Scientist 1995.

Hastings Donnan is Professor of Social Anthropology at The Queen's University of Belfast. He is the author of *Marriage among Muslims* and co-editor of a number of books including, most recently, *Irish urban cultures, Islam, globalization and postmodernity* and *Family and gender in Pakistan*. He was the editor of *Man: the Journal of the Royal Anthropological Institute* from 1993–95.

Kate Ingram obtained a BA in Philosophy with English and American Literature from the University of Kent at Canterbury and a Diploma of Education from the University of Edinburgh. She has an MSSc in Irish Studies from The Queen's University of Belfast and has worked on a variety of research projects. She is currently the administrator of an arts project with disabled people and her most recent research focuses on community involvement in the arts.

Colin Irwin completed his interdisciplinary doctoral degree in social science in 1985 at Syracuse University, on the topic of human conflict. He has worked for native organisations in Canada, and produced the critical report *Lords of the Arctic: wards of the state* (1989) for the Canadian Ministry of Health and Welfare. He has completed studies in Israel and Northern Ireland, and is presently a Research Fellow in the Institute of Irish Studies at The Queen's University of Belfast. His current research is funded by the Joseph Rowntree Charitable Trust and focuses on peace-building and public policy in Northern Ireland. Through the use of public opinion polls and articles in the popular press, this project aims to establish a middle ground on the social, cultural and political issues which continue to frustrate accommodation in this deeply divided society.

Neil Jarman is carrying out research into disputed parades in Northern Ireland. He is the author of *Material conflicts* and *Displaying faith*. He is a research officer at the Centre for the Study of Conflict at the University of Ulster at Coleraine.

Gordon McCoy holds a doctorate from the Department of Social Anthropology at The Queen's University of Belfast. His doctoral research was on Protestant students of Irish, and he is interested in cultural politics in Ireland, the anthropology of language, minority language issues, and ethnic revivals.

Graham McFarlane is Senior Lecturer in Social Anthropology at The Queen's University of Belfast. He has been working on issues of identity in Northern Ireland, and is currently extending this research on identity in Greece as a consequence of his involvement as co-ordinator of a project on Greek and Irish farming households. He is co-editing a collection of essays entitled *Dimensions of difference: an introduction to Northern Irish studies*.

Eithne McLaughlin is Professor of Social Policy at The Queen's University of Belfast. She was previously a Reader and Lecturer in Social Policy at Queen's and a Research Fellow at the University of York. She has published across a range of areas including labour supply, unemployment and social security, equal opportunities policies, and family and community care policies: for example, *Policy aspects of employment equality in Northern Ireland* (1996, ed. with P. Quirk), *Paying for care—lessons from Europe* (1993, with C. Glendinning), *Understanding unemployment* (1992), *Women, employment and social policy in Northern Ireland* (1991, ed. with C. Davies), and *Social security and community care* (1991).

Iain Macaulay was a Research Assistant on the Changing Farm Economies and the Competitive Agriculture in Marginal Regions of Europe projects between 1991 and 1995, as well as a local activist for rural development in County Fermanagh, Northern Ireland. He has an MA in Social Anthropology from the University of Edinburgh.

Kay Milton is Reader in Social Anthropology at The Queen's University of Belfast. Her main research interest is in environmental issues, particularly the culture of environmentalist ideologies. Her publications in this field include *Environmentalism and cultural theory* (Routledge 1996), and two edited volumes: *Environmentalism: the view from anthropology* (Routledge 1993) and, with S. Baker and S. Yearley, *Protecting the periphery* (Frank Cass 1994).

Jude Stephens works at The Rural College in Draperstown where she co-ordinates the College's input to the MSc/Postgraduate Diploma in Rural Development with the Centre for Rural Studies at Queen's University. She is currently working on a European Union programme to promote the take-up of renewable energy opportunities in rural Northern Ireland, and she is actively involved in a number of environmental and alternative energy projects. She holds a PhD in social anthropology from The Queen's University of Belfast.

1   Cultural perspectives on public policy in Northern Ireland

Hastings Donnan and Graham McFarlane

This book is about the role which culture plays in mediating the impact of, and responses to, public policy in Northern Ireland. It presents the results of work recently carried out by anthropologists in the policy domain in areas which range from Green politics to integrated education, and from Irish language to unemployment. In all of these areas culture is shown to have a critical influence on the effectiveness and acceptability of public policy initiatives, which are inevitably shaped by and moulded to a variety of local circumstances and particularistic local understandings. A major goal of the book is thus to make available the substantive results of a perspective on policy issues which privileges culture as a focus.

But more than this, the book is also concerned to reflect upon the form which a cultural perspective on policy might take, or at least, upon the form which it has taken in the particular context of Northern Ireland. Culture has long been a central concept in anthropology and more recently has begun to inform approaches in the other social sciences. Despite its long pedigree, it is not easy to provide a definition of culture upon which all anthropologists would agree. Nevertheless, it is possible to identify a critical difference between anthropological usage of the term and the way in which it is employed by other social scientists.

> For many social scientists, culture has been seen as something on the periphery of the field as, for example, we find in conceptualizations which wish to restrict it to the study of the arts. Even when this view became extended to incorporate the study of popular culture and everday [sic] life, culture was still regarded by many as esoteric and epiphenomenal . . . Culture was . . . regarded as readily circumscribed, something derivative which was there to be explained (Featherstone 1992: vii).

Such a view could not be further from anthropological conceptions of culture, for in anthropology—at least in its contemporary form—culture is not just one variable which must be incorporated into the analysis alongside other variables such as the economic and political, but is regarded as the central factor through which all else is mediated and articulated. In this view culture is therefore not a residual category when everything else is sifted out, something left behind when more obviously 'economic', 'ecological' and 'political' factors have been dealt with, but a key element which inflects the entire social field.

While the concept of culture is central to its practice, contemporary anthropology is generally considered to have a number of defining characteristics: it is globally comparative, concerned with worlds of meaning as they are constructed by people; it is fundamentally humanistic and reflexive in its attempt to deconstruct or analyse these worlds of meaning and the social action connected to them; and it is perpetually rethinking how it uses its concepts, especially its central concepts like society and culture. Anthropology is not, as some suppose, simply definable by its research 'methodologies' and research 'techniques', since despite the mystique still attached to ethnographic 'fieldwork' in some quarters, everyone within the discipline is aware that fieldwork is a gloss for a promiscuous blend of all sorts of quantitative and qualitative research styles, none of which is the exclusive property of anthropology (different versions of 'ethnography' have become very popular in many social science disciplines). Nor is anthropology definable by a third world subject matter, since it is concerned with the thinkings and doings of all people everywhere.

Anthropologists engaged with the world of social policy in one way or another recognise this vision of anthropology just as much as do those securely ensconced in the academy. But there are important differences and even tensions between the two, which largely stem from the different set of operational imperatives under which each work, and from the fact that they have only partly overlapping sets of aims and objectives. For those in the academy, heavier doses of 'direct policy relevance' and 'engagement with real issues', ideally worked out in conjunction with other disciplines, have since the 1980s been increasingly presented as elements in the prescription for lifting anthropology out of its supposed states of theoretical malaise and ongoing crisis (e.g. Firth 1992; Rappaport 1993). Some of those in the academy have thus turned their attention to the analysis of the world views, practices and ideologies of policy makers and other policy professionals, as an adjunct to the many studies of the localised effects of their policy initiatives (see Herzfeld 1992). Out of this will hopefully come an anthropology of public policy which will involve comparative studies of the social practices of policy formulation, delivery, and evaluation, together with studies of the ideological groundings of these processes; in short, an anthropology of policy which is willing to engage with other disciplines, but which is certain of its disciplinary core and unwilling to compromise its central questions and ways of answering them.

For those in the policy field, on the other hand, whose practice is in large measure determined by externally imposed deadlines, demands for deliverables in the form of policy recommendations, and by a pre-formulated research agenda, the quest for global comparison and refinement of theoretical concepts can seem at best a luxury and at worst an irrelevance, however much they might appreciate the apparent support for their work from colleagues in academic positions. As a result, those engaged with the policy arena can feel that their practice falls short of the ideal of providing the kind of anthropology of public policy envisaged by the academy. In other words, studies in the policy field can appear as somehow compromised or truncated versions of the anthropological vision, in so far as a commonsense view of culture replaces the theoretical sophistication which this concept has acquired in anthropology more generally, and in so far as global comparisons are eschewed in favour of more parochial accounts. This has sometimes seemed to be the case with anthropological research on public policy in Northern Ireland. Although many aspects of life in Northern Ireland seem conducive to the development of the anthropology of public policy, although the track record of anthropologists involved in policy fields there is impressive, especially in the field of policy evaluation, and although everyone involved in this research can express the vision of anthropology we have described, ethnographic research on policy issues has sometimes diverged from the ideal in ways we outline below.

First, however, we should stress here that by drawing attention to these differences we do not mean to suggest that one or other of these versions of anthropology is somehow better anthropology (though there are undoubtedly some who would make such a claim): both are equally valid forms of anthropological practice in the contexts in which they occur, and which operate to some extent under different circumstances and constraining or facilitating influences. Rather, we draw attention to their difference in an effort to understand the ways in which anthropology is fashioned through its encounters with those outside its own disciplinary field; in this sense, our interest could be said to touch upon the sociology of knowledge. Moreover, and more importantly in the present case, we do so in the belief that these two styles in the anthropology of engagement can meet in mutually enriching dialogue. Sometimes it seems to us, and to the contributors to this collection, that anthropology is only now beginning to realise and identify its full potential in this regard. We begin by sketching the context within which policy research in Northern Ireland has developed and is carried out.

The context for policy research in Northern Ireland

Northern Ireland has what some have considered to be a unique set of social, economic and demographic problems relative to the rest of the United Kingdom. The most widely reported and most visible of these problems has been the sectarian violence and widespread political unrest which has characterised the region since 1969. Certainly it has been violent conflict which has preoccupied many of the local and international scholars researching in Northern Ireland, who have used the region as a testing ground for general theories on, for instance, nationalism, ethnicity, identity, and conflict. Assessing the mass of research carried out during this period, and while praising its generally high standard, Whyte (1990) lamented its comparative lack of practical impact in finding 'solutions' to the problem, pointing out that nothing much seemed to have changed as a result of all the effort.

In retrospect, it could be argued that part of the problem in identifying policy relevance in this work was the existence of a scholarly culture in which there seemed to be an ideological separation between, on the one hand, research on the politics of division and debates about its various causes and consequences, and, on the other hand, social research dealing more directly with the kinds of policy issues affecting nation-states throughout the industrialised world, research in which the local sectarian/ethnic division was treated as a backdrop. For a long time these two research trajectories were maintained as more or less distinct, something which State research funding in the 1980s tended to encourage by allocating grants for research projects not focused solely on the analysis of division (see Jenkins 1989). Of course, all researchers knew that all policy-related arenas and issues in Northern Ireland were affected to different degrees by the local 'Troubles', but they also knew how to play the game of obtaining grants by being less explicit about this fact. However, there was a kind of sea change in the rhetoric in the late 1980s, when researchers in Northern Ireland began to be more explicit about the inadequacy of compartmentalising sectarianism from other areas of social life, rejecting in their rhetoric the artificial division between conflict research and research into other aspects of local society and culture. As one writer argued, the province's distinctiveness within the United Kingdom lay not 'simply in the Troubles, nor in the nature of communal division, but in the way [these] interact with "normal" social issues' (O'Dowd 1989: 15). This view has permitted a more realistic purchase on policy issues, since it demands productive comparison of similarities and differences between the policy fields of Northern Ireland and those relating to the rest of western Europe and beyond.

Anthropologists have been involved in all these debates, as one kind of voice among many. One distinguishing feature of anthropology in Northern Ireland, compared for instance to anthropology elsewhere in the United Kingdom, has been its central concern with the anthropology of the region in which its institutional base is located. Ever since a Department of Social Anthropology was established at Queen's University Belfast in 1971, under the leadership of Professor John Blacking, a growing body of local and locally-trained anthropologists has directed its attention to issues and questions of concern to the society in which it lives and works, and not only to the study of those overseas communities with which anthropology is sometimes more commonly associated. This twin track of local and foreign study arguably gives to anthropological research in Northern Ireland its particular shape and form, and potentially distinguishes its insights from those of other types of social research in the region.

There have been numerous overviews of the strengths and weaknesses of anthropological research in Ireland, north and south (see, for instance, Curtin, Donnan and Wilson 1993; Donnan and McFarlane 1983; 1986; Wilson 1994). As we suggested in a volume dealing explicitly with policy-related research (Donnan and McFarlane 1989), anthropologists researching in Northern Ireland have been drawn to research in the policy field by many of the same factors which have influenced the entry of anthropologists to this field elsewhere: partly out of a sense of personal commitment and a genuine desire to contribute to debates of practical concern and, more cynically, partly because this has often been where jobs could be had, especially for those recently graduated in the discipline. But a number of more specific local factors which encourage participation in policy research also operate in Northern Ireland, and these factors affect social anthropologists as well as other social researchers.

The small scale and dense networks of Northern Irish intellectual and political life seemed to hold out reasonable hope that the academic voice would be heard in the corridors of power. At the level of rhetoric at least, those in the corridors of power have proclaimed themselves open to academic advice on social affairs, whether this advice is based on quantitative and supposedly representative surveys of attitudes and opinions, or on more qualitative research methodologies. Over the last decade, social scientific research has provided the intellectual rationale for various policy initiatives which have resulted in the setting up of a Central Community Relations Council and the Opsahl Commission (looking for paths to resolving the conflict), and has contributed to the introduction and refinement of Fair Employment and Equal Opportunities legislation (see, for instance, Crozier 1989; 1990; Cormack and Osborne 1983). The influence of the small-scale and density of the network of academic researchers and policy professionals is manifest in how discussions within this network are framed even in formal settings. Here academics and government officials engage with one another as people known 'in the round', rather than as representatives of 'the state' or 'academia'.

In other ways too, the social context for policy research in Northern Ireland differs from that in Britain. Stimulated by a limited regional focus, there has been an increasing degree of interdisciplinary collaboration in policy research in Northern Ireland. Just as social scientists working in the policy field often know personally those who may sponsor their research, so they also know, and meet regularly at conferences, seminars and in less formal settings, academics from other disciplines with similar research interests as themselves. In these settings, there does seem to be an openness to the viewpoints of social scientists and an awareness of at least the potential of anthropological research.

Anthropologists interested in researching in the policy arena in Northern Ireland have thus to some extent been able to operate in an environment in which their voice might be heard, both by academic colleagues and by those who have the power to employ them or commission research.

It was against this apparently positive and welcoming background that anthropologists in Northern Ireland began to engage with the policy arena. Although one early policy-related study by an anthropologist was carried out in the 1940s (Mogey 1947), much of this work began in the 1980s, as we discuss in the following section.

Anthropology and policy research in Northern Ireland

Although we focus only on a selection of examples in this section, it may be helpful first to sketch out the range and extent of anthropological involvement in the
policy field in Northern Ireland. These are summarised in Table 1, which indicates
the content and geographical spread of policy-related anthropological projects in
the region. Few of these projects have been initiated by the researchers themselves, and where researchers have not been approached directly to do such
research, their involvement has usually been in response to newspaper advertisements or invitations to tender.

Despite those features, mentioned above, which to some extent make the
practical aspects of policy involvement in Northern Ireland distinct, researchers
working there have been preoccupied with many of the same policy issues which
have concerned researchers throughout the United Kingdom. Since the 1980s,
Northern Ireland has witnessed the involvement of many social scientists, including anthropologists, in the evaluation of the various processes of delivery of recent
governmental policy initiatives. As Table 1 indicates, policy research in Northern
Ireland tends to have been dominated by projects which focus on aspects of economic restructuring, of unemployment, of gender and ethnic discrimination in the
workplace, of housing, and of education. These studies do take on a local flavour,
one inevitably and necessarily sensitive to—and often arising out of—the wider
sectarian division which pervades Northern Irish life. Thus one study (Irwin 1991)
evaluated the role of education in promoting social integration between Catholic
and Protestant, while a study of the impact of state capitalisation on the fishing
industry demonstrated how government grants for improving the quality of the
fishing fleet reinforced sectarian segregation and increased the chances of
Protestants acquiring modern vessels (Dilley 1989).

However, it is the complex *interplay* between local factors, such as sectarianism, and other factors such as unemployment or gender, which constitute the
foci of several other studies. In a series of publications, Howe (1989b; 1990; 1994)
has examined the experience of unemployment in two Belfast housing estates, one
Catholic the other Protestant, showing how the daily realities of being unemployed are shaped not so much by the cultural preconceptions of Catholics and
Protestants *per se* as by the structure of State economic development policy, and
its inevitably localised consequences for the sectarian geography of the north.
Stepping back even further from essentialist arguments about cultural differences
between Catholics and Protestants, Howe (1985; 1990) has also examined the
bureaucratic administration of welfare benefits and their delivery at the cultural
boundary between those responsible for enacting policy and their 'clients', documenting how in social security offices the widely held distinction between
'deserving' and 'undeserving' claimants is confirmed and reproduced in everyday
practice. This interface between client and policy professional, especially at those
points where there is correspondence or disjunction in cultural assumptions, has

been a central theme in Donnan's and McFarlane's work on counselling provision for the long-term unemployed in a socially heterogeneous area of Belfast (Donnan and McFarlane 1988; see also, this volume). Although their research does not identify any serious differences in the ideal models of what constitutes 'counselling' held by the professionals and their clients nor, indeed, any sharp disagreement between Catholics and Protestants, it does indicate that there are cultural barriers to the take-up, delivery and perceived relevance or usefulness of 'counselling' services, located in both organisational and client world views. The somewhat parochial view of Northern Ireland was again challenged in a report commissioned by the Northern Ireland Equal Opportunities Commission, which argued that it is a more global cultural construction of 'training', and associated cultural constructions of 'skill', which underlie and explain the relatively disadvantaged position of women in the Northern Ireland clothing industry. Arguing against the parochial 'victimology' practised by members of the two main ethnie in the north, the authors of this report stress that gender inequality at work may well be greater than inequalities based on ethnic or sectarian identity in Northern Ireland (McLaughlin and Ingram 1991; see also, Davies and McLaughlin 1991 and Ingram, this volume). The issue of ethnicity is mainly irrelevant in Milton's work on rural and urban planning policy (see Milton 1990; 1993a; 1993b; and this volume).

So, while much of the policy research carried out in Northern Ireland is inevitably sensitive to issues of sectarian or ethnic division, much of it also shows that it is not sufficient to treat Northern Ireland as unique, simply because it is divided along sectarian lines. Northern Ireland has been affected by the same problems as the rest of Europe, and social anthropologists have made a contribution to the understanding of the consequences of these problems.

However, if circumstances in Northern Ireland seem favourable for the production of effective policy research, we feel that anthropology has apparently not always fulfilled its potential. For amidst all the bustling research and interdisciplinary communication, anthropology has usually been the quiet voice, a voice which, while recognised by both policy makers and other social scientists as having something *potentially* important to contribute, is one that has somehow not quite been able to deliver the goods in a manner which is anthropological in the pure sense, in the eyes of some disciplinary colleagues at least.

The fate of anthropological policy-related research, and the reasons for it, are often particularly apparent where anthropologists work in multi-disciplinary teams. It is common in such collaborative endeavours, at least in the planning stages, to consider the difficulties and opportunities involved in trying to reach general conclusions from different disciplinary perspectives and with different research tools. One form which this can take when anthropologists are involved with other types of researcher such as economists is the expression of a desire to break out of what McLaughlin (1991) has called the 'oppositional poverty' of confronting quantitative with qualitative research methods, of defining the two sets of

Table 1:   **Policy-related research by anthropologists in Northern Ireland by topic, date and location**

	Armagh	Antrim	Down	Fermanagh	Derry	Tyrone	Province-wide
1940s							Rural economy (1)
1980							
1981							
1982					Travellers (2)	Travellers (2)	
1983		Unemployment (3)					
1984			Fishing (4)		Community care (5)		
1985					Unemployment (6)		
1986		Unemployment (7)					
1987		Housing (8)					
1988		Unemployment (9)					Environment (10)
1989							Clothing industry (11)
1990							
1991		Education (12)	Farming (13)	Farming (14)			Community relations evaluation (15)
1992							Tourism (16)
1993							
1994	Political parades (17)						Political parades (18)

Key to Table 1: Researchers and publications

Researcher (s)	*Publications*
(1) Mogey	Mogey 1947
(2) Butler	Butler 1985
(3) Howe	Howe 1985; 1988; 1989a; 1990
(4) Byron & Dilley	Dilley 1989; Byron & Dilley 1988a, 1988b
(5) Cecil et al.	Cecil et al 1985; 1987; Cecil 1989
(6) McLaughlin	McLaughlin 1989; Davies & McLaughlin 1991
(7) Blacking et al.	Blacking et al 1989
(8) Ogle	Ogle 1989
(9) Donnan & McFarlane	Donnan & McFarlane 1988
(10) McLaughlin & Ingram	McLaughlin and Ingram 1991
(11) Milton	Milton 1990; 1991; 1993a; 1993b
(12) Irwin	Irwin 1991
(13) Dawson et al.	Dawson (this volume)
(14) Dawson et al.	Macaulay (this volume)
(15) Hughes	Knox et al. 1992
(16) Wilson	Wilson 1993
(17) Bryan et al.	Bryan, Fraser and Dunn 1995
(18) Jarman and Bryan	Jarman and Bryan 1996

methods as if the two were irreconcilable, being inextricably anchored in two different social scientific worldviews (cf. Robertson 1987: 8). Linked to this may be
a receptivity to the potential of the anthropological blend of research techniques
and its hallmark of close involvement with people. This is probably not a surprising attitude where rural sociologists and political scientists are involved in a
research team, since when one looks across the academic boundaries towards
rural sociology and political science, it would seem that over the last decade or so
abstract empiricism has been displaced from the centre of those disciplines by
sophisticated theoretical and methodological projects focusing on the central
question of how to connect studies of creative agency with studies of large scale,
encompassing structuring processes. In trying to formulate answers to this question, more narrowly defined studies of people's activities, carried out in the context of their complex networks of relationships, have become *de rigeur* in both
rural sociology and political science. So too has an awareness of the mediating
significance of something called 'culture'. But the common ground which apparently exists to facilitate meaningful dialogue in such settings is all too often belied
by what becomes of the anthropological contribution as such projects progress to
the final report stage.

For instance, anthropologists who work in teams frequently report how their
fieldwork 'findings' are drawn upon to help explain correlations in survey data; at
other times the correlations seem to be interpreted in an apparently *ad hoc* fashion, or at least interpreted in relation to the commonsense, extra-project, knowledge held by the team members and by the policy makers to whom the research is
addressed. While initial generalisations and conclusions from fieldwork may provoke nods of agreement and recognition, they are just as likely to be challenged
as being odd, or somehow 'unrepresentative' in the light of survey findings, such
talk signalling a deep-seated adherence to a view in which one can grasp the world
through quantitative analysis of representative survey responses which, of course,
is an aspect of that hankering 'for a "real" positivist hold on a world of slippery
intangibles' (Wright 1994: 3). Demands on anthropological team members for
more information about an array of issues may reflect not so much a serious
acceptance of the theoretical assumption that everything is culturally mediated as
a less refined assumption that the qualitative approach adopted as one strand of the
research is simply a way to get at some complex or sensitive issues. In the process,
anthropology is constructed as a methodology or, even worse, as a kind of
research technique.

Such experiences will be familiar to any anthropologist who has had to negotiate their contribution as a project develops. So too will be the manner in which
anthropological insights and findings are frequently incorporated into a research
team's final report. The result is usually a final report which reflects a somewhat
truncated version of 'anthropology', a version which, while perhaps most acutely
evident in team research, is typical of much policy-related anthropological work
in Northern Ireland. When purveyed, usually by default, this truncated version of

anthropology is potentially detrimental both for the contribution which anthropology might make to policy debates, and for the standing of 'policy research' within the discipline more generally.

'Truncated' anthropology and project reports

We would argue that the final product of the research described above is but one instance of a more general trend in anthropological writing about policy concerns in Northern Ireland. Faced with sponsors and, in multidisciplinary teams, colleagues, who want to get what they think is usable knowledge, presented in a way which is readable and on time, anthropologists have adapted pragmatically by compromising theoretical concepts, epistemological principles and methodological rigours which they would otherwise take for granted in more academic arenas.

The environment in which anthropologists find themselves working is one where there is, perhaps inevitably, a skewed vision of what anthropology is 'about' among policy professionals and members of other disciplines. In this environment certain key words form part of a shared vocabulary, but the meanings attached to these words diverge radically between the different parties involved. As any anthropologist would expect, a term for which there are multiple meanings is 'culture'. For the policy professionals, and members of other disciplines, anthropologists are experts on 'culture', but for the non-anthropologists who use and think about the term, 'culture' still has the definitional attributes which anthropologists have been calling into question since at least the 1960s. For the non-anthropologists, 'culture' seems to be thought of as a relatively discrete collection of essential or fundamental beliefs, values, assumptions and behavioural traits, passed on like a tradition from generation to generation, in an only slowly changing form. This 'culture' is attached to, or belongs to, identifiable categories of people; and in Northern Ireland there are many possible sub-cultures based upon ethnicity, class or occupation, locality and gender, all nesting in complex ways within the larger weave of Northern Irish society and, for the less parochial, in networks of relationships beyond Northern Ireland.

All anthropologists working in Northern Ireland are obviously aware of the on-going debates about the concept 'culture' within the discipline, and the deconstructionist, anti-essentialist trend within these debates. Indeed, most anthropologists working in the policy field would question the version of culture expounded by the non-specialists with whom they are involved, in discussion with colleagues. Furthermore, the ethnography of the ethnic conflict in Northern Ireland, for all its shortcomings, has consistently argued that it is much too simplistic to understand the ethnic conflict simply in terms of a competition between discrete ethnic blocs, each holding discrete cultures or traditions (for one of the latest statements, see Buckley and Kenney 1995). Since serious anthropological interest in the ethnic conflict developed in the 1970s, terms like 'Catholic' and 'Protestant' have been used in analysis, but they are used as generalisations to be unpacked and decon-

structed in pursuit of complex particularity (see Bryan and Jarman, this volume).
Indeed, this deconstructionist thrust in anthropological work on the ethnic division has provided the basis for a thoroughgoing critique of the state-sponsored
Community Relations/Cultural Traditions initiatives, which see at least partial
solutions to the Northern Ireland 'problem' to lie in the establishment of greater
mutual understanding and contact between the two major ethnic blocs (Ruane and
Todd 1996: chapt. 7): this is very similar to the anthropological critique of 'multiculturalism' in the United States (see Segal and Handler 1995).

However, when anthropologists (often the same anthropologists) are working
in the policy field, much of this theoretical understanding has tended to get set
aside. The idea of culture can appear as little more than a gloss for the various spoken and unspoken attitudes and worldviews held by, for example, 'the unemployed', 'counsellors', and 'fishermen' about the policy issues and domains in
which they are involved, or even, more generally, as a gloss for some more undif-
ferentiated collectivity's attitudes and perceptions towards issues like being 'a
good neighbour'. The use of 'culture' in this way provides a kind of contextual
flavour to the discussion of more real 'structural' (usually economic or political)
processes. In short, culture becomes a residual category in the manner mentioned
earlier.

In relation to the policy environment in Northern Ireland, since the central
anthropological concept culture can end up being thought about, and indeed written about, by all parties involved with projects in much the same way (as local
flavour and as a gloss for people's attitudes and perceptions), it is hardly surprising that anthropology has come to be seen less as a discipline with its own distinctive theoretical concepts, concerns and questions, and more as a collection of
research techniques, essentially qualitative in nature. For some, both within and
outside anthropologists' networks, anthropology seems close to a kind of journalism (especially whenever residential fieldwork is not possible). We do not see any
real problems with this association between journalism and anthropology, especially when the association is made between anthropology and *good* journalism.
However, for others more concerned with the specific contribution which anthropology can make to the field of policy, this is very worrying. Anthropology, as they
like to think of it in seminars and elsewhere, seems to dissolve away on engagement with policy issues.

This is a tendency to be found throughout anthropological work in the field
of public policy, and it is certainly not unique to Northern Ireland. In general, the
tendency is driven by a kind of compromise and what one can read as a mutual
suspension of disbelief between anthropologists and policy professionals. Those
who sponsor or otherwise support anthropological research in policy fields know
as well as anthropologists that the world is a complex place, with no single issue
reducible to a set of key variables which can be manipulated to produce 'true'
accounts. But since these people see their jobs as entailing identifying just such
variables (in pursuit of approximate truths or a plausible account in the light of

their commonsense knowledge of what people are like), of necessity they must engage in a compromise: they must suspend their disbelief that the world can be understood in fairly simple positivistic ways. Anthropologists must suspend their disbelief too, if they want their reports to be read (and indeed to be employed again), and to signal their suspension of disbelief, they must produce research summaries which generalise a way through the 'slippery intangibles' and complexity. The non-theorised version of 'culture' which pervades project literature helps to provide summarisable and generalised accounts of the complex reality with which we all have to deal.

We emphasise that this is a general tendency, but there may be features in the Northern Irish scene which exaggerate the tendency there. The pressure to engage in this mutual suspension of disbelief in the Northern Ireland context may be increased, ironically, because of one of the very features of Northern Irish academic life which we have presented as being conducive to letting anthropology's more reflective and perhaps louder voice be heard. It is the very existence of a world of close personal relationships which pull together academics and policy professionals which may make it difficult (not least for career reasons) for anthropologists to question loudly the vision of the world which they have been involved in reproducing.

This volume is an attempt to find some way out of this impasse. The chapters are each the result of a long series of conversations, not least between those who are relatively secure in the academy and those who are not. The conversations started early in the 1990s at a workshop held at Queen's University, at which participants were encouraged to think about the specific contribution which anthropology might make to policy concerns in Northern Ireland, and to think about this issue beyond the limiting frameworks imposed by those who had in various ways commissioned their work. It became clear that the issue of 'culture' in all its theoretical complexity was to be the dominant focus of the discussions, a fact that is hardly surprising given the extent to which 'culture' had featured in the ways in which the participants had defined themselves as anthropologists. This is not to say that all participants agreed on how we should conceptualise 'culture', but at least they did agree that their identities as anthropologists were definable more by their focus of interest than by their research techniques. The contributors to this volume, each in their own way and in relation to a range of settings, thus try to recover a more theoretically sophisticated notion of culture in their analyses. These analyses address issues which have concerned anthropologists working in the policy arena for some time—unemployment and the labour market (Donnan and McFarlane, Ingram, McLaughlin), education (Irwin), and rural development and conservation (Dawson, Macaulay, Milton)—as well as open up new areas for policy research in Northern Ireland in relation to reproductive health (Cecil), language (McCoy), street politics (Bryan and Jarman) and alternative political movements (Stephens). In this regard, this volume represents a temporary entextualisation of these conversations.

Note

This introduction is a modified version of a chapter to appear in Cris Shore and Sue Wright (eds.), *The anthropology of policy* (London: Routledge).

References

Blacking, J., K. Byrne and K. Ingram 1989. Looking for work in Larne: a social anthropological study. In H. Donnan and G. McFarlane (eds.), *Social anthropology and public policy in Northern Ireland.* Aldershot: Avebury.

Buckley, A.D. and M.C. Kenney 1995. *Negotiating identity: rhetoric, metaphor and social drama in Northern Ireland.* Washington: Smithsonian Institution.

Butler, C. 1985. *Travelling people in Derry and Tyrone.* Londonderry: World Development Group.

Byron, R. and R. Dilley 1988a. *Ulster fishermen: a study in social organisation and fisheries policy.* Belfast: Policy Research Institute.

Byron, R. and R. Dilley 1988b. Social and micro-economic processes in the Northern Ireland fishing industry. In R. Jenkins (ed.), *Northern Ireland: studies in social and economic life.* Aldershot: Avebury in association with the Economic and Social Research Council.

Cecil, R., J. Offer and F. St. Leger 1985. *Informal welfare in a small town in Northern Ireland: a report to the Department of Health and Social Services, Northern Ireland.* Coleraine: University of Ulster.

Cecil, R., J. Offer and F. St. Leger 1987. *Informal welfare: a sociological study of care in Northern Ireland.* Aldershot: Gower.

Cecil, R. 1989. Care and the community in a Northern Irish town. In H. Donnan and G. McFarlane (eds.), *Social anthropology and public policy in Northern Ireland.* Aldershot: Avebury.

Cormack, R. J. and R. D. Osborne (eds.) 1983. *Religion, education and employment.* Belfast: Appletree Press.

Curtin, C., H. Donnan and T.M. Wilson (eds.) 1993. *Irish Urban Cultures.* Belfast: Institute of Irish Studies.

Crozier, M. (ed.) 1989. *Varieties of Irishness.* Belfast: Institute of Irish Studies.

Crozier, M. (ed.) 1990. *Varieties of Britishness.* Belfast: Institute of Irish Studies.

Davies, C. and E. McLaughlin (eds.) 1991. *Women, employment and social policy in Northern Ireland: a problem postponed?* Belfast: Policy Research Institute.

Dilley, R. 1989. Boat owners, patrons and state policy in the Northern Ireland fishing industry. In H. Donnan and G. McFarlane (eds.), *Social anthropology and public policy in Northern Ireland.* Aldershot: Avebury.

Donnan, H. and G. McFarlane 1983. Informal Social Organisation. In J. Darby (ed.), *Northern Ireland: The Background to the Conflict.* Belfast: Appletree Press and Syracuse University Press.

Donnan, H. and G. McFarlane 1986. 'You get on better with your own': Social continuity and change in rural Northern Ireland. In P. Clancy, S. Drudy, K. Lynch and L. O'Dowd (eds.), *Ireland: A Sociological Profile.* Dublin: Institute of Public Administration.

Donnan, H. and G. McFarlane 1988. *Counselling and the unemployed in Belfast.* Belfast: Policy Planning and Research Unit.

Donnan, H. and G. McFarlane (eds.) 1989. *Social anthropology and public policy in Northern Ireland.* Aldershot: Avebury.

Featherstone, M. 1992. Preface. Cultural theory and cultural change: an introduction. In M. Featherstone (ed.), *Cultural theory and cultural change.* London: Sage.

Firth, R. 1992. A future for anthropology? In S. Wallman (ed.), *Contemporary futures: perspectives from social anthropology.* London: Routledge.

Herzfeld, M. 1992. *The social production of indifference: exploring the symbolic roots of Western democracy.* Oxford: Berg.

Howe, L. 1985. The 'deserving' and the 'undeserving': practice in an urban, local social security office. *Journal of Social Policy* 14: 49–72.

Howe, L. 1988. Doing the double: wages, jobs and benefits in Belfast. In R. Jenkins (ed.), *Northern Ireland: studies in social and economic life.* Aldershot: Avebury in association with the Economic and Social Research Council.

Howe, L. 1989a. Social anthropology and public policy: aspects of unemployment and social security in Northern Ireland. In H. Donnan and G. McFarlane (eds.), *Social anthropology and public policy in Northern Ireland.* Aldershot: Avebury.

Howe, L. 1989b. Unemployment, doing the double and labour markets in Belfast. In C. Curtin and T. M. Wilson (eds.), *Ireland from below: social change and local communities.* Galway: Galway University Press.

Howe, L. 1990. *Being unemployed in Northern Ireland: an ethnographic study.* Cambridge: Cambridge University Press.

Howe, L. 1994. Ideology, domination and unemployment. *The Sociological Review,* 42 (2), 315 - 340.

Irwin, C. 1991. *Education and the development of social integration in divided societies.* Belfast: Policy Planning and Research Unit.

Jenkins, R. (ed.) 1989. *Northern Ireland: Studies in Social and Economic Life.* Aldershot: Avebury in association with the Economic and Social Research Council.

Knox, C., J. Hughes, D. Birrell and S. McCready 1992. *Evaluation of district council community relations programme: report to the liaison committee.* Coleraine. Centre for the Study of Conflict.

McLaughlin, E. 1989. In search of the female breadwinner: gender and unemployment in Derry city. In H. Donnan and G. McFarlane (eds.), *Social anthropology and public policy in Northern Ireland.* Aldershot: Avebury.

McLaughlin, E. 1991. Oppositional poverty: the quantitative/qualitative divide and other dichotomies. *The Sociological Review* 39, 292–308.

McLaughlin, E. and K. Ingram 1991. *All stitched up: sex segregation in the Northern Ireland clothing industry.* Belfast: Equal Opportunities Commission for Northern Ireland.

Milton, K. 1990. *Our countryside, our concern: the policy and practice of conservation in Northern Ireland.* Belfast: Northern Ireland Environment Link.

Milton, K. 1991. Interpreting environmental policy: a social scientific approach. In R. Churchill, L. Warren and J. Gibson (eds.), *Law, policy and the environment.* Oxford: Blackwell.

Milton, K. 1993a. Belfast: whose city? In C. Curtin, H. Donnan, and T. M. Wilson (eds.), *Irish urban cultures.* Belfast: Institute of Irish Studies.

Milton, K. 1993b. Land or landscape—rural planning policy and the symbolic construction of the countryside. In M. Murray and J. Greer (eds.), *Rural Development in Ireland: a challenge for the 1990s.* Aldershot: Avebury.

Mogey, J. M. 1947. *Rural life in Northern Ireland.* Oxford: Oxford University Press.

O'Dowd, L. 1989. Ignoring the communal divide: the implications for social research. In R. Jenkins (ed.), *Northern Ireland: studies in social and economic life.* Aldershot: Avebury in association with the Economic and Social Research Council.

Ogle, S. 1989. Housing estate improvements: an assessment of strategies for tenant partici- pation. In H. Donnan and G. McFarlane (eds.), *Social anthropology and public policy in Northern Ireland*. Aldershot: Avebury.

Rappaport, R. 1993. The anthropology of trouble. *American Anthropologist* 95: 295–303.

Robertson, A. F. 1987. The Dal Lake: reflections on an anthropological consultancy in Kashmir. *Anthropology Today* 3 (2), 7–13.

Ruane, J. and J. Todd 1996. *The dynamics of conflict in Northern Ireland: peace, conflict and emancipation*. Cambridge: Cambridge University Press.

Segal, D.A. and R. Handler 1995. U.S. multiculturalism and the concept of culture. *Identities* 1, 391–407.

Whyte, J. 1990. *Interpreting Northern Ireland*. Oxford: Oxford University Press.

Wilson, D. 1993. Tourism, public policy and the image of Northern Ireland since the troubles. In B. O'Connor and M. Cronin (eds.), *Tourism in Ireland: a critical analysis*. Cork: Cork University Press.

Wilson, T.M. 1994. A question of identity. In T. M. Wilson (ed.), *The unheard voice: social anthropology in Ireland*. Belfast: Fortnight (Supplement 324).

Wright, S. 1994. Culture in anthropology and organizational studies. In S. Wright (ed.), *Anthropology of organizations*. London: Routledge.

2   Modernity and postmodernity in the Northern Irish countryside

Kay Milton

The relationship between the 'macro' social processes on which sociologists have often focused, and the 'micro' processes that form the traditional objects of anthropological analysis, is often unclear. And yet if the sociological models are accurate representations of what is 'really' going on, they should be reflected in observable sequences of interaction; large-scale changes in the nature of society should be discernible in terms of who does what with whom. The study of public policy provides an appropriate opportunity for making this kind of connection. By its very nature, public policy is intended to have a widespread and general impact; if it works, it might contribute to the transformation of society. But this can be realised only through the compliance and co-operation of individuals and groups, so people's responses to public policy can tell us something about their role in wider social transformations.

In this chapter I examine the connections between a particular policy debate in Northern Ireland and what social theorists have identified as a major transformation in western society, the shift from modernity to post-modernity (Harvey 1989). The debate over access to the countryside in Northern Ireland, while it might not be among the region's most pressing issues, embodies some of the tensions identified by sociologists as central in the shift to postmodernity. In particular, it mobilises cultural oppositions between work and leisure, production and consumption; oppositions which, I suggest, are expressed in the conflicting models of the countryside as 'land' and 'landscape'. In an earlier paper (Milton 1993) I showed how these models interact in the debate over rural planning in Northern Ireland. My purpose here, by examining their role in the access debate, is to show how the general shift from a modern to a post-modern condition is shaped by local concerns and circumstances.

Modernity and postmodernity

> In some ways it is difficult to address the topic of postmodernism at all. It seems as
> though the signifier 'post-modern' is free-floating, having few connections with
> anything real, no minimal shared meaning of any sort. (Urry 1990: 83)

There is plenty of evidence, in the sociological literature, of the difficulty
referred to by Urry in the above quotation. There is no consensus among social
theorists about what is meant by 'the post-modern'. According to Harvey, the only
agreement on postmodernism is that 'it represents some kind of reaction to, or
departure from "modernism"', and yet, as he went on to point out, this tells us little, for the meaning of modernism itself is also confused (Harvey 1989: 7; cf.
Miller 1994: 59). The boundaries of the modern and the post-modern, as analytical categories, are elusive, and can appear to shift and bend at the whim of the ana-
lyst. Thus an account of modernity (e.g. Miller 1994) can focus on characteristics
such as consumption, which other analysts (e.g. Urry 1990) associate primarily
with postmodernity, and an account of post-modern traits may emphasise their
basis in modernity (Featherstone 1992). This means that if an account of modernity and postmodernity is to be both clear and analytically useful, it has to be
selective. The following brief outline draws mainly on the work of Urry (1990;
1995) and Lash (1990) and focuses on those aspects of the modern and the post-
modern which appear most relevant to the debate over access to the countryside.

Modernity is seen as a product of class-based capitalism. There are sharp distinctions between capital and labour, middle class and working class, and their
associated tastes and values. In modern terms, it is possible to talk about 'high'
and 'low' culture, about 'good' or 'real' art, music, literature, as distinct from
baser, more popular, and therefore more common, versions of these things.
Snobbery, inverted or otherwise, is a modern characteristic. People's social identities depend on their roles in production, but these roles and identities are not
fixed. Unlike the pre-modern, feudal distinctions, modern boundaries can be
crossed, social mobility is achievable. Modernity is therefore dominated by a
work ethic which assumes that rewards are earned, that the future will be, or can
be, better than the present, if sufficient effort is expended. Gratification is expected
and hoped for in the future, rather than being demanded of the present.

Postmodernity arises out of the breakdown of class-based capitalism. In particular, it is generated by the expansion of the middle classes, fed both from above
(as the former owners of capital have turned to paid employment) and from below
(as the working classes have acquired economic capital and the capacity to engage
in 'middle class' pursuits). It is also generated by the presence of large sectors of
the population—the unemployed and service sectors—not engaged in material
production. These sectors have contributed in different ways to the post-modern
condition. The service sector (education, medicine, the social and civil services),
and the expanding middle class to which this sector belongs, are not characterised
by the labour-capital dichotomy that pervaded the early development of manufac-

turing industry, and therefore neither create nor sustain the cultural distinctions that characterise modernity. The criteria that define 'high' and 'low' culture lose their meaning, as the social distinctions they protect dissolve. Instead of good and bad taste, there is simply taste, whose infinite variations are all equally valid.

At the same time, the growth in unemployment, and its impact at every level of industry (top and middle management as well as factory floor), makes the future uncertain. Work can no longer be relied upon to lead to reward; it might lead only to redundancy. This uncertainty, particularly when added to the other contemporary dangers of war, crime and environmental catastrophe, creates a cultural climate in which gratification cannot be deferred, for fear that it might never come. Thus work is expected to be fulfilling in itself, rather than being a means to later fulfilment (in the form of wealth and a comfortable retirement). Pleasure is sought in all experiences; aesthetic and emotional satisfaction is demanded from food as much as from art or music. Having fun becomes both a moral obligation (Bourdieu 1984: 367) and a basic right; consumption takes over from production as the basis of social identity. Zukin described the expression of this new identity in the 'post-modern urban landscape': '. . . the restoration and redevelopment of older locales, their abstraction from a logic of mercantile or industrial capitalism, and their renewal as up-to-date *consumption* spaces behind the red-brick or cast-iron façade of the past' (Zukin 1992: 222, emphasis added).

Generally speaking, the terms 'modern' and 'post-modern' are not used by analysts to refer to whole societies. The cultures of most contemporary capitalist states are seen as encompassing both modern and post-modern characteristics (and often pre-modern ones as well). Where modern forms of organisation (such as a class-based or hierarchical manufacturing sector) exist alongside post-modern forms (such as an expanding service sector), we can expect to find a corresponding degree of cultural complexity—a variety of perceptions, values and attitudes. The particular aspects of this diversity that are most relevant for the analysis that follows are the ways people perceive the countryside, and the relationship of those perceptions with attitudes to work and leisure.

Modernity, postmodernity and the countryside

The aesthetic appeal of the countryside has a long history in British culture, and was a feature of the pre-modern, as well as modern and post-modern conditions. In pre-modern times, it is assumed, the aristocracy and gentry were the principal consumers of this appeal, fashioning the grounds of their country houses to their own taste, treating even the trappings of subsistence agriculture (cows and sheep tastefully dotting a hillside) as objects to be gazed upon. Under modern conditions, the sharp dichotomy between the urban and the rural became a central distinction. The countryside came to be seen by the urban population as somewhere to escape to and its benefits defined in terms of health (fresh air and clean water as opposed to the smog-filled atmosphere and polluted rivers of the urban indus-trial environment), as well as beauty. The countryside as an object of enjoyment remained, for the most part, the preserve of the wealthy and middle classes, while some coastal resorts, particularly with the advent of the holiday camp, catered for the masses (see Urry 1990: 16ff.). What is different about the post-modern coun-tryside is that, in the absence of distinctions in taste, its aesthetic appeal is expected to be universal. It is seen as a communal resource which everyone has the 'right' to enjoy. And in view of the post-modern expectations of pleasure from all experiences, it is no longer sufficient for merely the mountains and moorlands to look beautiful; all views must please the eye.

What constitutes an attractive countryside has been shaped by many factors: landscape painting, romantic fiction, travel brochures. It is also heavily influenced by environmentalist concern. To be attractive, an environment must be healthy, and environmental health is seen as depending on diversity. The conservation of 'biodiversity'—of the greatest possible variety of life forms—has become the object of international treaties (for instance, at the Rio Earth Summit in 1992), and of national government policies (HMSO 1994a). Conservation organisations con-centrate their efforts on protecting the greatest possible diversity of wildlife and habitats. A countryside that looks diverse, that contains a visible mix of fields and hedgerows, scrub and woodland, ponds and streams, is the embodiment of health and attractiveness. It is a countryside in which, it can be assumed, the birds will sing, the flowers will bloom and the trees will cast their dappled shade. It offers the complete aesthetic experience.

Alongside these post-modern values, a modern perception of the countryside is seen as persisting among those who depend upon it for their material wealth. For the farming, forestry and mining industries, among others, the countryside is an economic resource. Its potential to produce material wealth depends on the effi-ciency with which it is managed. Its appearance is irrelevant to this process, and the features that make for a diverse and attractive countryside are seen as obsta-cles to efficient management. Hills are whittled away to produce materials for the construction industry. Commercial forests of single species are planted in straight lines to suit modern machinery. Non-productive land is seen as a wasted resource, so scrub and woodland are cleared and wetland is drained. Small, irregular fields with hedgerows do not suit large equipment, so hedges are removed, surfaces lev-elled. The industrialisation of agriculture in the post-war years (when the aim was national self-sufficiency in food production), and later through the European Community's (now European Union) Common Agricultural Policy (CAP) has been well documented (see, for instance, Newby 1985). It is also well known that this process proved too successful, generating huge surpluses of agricultural pro-duce and leading to reform of the CAP, on which post-modern interests (in the form of environmental and amenity groups) have struggled to exert an influence.

The modern understanding of the countryside sees it, not only as an eco-nomic resource, but also as a private resource, as something that is owned by individuals, families and companies. It represents the future material security of these interests, to be inherited or ultimately sold for profit. The effort put into its management is therefore expected (in accordance with modern values) to reap material rewards, and the rights to enjoy those rewards are seen as belonging to those who expend the effort, who bear the costs of the investment. Anything that might interfere with those rights, like the suggestion that the countryside is a communal resource to be enjoyed by all, is resented and resisted.

Land and landscape, work and leisure

> . . . a working country is hardly ever a landscape. The very idea of landscape implies separation and observation. (Williams 1973: 120)

The modern and post-modern models of the countryside are encapsulated in the concepts of 'land' and 'landscape' (see Milton 1993). Land is a tangible resource that is worked for material profit; it can be mined, cultivated, sown, grazed, inherited, bought and sold, built upon; it is personal wealth that can be used to generate more personal wealth. Landscape is an intangible resource defined primarily by its appearance; it is viewed rather than worked, a commodity to be consumed rather than a factor in material production. Landscape is available to all who can see it, and is therefore owned communally rather than privately. The principal properties of land and landscape can be summarised as follows:

Land	*Landscape*
Private property	Communal property
Personal heritage	Communal heritage
(owner's family)	(future generations)
Place of work	Place of leisure
Production	Consumption
Functionality	Appearance

The opposition between work and leisure is particularly relevant to the debate over access to the countryside. Strictly speaking, this opposition itself belongs to modernity, for 'the very notion of "leisure" as a finite set of activities done in specialised sites for specific periods of time, is itself a quintessentially "modern" activity' (Urry 1995: 212). In the modern world view, work and leisure, production and consumption, are sharply divided by time and place. The countryside can be either a place of work or a place of leisure but not both. In the post-modern world view, work and leisure merge seamlessly. Our lives are no longer dominated by 'clock-time', in which work for fixed periods earned the reward of equally fixed periods of leisure (see Adam 1990, cited in Urry 1995: 216); instead, continuous rewards are demanded of both work and leisure. Similarly, places of work and leisure are no longer mutually exclusive. Working from home is a growing phenomenon, and workplaces themselves, in the form of industrial museums and open farms, are put on view, to be consumed as part of the leisure experience. In this context it is expected that the countryside, including those parts of it that retain a productive role, will be made available to all as a source of enjoyment.

Access to the countryside in Northern Ireland

Public access to the countryside became a subject of government policy in Northern Ireland in the early 1980s. Until then there was no formal legal recognition of public rights of access to private land, except where such land was dedicated for recreation purposes. Some rights of way, established by public use over a long period, were informally recognised, but not administered by any authority. In the early 1980s, the government introduced legislation similar to that which had existed in England and Wales since 1949 and in Scotland since 1967. The new Northern Ireland legislation thus standardised the legal provision for access to the countryside throughout the United Kingdom, with a few minor differences to take account of regional variations in administrative structures.

The legislative process

The new legislation, the Access to the Countryside (Northern Ireland) Order 1983, was drafted during the lifetime of the Northern Ireland Assembly (NIA), a non-legislative elected body which had been set up in an attempt to encourage power-sharing between Northern Ireland's loyalist and nationalist communities. One of the NIA's roles was to scrutinise proposed draft legislation and make recommendations to the government on possible amendments. Such scrutiny was carried out by the Assembly's statutory committees, which could invite public comment and hold public hearings to air the relevant issues. The relevant committee would then issue a report which was debated by the full Assembly and accepted, with or without modifications, as the NIA's Report. The government would then produce a Draft Order which was considered by Parliament and either accepted or rejected. The government would also respond directly to the NIA Report, detailing which of its recommendations had been accepted. This rather complex process provides a researcher with a great deal of valuable information. The NIA Reports contain (as appendices) written and spoken evidence provided by those who participated in the scrutiny of the draft legislation, and the debates on NIA Reports, where many of the main issues are revisited, are reproduced word for word in the Assembly's proceedings.

In December 1982, a proposal for a Draft Access to the Countryside (Northern Ireland) Order was published by the Department of the Environment (NI) and presented to the NIA. The Assembly's Environment Committee invited written responses from the public and held a public hearing on 1 February 1983. The Environment Committee's report on the proposed Draft Order was debated by the Assembly on 15 February (NIA 1983–4: 279ff.), when it was accepted, without modification, as the NIA Report (NIA 1983). This was sent to the Secretary of State for Northern Ireland on 16 February. The government's response to this report was presented to the Assembly on 26 October 1983 and the Draft Order went through Parliament just before the Christmas recess. The Access to the Countryside (Northern Ireland) Order 1983 finally came into operation on 22 March 1984.

The policy content

The Access Order contains two main sets of provisions, one relating to rights of way and paths and the other to 'open country'; these are contained in Parts II and III of the Order respectively. It also charges district councils, the only layer of local government in Northern Ireland, with the major role in implementation. Under Part II of the Order, district councils are obliged to assert and keep open existing public rights of way, and to keep maps and records of them. Rights of way may be diverted to allow for ploughing, but only temporarily. District councils may also create new public paths, either by agreement with landowners, or compulsorily, by order, and establish, with the agreement of the Department of the Environment (NI), long-distance routes for recreational use.

Part III of the Order provides for public access to open country, which is defined (in Article 25) as, 'land appearing to the district council or the Department to consist wholly or predominantly of mountain, moor, heath, hill, woodland, cliff, foreshore, marsh, bog or waterway'. Land used for agriculture, and land designated as nature reserve, is exempted from this classification. District councils may secure public access to open country by agreement with landowners, by order, or by compulsory acquisition.

In order to understand the points of view expressed in the debate that accompanied the government's policy on access, it is important to appreciate the potential impact of the Access Order. It promised to affect public rights of access in two main ways: through the formal recognition of existing rights, and through the extension of rights into areas where they had not previously existed. The Order was thus an instrument, both for controlling public access to the countryside, and for increasing such access. The distinction between these two aspects of the Order introduced an element of ambivalence, by presenting groups and individuals with different grounds for supporting or opposing the government's policy. Landowners, for instance, who resented the extension of rights of access into new areas, were nevertheless attracted by the prospect of greater control over existing rights of way. The published responses indicate that, while there was support from all parties for the control of public access to the countryside, there were sharp differences of opinion on whether such access should be increased or encouraged. Thus the debate which accompanied the introduction of the Order lined up those interests which broadly supported the promotion of regulated public access to the countryside, and which therefore supported the Order as a whole, against those who were opposed to any promotion or extension of such access.

The protagonists

In the explanatory document for the original proposed Draft Access Order, the Department of the Environment (NI) (henceforth referred to as 'the Department') stated that the proposal had been initiated, 'in response to representations received from District Councils, the National Trust, and various amenity and rambling societies in Northern Ireland' (NIA 1983: Appendix I). This seems to imply that these organisations were strongly in favour of the new legislation on access, that they might be seen as constituting a pro-access lobby. However, the written and oral evidence provided to the NIA's Environment Committee reveals a different picture. There is no record, in the NIA's published proceedings, of representations from the rambling societies (who might have thought that their views could be adequately expressed by the Northern Ireland Sports Council). It was admitted by a Department representative that the district councils desiring a change in the legislation could well be in a minority, and that their demands had consisted of 'oral representations . . . over the years' (NIA 1983, Appendix XII: 4). The National Trust's concern for a change in the law also seems to have been more muted than the explanatory document suggested, being confined largely to the creation and maintenance of paths, and having been expressed in rather oblique terms: 'Our [the Department's] discussion with them would suggest that they have felt on occasion that they had some difficulty . . .' (NIA 1983, Appendix XII: 4). Nevertheless, the National Trust generally welcomed the proposed Order (NIA 1983: Appendix V).

Of those organisations that submitted written and/or oral statements to the NIA Environment Committee, three expressed strong support for the Access Order. Two of these were statutory bodies. Representatives of the Northern Ireland Sports Council said that they had been campaigning for new legislation 'for quite a long time' (NIA 1983, Appendix XII: 27). The Ulster Countryside Committee (UCC), which advised the Department on matters of landscape amenity and conservation (and which has since been replaced by the Council for Nature Conservation and the Countryside), was claimed by its Chairman to have long felt 'that there would be considerable value in having this legislation enacted here in Northern Ireland' (NIA 1983, Appendix XII: 41). The remaining group expressing support was the Ulster Society for the Preservation of the Countryside (USPC), one of the longest standing voluntary conservation bodies in Northern Ireland, which welcomed the proposed Order and claimed to have been pressing for some such legislation for the previous 25 years (NIA 1983, Appendix XII: 12). The Sports Council and the USPC had been responsible for setting up the Ulster Way, a long-distance walking route around Northern Ireland, and therefore had been directly involved in the negotiation of public access to private land. These representations expressed support both for the formalisation of existing rights and for the general promotion of public access to the countryside for recreation purposes, and it seems reasonable, therefore, to treat them as indicating a pro-access lobby, albeit one with a slightly different composition than that described by the Department in its explanatory document.

The anti-access lobby is more easily identified. The strongest representations against the Access Order came from farming interests. Mr S. Porter, a farmer who spoke on his own behalf but claimed that his view was shared by a high percentage of the farming community, suggested that the Order should be scrapped (NIA 1983, Appendix XII: 34). A representative of the Ulster Farmers' Union (UFU), when giving oral evidence to the NIA Environment Committee, stated, '. . . when the subject of access to the countryside is talked about, the reaction of almost every farmer to whom one talks is: "we want nothing at all to do with the thing"' (NIA 1983, Appendix XII: 17). The UFU itself, however, was more moderate in its opposition, arguing, not against the Order as a whole, but against some of its provisions. In their view, the existing network of country roads provided adequate opportunity for people to enjoy the countryside without needing to enter fields: 'access to enclosed agricultural land should be visual access rather than physical access' (NIA 1983, Appendix III). They expressed strongly the view that the assertion of rights of way and the creation of any new paths across private land should be by agreement and not by order. In giving oral evidence, a representative stated that the UFU had favoured legislation because it seemed to offer the opportunity of formally extinguishing old rights of way that were no longer used. The UFU was particularly concerned that farmers should not incur any additional burden of finance or responsibility as a result of the new law, and argued that the district councils should meet maintenance and insurance costs. The NIA's Agriculture Committee approved the proposed Draft Order, but argued that it should give greater recognition to farmers' rights and contain adequate protection for their interests. In its report, the NIA broadly concurred with this view; out of 12 recommended amendments, five were aimed directly at increasing the protection of farming interests.

Defending the land: the language of modernity

I suggest that the debate over the Access Order can be seen as a struggle between modern and post-modern evaluations of the countryside. Those in favour of promoting public access to the countryside, including the Sports Council, the UCC, the USPC and the Department itself, employed a post-modern understanding of the countryside as landscape, a communal heritage which all have the right to enjoy. The Access Order, which provided for farmland, as well as 'open country', to be made accessible for recreation, was a clear expression of this model. The anti-access lobby can be seen as a bastion of modern resistance against this post-modern threat. Their model of the countryside is one of land rather than landscape. Its essentially modern character is indicated by its use of the oppositions between rural and urban, and work and leisure, and by its emphasis on land as a private economic resource.

Rural and urban, work and leisure

In the arguments presented by the anti-access lobby, the rural-urban and work-leisure oppositions are combined. It was assumed that the urban population would regard the countryside as a place of leisure, while the rural population would see it as a place of work; the analogy with a factory floor was made frequently (NIA 1983–4: 283, 288; NIA 1983, Appendix XII: 18). It was assumed that those wishing to enjoy the countryside would be entering it from the towns, and the Access Order was therefore seen as meeting the needs of an urban population (NIA 1983, Appendices III and X).

While it was conceded that many people wishing to spend their leisure in the countryside would be both responsible and well-intentioned, the urban environment was seen as the source of a small minority of vandals who would deliberately damage property. But the greatest potential threat was expected to come from the ignorance of urban dwellers unfamiliar with 'country matters', who might not appreciate the consequences of lighting fires, leaving gates open, dropping litter and failing to keep dogs under control (NIA 1983–4: 287). This concern was graphically described by the Chairman of the NIA Environment Committee in his presentation of the Committee's report to the full Assembly: '. . . the prospect of thousands of hedge-jumping, crop-destroying, livestock-chasing, rubbish-dumping, graffiti-writing townies being exported into the countryside is a real fear haunting the minds of some farmers' (NIA 1983–4: 279).

The division between work and leisure was defined in terms of time as well as place. It was suggested that, if farmland had to be opened up for recreation, then there should be opening times and closing times, as there are for leisure facilities provided by local authorities and other organisations. This argument was aimed partly at protecting the sanctity of the farmers' leisure, which was confined to Sundays and the hours of darkness (NIA 1983, Appendix VIII).

Underlying the opposition between work and leisure was the implicit assumption that the former is more worthy than the latter. Work is important economic activity—the importance of agriculture to the economy of Northern Ireland was mentioned several times—and therefore confers stronger rights. It was assumed that those who work in the countryside, who invest daily effort in its management, have a much greater right to it than those who merely play in it. The important daily business of farming should not be disrupted, or even inconvenienced, in order to accommodate mere leisure pursuits. In any conflict of interests, therefore, between farming and recreation in the countryside, it was argued that farming should take priority, and that the legislation should ensure this.

The farming lobby's perceptions of the divisions between work and leisure, rural and urban, are neatly illustrated in an anecdote which was told during the NIA discussion on the Access Order, and repeated to me several years later in research interviews with farmers' representatives (quoted in Milton 1993: 137). A farmer approached a family picnicking in one of his fields, intending to 'chide them gently' for not having asked his permission. He met with a hostile reception, however, and retaliated by taking his family to picnic in their front garden the following Sunday afternoon (NIA 1983–4: 284). This story contrasts the reasonable, virtuous farmer (who took his leisure only on a Sunday) with the argumentative and unreasonable urban dweller. It also makes an important point about ownership. The urban dweller was unreasonable because he failed to recognise that the farmers own their fields just as much as he owns his front garden. Probably the most fundamental fear generated by the Access Order was that of losing control over private property.

Land as a private economic resource

The Access Order was seen by farmers as a direct challenge to private ownership. As far as they were concerned, their ownership of the land was a legal fact, established through purchase or inheritance. And yet here was a law that appeared to dispute that fact, by implying that non-owners had rights to use the land for their own purposes, and to restrict the farmers' own use of it. It is difficult to construct arguments against so fundamental a challenge, and at least one member of the anti-access lobby resorted to dogmatic assertions of ownership: 'this Order is really an infringement on us, the owners of the land. We are actually the owners and therefore it is a very great infringement' (NIA 1983, Appendix XII: 30); 'we have to assert our ownership and we have to see that the thing is completely scrapped' (NIA 1983, Appendix XII: 34).

The defence of ownership, however, was not merely dogmatic, but was also couched in economic terms. Land is the farmers' main security for the future; it is their store of personal wealth and their means of increasing that wealth. The anti-access lobby argued that farmers should suffer no financial loss as a result of the new legislation. They were concerned about facing claims for damages should members of the public be injured on their land, about the possible costs of maintaining paths and stiles, and about the cost of fencing needed to keep the public on the paths and out of the fields (NIA 1983, Appendices III and X). There was also concern about the effect that rights of way and public paths might have on the value of their land and their ability to develop it for future profit (NIA 1983–4: 303). An additional perceived threat was the possibility of farmers' land being used by others, such as riding schools and horse trainers, for their own economic benefit (NIA 1983, Appendix VIII).

These arguments imply an understanding of the farmers' role and identity which further confirms their allegiance to modern values. Farmers are primary producers in the modern economy, and the land is a factor in production, not itself a product to be consumed. If, however, the (urban) public wish to consume the countryside itself, then its status as a product of the farmers' labour should be acknowledged. It should be paid for, like any other agricultural product is paid for, and the conditions of its supply should be formally established, with the producer having some say in the matter. Thus, faced with a view of the world in which consumption is considered both a right and a duty, farmers seek to maintain their identity as producers.

From policy to practice

The debate that surrounded the introduction of the Access Order can tell us something about the distribution of modern and post-modern values in Northern Irish society at that time. By examining the subsequent implementation of the Order, or lack of it, we can learn more about how these values influence political realities, and in particular their differential impact on local and central government.

It is significant that the principal implementing authorities for the Access Order were the district councils. There are twenty-six such councils in Northern Ireland, created in the early 1970s. This was part of the wholesale reorganisation of government following the outbreak of political unrest in the late 1960s. The Northern Ireland Parliament was dissolved and direct rule imposed from Westminster, making central administration the responsibility of the Secretary of State for Northern Ireland and a team of five ministers. Because these posts are reallocated quite frequently, and because those appointed are often unfamiliar with Northern Ireland, a heavy burden of responsibility for the process of government falls on the Northern Ireland Civil Service.

As part of the reorganisation of government, most of the functions that had been the responsibility of local councils (planning, roads, water supply, sewerage, housing, social services and education) were either transferred to central government or else allocated to specially created public bodies (such as the Housing Executive and the Education and Library Boards). This left the new district councils with responsibility for waste disposal, public health, recreation and tourism. It was therefore entirely appropriate that the task of implementing the Access Order at the local level should fall to the district councils, since its purpose was to provide for public recreation. However, the overall responsibility for promoting public enjoyment of the countryside, and administering the provision for access, lies with the Department of the Environment. Thus, while the district councils have largely been left to get on with implementing the Order, the Department has maintained an interest in their progress.

Until the Access Order was introduced, the provision for recreation by the district councils generally took the form of managing public parks and playgrounds. A few councils (notably Craigavon) had taken up the additional challenge of expanding opportunities for rural recreation, but most had done very little in this respect. The Access Order both imposed a duty to do more (by asserting rights of way) and provided an opportunity to do more (by creating new paths and access to open country). Studies undertaken in 1989 and 1993 have shown that the councils' responses to this challenge have been extremely variable.

The councils' response

In 1989, as part of a wider study of conservation policy and practice in Northern Ireland, district councils were sent a list of questions asking about their implementation of the Access Order (see Milton 1990: 89). Thirteen of the 26 councils responded, some providing more information than was asked for. The most progress appeared to have been made in two areas. First, eight of the thirteen councils had appointed rangers or footpath officers (various job titles were used) to undertake some of the tasks imposed by the Order, and a further two were in the process of making such appointments. Additional comments indicated that some councils considered this a necessary first step, feeling unable to implement the Order without additional staff. Financial assistance for these appointments was available from several sources, including the Department, and ten of the councils had, at that time, applied for such assistance. Second, eight of the 13 councils had made maps and records of rights of way and other areas accessible to the public, and a further two had taken steps towards this. Again, additional comments from some councils indicated that they considered it necessary to assess and record what already existed by way of access provision, before attempting to provide more.

The debate on the Access Order had indicated that its most contentious provisions were likely to be the 'assertion' of rights of way (the farming lobby had hoped that some might be eliminated) and the creation of new paths. Only six of the 13 councils had asserted rights of way (or were in the process of doing so); the record of Down District Council, in asserting 24 rights of way, was exceptional, as was the record of Craigavon, which had formally established both rights of way and public paths before the Order was introduced. Seven of the 13 councils had created new public paths (or were in the process of doing so). All this information has to be treated with caution, since no details were asked for; it was not revealed, for instance, how many of the asserted rights of way or new paths were across farmland, or whether any had been contentious. Nevertheless, as a partial record of the district councils' early responses to the Access Order, the survey showed that, at the very least, implementation had been patchy.

In 1993, a much more detailed study of access to the countryside in Northern Ireland was undertaken on behalf of the Department of the Environment (NI), the Sports Council for Northern Ireland and the Northern Ireland Tourist Board (Peter Scott Planning Services 1994).[1] One of the main components of the study was an evaluation of the implementation of the Access Order. This was conducted through a questionnaire, which was sent to all 26 district councils (20 responses were received) and through interviews with representatives of 16 councils. On the basis of this survey, the researchers divided district councils into two categories:

> *Approximately one-third of councils are proactive.* They are aware of the range of powers conferred by the Access Order, have achieved or are working towards the assertion of significant numbers of rights of way and are developing other routes or access opportunities. Most employ a full-time countryside officer.

> *The remaining two-thirds of councils adopt a reactive stance.* They have a poor understanding of their access duties and discretionary powers, are less motivated, take action only occasionally and have asserted few, if any, rights of way. (HMSO 1994b: 16, emphasis in original)

In addition, they noted the strong tendency of all councils to exercise caution where public access to private land is concerned, and, wherever possible, to secure access by agreement rather than by order. They noted that such agreement is often achieved on the farmers' terms, which usually means that it is informal and carries no long-term security (Peter Scott Planning Services 1994: 62).

The reluctance of most district councils to take a more proactive stance on public access to the countryside was attributed to several factors, including the legal and technical complexities of the issue and its tendency to absorb more time and effort than was considered worthwhile. The most important factors, however, were worries about public liability and pressure from farmers and landowners (Peter Scott Planning Services 1994: 63). Some district councils have farmers among their elected representatives, and all councils are aware of the farming community's hostility to increased public access (Peter Scott Planning Services 1994: 61). There was also a lack of pressure from the local community for increased access to the countryside, so the message generally received by district councils is that there would be no votes gained and possibly many lost in making more effort to implement the Access Order (Peter Scott Planning Services 1994: 65).

Contributory factors

The absence of local pressure may indicate that the modernist attitude to land is prevalent outside, as well as within, the farming community. The researchers in the 1993 study observed that 'deeply held values about private property . . . are part of the traditional culture of Northern Ireland' (Peter Scott Planning Services 1994: 62) and that some of the councils which had done little to implement the Access Order held doubts about the legitimacy of public access to the countryside (HMSO 1994b: 17). These observations, taken on their own, would seem to suggest a fairly strict polarity of values between central government and the majority of the population in Northern Ireland; that central government is attempting to impose a post-modern policy (in the shape of the Access Order) on a population whose view of the world is essentially modern, and whose sensibilities are reflected in their locally elected councils. It is clear, however, that the situation is not this simple, for the fact remains that a section of the population (the pro-access lobby in the debate on the Access Order) favours a post-modern countryside, aesthetically pleasing and accessible to all, and that the actions of a minority of district councils reflect this view. I suggest that this complexity can be understood in terms of a combination of factors, some of which have shaped central government's role in the access debate, and some of which have shaped the public response.

Influences on central government

First, it could be argued that, since the imposition of direct rule, central government policy in Northern Ireland has been heavily influenced by what takes place in Great Britain. This is not surprising, given that the government ministers appointed to serve in Northern Ireland sit in the Westminster Parliament and, for the most part, have been elected to represent constituencies in Great Britain. That they should be in closer touch with policy and practice in Great Britain than in Northern Ireland is to be expected, and, insofar as they regard the practice in Great Britain as good or appropriate, they might also be expected to want Northern Ireland to conform.[2] Thus some of the policies introduced into Northern Ireland have the effect, if not the explicit intention, of bringing Northern Ireland into line with the rest of the United Kingdom. The policy on access to the countryside was no exception to this, and it could be that the provisions of the Access Order were considered desirable by central government, partly because they reflected the situation already existing in England, Scotland and Wales.

Second, the apparent concern of central government in Northern Ireland to impose a post-modern model of the countryside, can be related to the growth of the leisure and tourism industries in other areas. Central government is, inevitably, concerned with the general state of Northern Ireland's economy, which has suffered severely due to the political unrest of the past 25 years. During this time, there has been virtually no incoming tourism (except that generated by visits among relatives), and the demands of the resident population for recreation have been met by what central and local government, together with bodies like the National Trust, could provide (in the form of Country Parks, Forest Parks, beaches and coastal footpaths, etc.). During the past few years, and particularly after the cease-fire was declared in 1994, there has been a dramatic increase in the number of visitors. It is assumed that, if Northern Ireland is to compete successfully in the tourist market, it must provide the kinds of facilities that tourists seek and find elsewhere (see HMSO 1994b: 10), and these include an attractive and accessible countryside. Thus a post-modern countryside, one that offers aesthetic enjoyment rather than simply producing food and raw materials, is now seen as profitable. That this is also recognised by the district councils, is shown by the fact that, in the 1993 study, they cited the wish to attract visitors and tourists as the strongest encouragement to promote access to the countryside. But, as indicated above, the political sensitivity of the access issue was sufficient, in most cases, to overcome this incentive.

Influences on the public

The public response to the access issue consists, not only of the resistance offered by the farming lobby, but also the support of the small but significant pro-access lobby and the general lack of interest apparently shown by a majority of the population. I suggest that both the farmers' hostility to access and the general lack of demand for it have their roots in the pattern of land ownership in Northern Ireland. This can be illustrated through a brief comparison with England, where the debate on access to the countryside has gained far more prominence.

The struggle for ownership of England's countryside has a long history. After the Norman conquest of 1066, the land in private hands was seized by the crown and parcelled out to knights and barons. The rights to common land remained, however, as well as a recognition that everyone should have free access even to private land. It was not until a capitalist economy began to replace the feudal system, and land came to be seen as a commercial asset (the beginning of modernism), that the exclusion of the public from the English countryside began in earnest. From the sixteenth to the nineteenth century, both through the legal process and through unlawful seizure (and with repeated and considerable public unrest), common land was progressively enclosed and rights of access to private land progressively eroded (see Shoard 1987: 48ff. for a detailed account).

In the twentieth century, the battle for public access to the English countryside has continued against the legacies of this historical process. While a percentage of the ancient rights of way still remain as public footpaths, many have been (and continue to be) destroyed in the interests of industrial agriculture. Large tracts of land remain in the hands of titled families, who have also exercised considerable influence over large landowning bodies such as the Forestry Commission and the National Trust.[3] Much of the remaining private land is owned by farming families for whom it remains, primarily, the main factor in the creation of personal wealth. Newby et al. (1978) have shown how these landowners constitute a ruling class, dictating, not only the management of their own property, but also important areas of public interest such as planning and local government resources. All these factors have combined to make the battle for access to England's countryside a modern as well as a post-modern phenomenon. The access issue has been defined in terms of the opposition between the holders of capital and the dispossessed masses (whose rights are seen as dating from the pre-modern era). Post-modern values (health and leisure for all, a universal right to enjoy) have added weight to what was an ancient and continuing class struggle.

In Ireland the historical pattern has been very different. Although large estates were established in the twelfth century by Anglo-Norman colonists, much of the land remained in the hands of the Gaelic population. The plantations of the late sixteenth and seventeenth centuries were more effective in transferring land ownership to immigrant families (including some aristocracy), mainly from England, but even then, many of the peasant communities in the west remained undisturbed (Aalen 1989: 100). Nevertheless, much of the island, from the seventeenth to the nineteenth century, was owned by landlords and either managed by them through a labour force or tenanted out to farming families.

The most significant development in land ownership came in the late nineteenth and early twentieth centuries. Rural Ireland experienced major fluctuations of fortune during the nineteenth century. Initially, the success of Irish agriculture supported a rapid growth in population, but successive famines (the most well-known in 1845–7) demonstrated its fragility. The famines also weakened the large estate-holders and led to agrarian unrest in 1879–82. Over the next forty years, legislation was enacted which transferred the ownership of much of the land from landlords to tenants (Aalen 1989: 109). This established the pattern of landholding which Northern Ireland inherited on partition in 1922, and which has survived throughout the twentieth century. Most of rural Northern Ireland is divided into owner-occupied farms with an average area of less than 30 ha.; over half the farms have an area of less than 20 ha. (Department of Agriculture (NI) 1989: 39, 63).[4] This distribution of land has prevented access to the Northern Irish countryside from becoming a class issue. While the 'common people' in England have been dispossessed of their countryside, in Northern Ireland they have had it returned to them, and have felt no need to demand access to what is already theirs.

There remains the question of how a significant pro-access lobby, holding a post-modern view of the countryside, supporting the initiative of central government and influencing the actions of some local authorities, emerged in Northern Ireland. It is clear from the documentation on the access debate that support for access has a long history among some groups, such as the USPC. However, I suggest that the recent period of political unrest has played its part, in the sense that it has had contradictory consequences for the spread of post-modern values. On the one hand, as noted above, the development of leisure and tourism and their associated values and aspirations have been suppressed by the political unrest, but there have also been counter-trends that have had the opposite effect.

First, the sectarian violence created, for many people, a fear for their own physical security. Along with other factors (see Yearley and Milton 1990: 192), the political problems also brought about a rapid decline in the manufacturing sector and discouraged further commercial investment. This created high levels of unemployment, much of which has been long-term, adding financial insecurity to physical insecurity. Such conditions, according to theorists of postmodernity, foster demands for instant gratification and an emphasis on consumption, in the absence of a productive role. At the same time, as social and economic problems escalated and the process of government became more difficult, the service sector expanded, especially the medical, civil, security and social services. It is the service sector which, it has been suggested, provides much of the support for conservation and amenity organisations (see, for instance, Cotgrove and Duff 1981). Thus, it could be argued that Northern Ireland's political problems have accelerated the development of a consumer society with an expanding middle class, precisely those conditions in which, it has been suggested, post-modern values flourish. In these circumstances, it is not surprising to find some demand for a post-modern countryside in a region where the majority may feel more at home with modernity.

Notes

The 1989 study on conservation policy and practice, of which the brief survey of district councils was a part, was undertaken with financial support from the World Wide Fund for Nature (WWF).

1.   A summary of this study was published separately (HMSO 1994b).
2.   It was noticeable, for instance, that when the House of Commons Select Committee on the Environment examined environmental issues in Northern Ireland, they were most concerned that rural planning conventions did not conform with those in Great Britain (see HMSO 1990).
3.   Although the National Trust holds much of its property for the purposes of providing for public recreation, it has not been immune from battles over access to its land.
4.   This compares with an average farm size of over 60 ha. for Great Britain (Milton 1990: 41).

References

Aalen, F. 1989. Imprint of the Past. In D. Gillmor (ed.), *The Irish Countryside*. Dublin: Wolfhound Press.

Adam, B. 1990. *Time and Social Theory*. Cambridge: Polity.

Bourdieu, P. 1984. *Distinction*. London: Routledge & Kegan Paul.

Cotgrove, S. and A. Duff 1981. Environmentalism, values and social change. *British Journal of Sociology* 32 (1): 92–110.

Department of Agriculture (NI) 1989. *Statistical Review of Northern Ireland Agriculture 1988*. Belfast: Department of Agriculture (NI) Economic and Statistics Division.

Featherstone, M. 1992. Postmodernism and the aestheticization of everyday life. In S. Lash and J. Friedman (eds.), *Modernity and Identity.* Oxford: Blackwell.

Harvey, D. 1989. *The Condition of Postmodernity: An enquiry into the origins of cultural change.* Oxford: Blackwell.

HMSO 1990. *House of Commons Environment Committee First Report: Environmental Issues in Northern Ireland.* HC Paper 39, London: Her Majesty's Stationery Office.

____. 1994a. *Biodiversity: The UK Action Plan.* London: Her Majesty's Stationery Office.

____. 1994b. *Access to the Northern Ireland Countryside: Summary Report.* London: Her Majesty's Stationery Office.

Lash, S. 1990. *Sociology of Postmodernism.* London: Routledge.

Miller, D. 1994. *Modernity: An Ethnographic Approach: Dualism and mass consumption in Trinidad.* Oxford and Providence: Berg.

Milton, K. 1990. *Our Countryside Our Concern: The policy and practice of conservation in Northern Ireland.* Belfast: Northern Ireland Environment Link.

____. 1993. Land or Landscape—rural planning policy and the symbolic construction of the countryside. In M. Murray and J. Greer (eds.), *Rural Development in Ireland.* Aldershot: Avebury.

Newby, H. 1985. *Green and Pleasant Land? Social change in rural England.* 2nd edition, London: Wildwood House.

____., C. Bell, D. Rose and P. Saunders 1978. *Property, Paternalism and Power.* London: Hutchinson.

NIA 1983. *Northern Ireland Assembly Report on the Proposal for a Draft Access to the Countryside (Northern Ireland) Order.* Belfast: HMSO.

____. 1983–4. *Official Report.* Belfast: HMSO.

Peter Scott Planning Services 1994. *Access to the Countryside in Northern Ireland—for Walking, Cycling and Riding.* Edinburgh: Peter Scott Planning Services.

Shoard, M. 1987. *This Land is Our Land: The struggle for Britain's countryside.* London: Paladin.

Urry, J. 1990. *The Tourist Gaze: Leisure and travel in contemporary societies.* London: Sage.

Urry, J. 1995. *Consuming Places.* London and New York: Routledge.

Williams, R. 1973. *The Country and the City.* London: Paladin.

Yearley, S. and K. Milton 1990. Environmentalism and Direct Rule: The politics and ethos of conservation and environmental groups in Northern Ireland. *Built Environment* 16 (3): 192–202.

3 Identity and strategy in post-productionist agriculture: a case study from Northern Ireland

Andrew Dawson

In recent years rural areas have faced a situation of accelerating social, economic and environmental crisis. Governments throughout western Europe and beyond have responded with a policy sea-change, whose intention has been to bring about a restructuring of rural economic life. As the economic mainstay of most rural communities, few sectors have felt the impacts of change more than agriculture. Recent agricultural policy has effectively moved the sector into a new era, from 'productionism' to 'post-productionism' (European Society for Rural Sociology 1995), involving the inception of new production and land use strategies.

Reflecting the concern of much recent research with understanding the impact of policy in its local contexts, this chapter considers Northern Irish farmers' responses to restructuring.[1] More specifically, it focuses on the responses of farmers in County Down to calls for greater economic diversity and land transfer, strategies at the forefront of many local farmers' minds. It notes that farmers' responses are often diverse, and argues that the key to understanding such diversity lies in the conceptualisation of responses as strategies, in a recognition of the differing roles which ideas of tradition and identity play in strategising, and in an appreciation of the impact that recent social changes have had on processes of tradition and identity construction.

Agricultural restructuring: policy and research

Recent agricultural policy, especially in European Union member countries, has combined three key aims: protection of the environment, the reduction of food surpluses, and the assurance of a fair standard of living for agricultural populations. These aims are being pursued through the implementation of a combination of restructuring and welfare objectives and measures. A clear and stark logic can be identified here.

The logic calls for the transformation of agricultural production and land use. The intensive production of goods in which there are surpluses is to be curtailed through means such as the cessation of price guarantees and the implementation of production quotas. Alternatives to intensive production are encouraged. Extensification and diversification of production and the selective setting aside of land are promoted through the provision of grants and subsidies.

Welfare measures alone cannot be expected to compensate farmers for the inevitable loss of revenue that such changes entail. According to the logic, compensation must be generated from within the farms themselves. The two principal means by which this is achieved are different sides of the same coin. An agricultural 'shake-out', whereby consolidation and expansion of some, usually large farms, at the expense of other, usually small farms, should be accompanied by the development of pluri-active economic strategies (Bowler 1985). The first means is encouraged through agricultural policy measures which include the selective targeting of grants and the stipulation that quota may be floated on the open market. In contrast, pluri-activity can only be enhanced by wider development strategies which promote opportunities for waged employment and conditions for private enterprise to flourish in rural areas. These developments have been accompanied by the aim, in both political and academic circles, of understanding the restructuring of agriculture in its local contexts. This aim has emerged for a number of reasons: because the impacts of restructuring are as diverse as agriculture is heterogeneous; because heterogeneity in agriculture cannot be straightforwardly attributed to the wider forces of market and state (Tarrow 1977); because this heterogeneity can, in part, be put down to local differences in social organisation (Mansvelt Beck 1988); and because, in contrast to organisations such as the United Kingdom's rural development agencies, whose fulfilment of the aim reflects an ideology of state disengagement, effective policy and development strategy require a greater valorisation of local resources (van der Ploeg and Long 1994).

Attempts to understand restructuring in its local contexts have led to the development of research within academic territories more usually associated with anthropology. Cultural analysis and work on tradition and identity now proliferates. Unfortunately, the absence of anthropological expertise is often apparent. This chapter is written with some of the shortcomings of recent research in mind. Crucially, the chapter's substantive and critical remarks stem from a conceptualisation of responses to agricultural restructuring as 'strategies', culturally mediated and conscious decisions (Redclift 1986) in which ideas of tradition and identity play a central role.

First, in worst case practice many of the growing array of multi-disciplinary teams see 'cultural factors' as constituting a residual category; what is left over after the economists, political scientists and ecologists have identified their objects of study. In the case of rural sociology, this may be an understandable reaction to the all-encompassing and cataloguing approach to the understanding of rural social life that characterised the community studies genre (Winter 1991). Nevertheless, in contrast to the compartmentalising tendencies of some research, this chapter emphasises that all factors which impinge upon the farm household, and which play a part in farmers' responses to restructuring, are culturally mediated.

Secondly, in worst case theorising, tradition and identity are relegated to the status of epiphenomena or are conceptualised as unchanging belief, custom or narrative (Cole 1977). Thus they are seen, respectively, as having either a minimal or, more usually, a constraining impact on the ways that farmers respond to restructuring (Winter 1991; van der Ploeg and Long 1994). Echoing others, this chapter suggests that ideas of tradition and identity are central to the responses of farming people (Mormont 1990; Dawson 1994). It accepts the assumption of some observers that such ideas may act as constraints. However, as in much sociological and anthropological writing, it demonstrates that they may also be used inventively and resourcefully as central elements of strategy (Barth 1969; Boon 1982; Cohen 1989; Fischer 1986; Hobsbawm and Ranger 1983).[2] Indeed, such resourcefulness may include the strategic representation of tradition and identity as constraints (Ennew 1980; Dawson 1994).

The final and most important problem concerns the issue of human agency. There has been widespread recognition that within most social scientific research on agriculture agency has often been marginalised by an emphasis on the structural constraints which farming people confront (see, for example, Pile 1990; van der Ploeg and Long 1994). However, diagnosis has rarely been followed by remedy. While some research has accounted for cultural heterogeneity between local contexts, it has rarely considered the full degree of intra-local diversity. Even amongst the most vociferous proponents of actor-oriented approaches, structure is usually emphasised at the expense of agency. For instance, Pile (1990) describes how, in their 'readings' of the world, farming people unwittingly reproduce the very structural relationships which threaten farm survival. That this shortcoming is widespread is evident in ubiquitous references to the 'village voice', and in commonplace conceptualisations of the family farm as an 'organic entity' (Whatmore 1988). Such references imply uniformity; shared ideas of collective traditions and identities, a consensus of opinion and, in some cases, locally uniform responses to restructuring.

The focus in this chapter is on diversity. It highlights how ideas of collective tradition and identity are animated by human subjects. It emphasises that they are only sustained by the very idiosyncratic uses that individuals find for them and meanings that people invest in them (Cohen 1989). Diversity has, of course, long been of concern to anthropologists working on rural Britain and Ireland. However, while the bulk of that work has focused on diversity between individuals, on the multivocality of shared symbols of identity (see, for example, Cohen 1987), or on their diverse world views (see, for example, Rapport 1993), less attention has been paid to diversity within individual outlooks and responses to change. This chapter develops such a focus, in this case on the often marked contrasts between local farmers' representations of farming and their farming practices, their political and economic strategies, and their strategically constructed representations of identity.

It should be pointed out that this focus on diversity does not mean that the kind of structural issues which forms the central concern of most research on agriculture is omitted from analysis. Some anthropological work might lead us to suspect that this would be the case; for instance, those anthropological approaches to identity where the world is viewed as fanning out from individuals in concentric circles of greater and lesser degrees of sociality—from house to village, from village to tribe and from own tribe to other tribes (Sahlins 1968). In contrast, the findings presented in this chapter concur with recent anthropological work which has shown how, in the midst of social, economic and political changes, people are increasingly able to draw from beyond their most immediate sites of sociality on an ever-widening range of identity options and cultural resources in the construction of their traditions and identities. This process, which has been variously referred to as creolization (Drummond 1980) and cultural compression (Paine 1992), has potentially contradictory consequences, leading, often simultaneously, to the dissolution or the enrichment of traditional forms of identity and identity boundary.

Farming in North Ards: from productionism to post-productionism

North Ards, where field research was carried out between 1990 and 1993, is situated in County Down on Northern Ireland's eastern seaboard, a few miles to the south east of Belfast. It is close to the province's centre of economic activity, has largely escaped the worst sectarian violence, and enjoys favourable climatic conditions and high quality agricultural land. These geographical and political blessings lie at the root of several of the area's changing social characteristics.

The productionist years

Since the Second World War, North Ards has become an all too rare heartland of prosperity within Northern Ireland. Local farming was particularly well placed to prosper. The climate and land sustain a rich mix of market gardening, arable and livestock enterprises. Proximity to the province's key markets enables farms to enjoy low transportation costs and easy access to the contractors for whom they produce increasingly. By exploiting these conditions, local farming was able to develop in ways which conformed to the ideal image of the 'modern farm' encouraged by productionist agricultural policy (Gasson and Errington 1993). In essence, the majority of local farms became increasingly capitalised, modernised, specialised, intensive, productive and growth-oriented.

Over this period the area rapidly urbanised. An increasing city orientation in the lives of local people was accompanied by the influx of urban 'offcomers'. The peri-urban development which facilitated this can be attributed to a mixture of economic, political and cultural factors. Throughout 'the Troubles' much of the province's planning policy has reflected a concern to safeguard rural development and avoid the kind of restrictions that may condemn rural areas to economic depression. The mid-1980s were golden years for development. The push provided by relative economic prosperity was complemented by implementation of liberalising measures proposed in the Cockcroft report (1978).

Like much of contemporary rural Europe, the area became increasingly middle class (Lowe et al 1986), with increasing numbers of middle class offcomers joining the upwardly mobile sections of the local population, many of whom were farmers. Beyond specifically local reasons, such as the area's commutable distance from Belfast, the influx reflects a broader trend of exogenous investment in rural areas and in agricultural land (Pepinster 1996).

However, accounts offered by local people suggest considerable disjunction between the general and the farming populations in terms of several social transformations wrought by the growing prosperity, the changing class structure, the peri-urbanisation and their geographical and political causes. Several of the processes often associated with urbanisation had little impact on farming. As in much European farming, key traditional elements of the relations of production remained untouched (Gasson and Errington 1993). Most importantly, despite their increasing size, the majority of farms remained family owned and operated. Moreover, a disjunction in the ethno-religious composition of the area emerged. As the general population became more mixed, the farming population remained steadfastly Protestant. Also, like much of the east of Northern Ireland, the area experienced significant population growth, though the farming population dwindled.

There are several reasons for this. First, expansion of the majority of farms was achieved at the expense of smaller farms. Secondly, where once it was possible to accommodate several siblings on the family farm, more recent years saw it become increasingly difficult to accommodate more than one, if any. This was mainly due to the progressive substitution of labour by capital. Thirdly, upward socio-economic mobility brought negative consequences. Throughout Northern Ireland, there has been a steady reverse in patterns of migration. Once it was working class Catholics who left the province in large numbers. More recently, it has been middle class Protestants who have been leaving (Bruce 1994). Local farms were not immune to this change. The consequence for many was all too apparent. It became increasingly difficult to find suitable successors.

The post-productionist years

Despite the decline in the size of the farming population, agriculture has maintained its centrality within Northern Ireland's economy and society. Its contribution to the province's GDP is three times greater than it is in the United Kingdom as a whole (Phelan and Markey 1993: 58). Moreover, agriculture employs 7.8 per cent of the province's population, in contrast to only 2.4 per cent in the United Kingdom (DANI 1990). Consequently, Northern Ireland has been profoundly affected by the recent policy shift, North Ards included, where the impact of policy changes have manifest themselves in particular ways.

Many of the post-war social transformations have continued apace, but the once near certainty of increasing farm prosperity has not. While true of agriculture in general, there is considerable credence in a view widespread locally that recent agricultural policy has placed North Ards farms somewhere between a rock and a hard place. As predominantly 'modern', productive farms, North Ards farms are subjected to the anti-productionist elements of restructuring and offered little in the way of welfare support. Many farms have been adversely affected by the introduction of production quotas and the end of price guarantees. Measures designed to ensure income have been directed at enterprises more rarely found in the area. For example, few local farms have been able to reap the subsidies for mountain sheep production.

Nevertheless, most North Ards farms are well placed to adapt to the new visions of farming in the post-productionist era. Their high levels of modernisation and remuneration place them in a position to thrive in the shake-out. For instance, several local dairy farms have been able to raise the significant amounts of money required to qualify for modernisation grants and compete effectively in the market for quotas. Also, and most importantly, the area's proximity to Belfast has become increasingly significant. First, proximity to the key markets for employment and produce make pluri-activity and diversification more than a possibility. Secondly, farmers have benefited from the area's peri-urbanisation, which has enabled them to obtain planning approval where this might have been denied elsewhere in the province. The generally benign economic and political context has facilitated the growth of a 'speculative development culture'. Development and sale of land for development have been perceived increasingly as gainful economic pursuits, particularly during the 1990s when farm incomes fell and there was general economic recession. Yet despite these opportunities, there remains a profound pessimism among many local farmers. As one farmer stated:

> Now you see the typical farm in County Down . . . these edicts coming down from
> Brussels will be the death. They'll be the death of family farms like this one. Yes,
> it's bad and we certainly have rough times.

These words were spoken by a man who owns 285 acres of prime grassland (large for this area), 400 breeding ewes eligible for subsidies (rare in this area), 100 beef cattle, a highly profitable nursing home, income from an advisory position with a rendering company, two Range Rovers and a holiday home with land in the

Picos D'Europas. The level of wealth and degree of pluri-activity and production diversity may be somewhat untypical in this case, but the view expressed is not. Exaggerated images of the North Ards farmer as policy victim are widespread.

Such images might be regarded as a knee-jerk reaction to a bitter irony wrought by the transition from productionism to post-productionism. At one level the post-productionist model of the diversified and pluri-active farm resembles the mixed and part-time farm from which local farmers, encouraged by productionist policy, had tried successfully to escape. At another level the implementation of post-productionist measures aimed at curbing production means that local farmers have in effect been punished for pursuing successfully the kind of economic strategies encouraged by previous agricultural policies. As one farmer explained:

> First they said produce, produce, produce, and we did. The problem is they tell us to do something and we do it too well. The industry here is a victim of its own success . . . doing exactly what government has asked it to do over the years. They have decided that enough is enough.

Accounts such as this only partially explain the exaggerated images. In the context of North Ards, their logic lies in ideas of tradition and identity.

Tradition, identity, environmentalism and farm diversification

A central claim in much social scientific writing about Northern Ireland is that all politics there are identity politics. For example, in commenting on redistributive social policy, Bruce (1994) describes how measures are assimilated to visions of ethnic competition. The same is true of agricultural policy. However, in the context of North Ards at least, concerns extend beyond ethnicity. Here the visions are those of rural-urban competition as well as of Protestant-Catholic rivalry.

Conspiratorialist assimilationism: protection of the environment

At one level the assimilationist visions take on a conspiratorial form. Governmental consultation with inappropriate groups and representation of inappropriate interests have allegedly led to the mis-diagnosis of the problems affecting rural areas. This mis-diagnosis has led in turn to the development of inappropriate policy. The conspiratorial form of assimilationist visions shows through clearly in local farmers' views about the environmentalist aim in recent agricultural policy.

A sense of displacement rooted in the 'political vacuum' and in the ideological shifts of government is widespread. In essence, direct rule has shattered the once cosy relationship between the Protestant and large farmer dominated Ulster Farmers' Union and the British government. Today local farmers are forced to consult with ministers from mainland Britain who have little in common with Northern Irish farmers, and who, the farmers believe, see the province as a stepping-stone to promotion, or as a place of political purgatory. Moreover, in terms of their political autonomy and electoral constituency, the Thatcher and Major governments were radically different to most previous Conservative administrations. They implemented the measures of a supra-national body, the European Union, which has systematically favoured other 'less developed' countries. Some would argue also that the European Union tends to favour the Catholic countries which make up the majority of its members. Finally, and most importantly, as far as environmentalism is concerned, the national government is seen to represent an increasingly urban constituency (see Milton, this volume).

Few local farmers would disagree with the following resume of their views about the environmentalist aim and its emergence from the vacuum and the ideological shifts. Measures have, by and large, been set up to restrict farming practices. The designation of large tracts of local agricultural land in the 1980s as 'Areas of Special Scientific Interest' helped to crystallise this view. Government has been excessively attentive to the misinformed opinions of the public and an over-zealous environmental lobby. This lobby is seen as predominantly urban-based (Milton 1990). Farmers are represented as foes rather than friends of the environment. The reality is, however, somewhat different. The very beauty of the countryside that environmentalists seek to protect stands as evidence that farmers have been its responsible custodians. They possess a detailed knowledge of the micro-environments within which they work, and environmental protection has always played an integral part in farming practice. As such, policy should not set out to restrict and penalise farmers. Rather, in these times of declining prosperity, it should compensate them for the environmental services they have performed without payment.

Accidentalising assimilationism: farm diversification

At another level, and more commonly, the assimilationist visions take on what might be called an accidentalising form. Whether by sound governmental consultation and representation or not, the problems affecting rural areas have been diagnosed correctly. Consequently, the resultant policies are by and large appropriate. However, while some groups are predisposed to benefit from the new policy measures, some are not. The accidentalising form of assimilationist visions shows through clearly in local farmers' views about the policy aim of reducing food surpluses via promotion of the economic diversity route to farm survival, i.e. the promotion of pluri-activity and, above all, farm diversification. Expressions of a general reluctance to diversify are permeated with humour. Agri-tourism (or 'people farming') and organic farming are unambiguous cues for laughter. In the case of the former, the hilarity stems from the apparent problems of attracting tourists to an area that to outsiders is noted more for bombs than for beauty. In the case of the latter, it stems from the marginal and hippie sub-cultural connotations of the organic vegetable. Reluctance to engage in these activities is also expressed through the representation of mainstream farming as a 'way-of-life'. This term refers to the centrality of particular types of farming in the lives and life experiences of local farming people. By implication, it refers also to the wealth, or more usually the poverty, of the kind of life experiences which might be of value beyond these particular types of farming, experiences which might be of relevance for diversification. Humour often emerges at moments of unease and ambivalence. The unease in this context is double-edged. It stems from the fact that underlying the apparently objective reasons for reluctance to diversify, such as the limited market for tourism, are a plethora of often self-deprecating experiential reasons. It stems also from the fact that underlying the much celebrated Northern Irish culture of decency (Bufwack 1982) is a thinly veiled resentment that it is others who are seen to be best equipped for the new times in farming, equipped to diversify. The self-deprecating experiential reasoning and the resentment are permeated by stereotypical ideas of rural and urban, and Protestant and Catholic traditions and identities.

The reluctance to diversify is multi-faceted. It is rooted in ideas about occupation and status. For example, success in modern farming is considered widely in North Ards to be a key route to maintaining the integrity or public face of the family farm. The status attached to success in modern farming is manifested in a number of ways, including the prominence of large farmers within a myriad of local institutions.

Reluctance is also rooted in ideas of risk and the market place. Local accounts portray the mainstream agricultural economy as cyclical; stability followed by shake-out followed by stability. Such portrayals often employ commonsense rural metaphors; every cold winter is followed by a warm summer. In contrast, the markets for alternative agricultural goods are seen as inherently problematic; sometimes small, sometimes saturated, and almost always difficult to predict. However, they are only difficult to predict for some. Diversification requires a knowledge of the market for commodities that few local farmers see themselves as possessing. This prompts a cultural juxtaposition of the local farmer with an idealised and usually urban entrepreneur. Corollaries of this include the argument that if an idea for an alternative enterprise is viable, it will already have been developed by a businessman.

Reluctance to diversify is rooted in an awareness that diversification is facilitated by an ability to seek state assistance in the form of grants and subsidies. This ability is frequently seen as the unjust preserve of the urbanite. As one farmer explained:

> What a crazy situation, where you have got somebody who has maybe made through the business that they're involved in . . . they have maybe made a vast amount of money, and what have they done? They've come out into the country and they've bought maybe thirty or forty acres. They're hobby farms. They have a few cows, a few sheep . . . Those people are going to get all the money that's going from subsidies and there's going to be no attention paid to what money they're making elsewhere.

Sometimes it is seen as the unjust preserve of the Catholic. In this sense sentiments are often informed by vulgarised accounts of Weber's thesis on 'The Protestant ethic and the spirit of capitalism'. While the Protestant is industrious and self-reliant, the Catholic is lazy and a skilled manipulator of the state. Bruce (1994:61) sums up well the import of such accounts within many rural Protestant outlooks on the present day rural economy:

> The typical Free Presbyterian knows how to run the family farm or the small chain of shops. He does not know how to bid for the International Fund for Ireland and he is resentful of those who do.

Reluctance is also rooted in an awareness that diversification requires economic flexibility. Central among a range of concerns in this respect is doubt about local farmers' abilities to cope with change that a new enterprise might bring to the economic cycle of the farm. This concern is usually substantiated with reference to the cautionary tale of many Northern Irish dairy farms. Enticed by subsidies and the lure of cashing in on the sale of milk quotas, they cut down on their dairying and incorporated other livestock enterprises in the farm. In some cases demise came about because of an inability to cope with financial change. Where once they received a more or less constant and weekly income in the form of a creamery cheque, now they became part dependent on the less frequent and more varied payments from subsidy and sale on the open market. The idea of ethnic differentiation in the propensity for economic flexibility is commonplace. Justification for this idea is found in a perverse reading of post-Plantation history which represents the unequal ethnic distribution of quality land as a contemporary dubious legacy. In essence, in the predominantly Protestant parts of the province the land enabled the establishment of full-time and specialised farming as the norm. In the predominantly Catholic areas a tradition of part-time and mixed farming came to predominate out of necessity. The corollary of this should be clear. Economic flexibility is often seen as a preserve of the Catholic farmer.

Finally, reluctance is rooted in an awareness that diversification requires participation in information and assistance networks. The value of such networks has grown recently as, according to much local opinion, there is a lack of effective advice emanating from the state. Many official agricultural advisors are still in the 'production mind-set'. Ethnic differences in predisposition towards participation in such networks have been recorded by current sociological research. For

Protestants, contact is usually low level and fragmented (Shortall 1994). Local accounts explain the difference in terms of politics and culture; in terms of, paradoxically, Catholic rejection of and by the institutions of the British state, a Catholic culture of collectivism and conformity, and, above all a Protestant culture of non-conformity and individualism. The centrality in Protestant thinking of non-conformity and individualism has been well documented (Crotty 1986). What is important to note here is that their meanings are often contextually specific. For the farmers of North Ards, they are generated by the solitary as opposed to collective working practices inherent in specific types of farming. They are also rooted in readings of the political context. Images of the farmer as a loner, working the land in solitude, have particular resonance in contexts where the preservation of ethnic and national territory is an ongoing issue (Herzfeld 1985). This is as true for the Protestant farmers of North Ards as it is for those in the border counties.

Bruce suggests that the idea that 'late capitalist economies no longer need the "Protestant ethic"' is central within many rural Protestant visions (1994: 62). The idea is certainly widespread amongst North Ards farmers. The terms 'modern farmer' and 'new farmer' (or 'CAP man' [3]) have some currency in local discourse. The former refers to the farmer who operates by productionist logic, a logic which encourages modernisation, intensive production and farm growth. The latter refers to the farmer who has adapted to recent post-productionist policy and its emphasis on economic diversity. Stereotypically, the former is rural and/or Protestant and the latter urban and/or Catholic. In local visions productionism was the era of the ruralite and Protestant, and post-productionism the era of the urbanite and Catholic.

Tradition, identity and land transfer

In North Ards land transfer takes place within a context of particularly high land prices. There are several reasons for the high prices. They include the increasing demand for farm land amongst groups not traditionally associated with farming (Pepinster 1996), the high social value of land in Northern Ireland (see below), the unusually high quality of North Ards farming land and, above all, the high potential for non-agricultural land use in the area. In this increasingly peri-urban area, land with planning approval is at a premium. Given this, it is not surprising, as already mentioned, that a culture of speculative development has developed in local farming. Even amongst the relatively small group of farming people who were the focus of this research, a wide range of projects had been executed or considered. These ranged from sale of land for housing to the proposed development of a commercial airport. Clearly, land transfer through rent or sale constitutes a considerable economic opportunity.[4] However, for the opportunity to be realised, transfer has to be negotiated against a background of pervasive social imperatives.

The social imperatives of land holding: providing for the family and maintaining the social composition of the area

In North Ards, as in much of Northern Ireland, land is associated almost inextricably with an array of social groups, from the family to the ethnic group. The associations are reinforced through a number of means; through codified land transfer practices, through the mnemonics of landscape, and through the distribution of status and sanction. These means of reinforcement serve to ensure that two key social imperatives are met; provision for the family, and continuity of the traditional social composition of the area. Clearly, the social imperatives are related. For example, even though there is a farm succession problem in the area, provision for the family in the form of land and property is usually regarded as a means of ensuring their continued residence in the area. It is in these senses that land in Northern Ireland is often described as having a high social value.

The family-land association is evident in 'keeping the name on the land', an idealised code of land transfer practices. In essence, farming people are compelled to ensure ancestral continuity on the land. Where there is no immediate direct descendant, the nearest blood relative, even if his/her ancestral tie to the owner is tenuous, have the option of using, renting, buying or inheriting the farm. For some people, operation of the family land transfer code is regarded as a way of sustaining endogamy. The notion of a self-perpetuating core of Protestant families who have dominated local land ownership, farming and residence is widespread. Reminders of the code and the idea of endogamy are ever present in the landscape. The name is kept on the land quite literally. Natural features are named after the members of core families, and belonging is proven by the ability to recite complex land ancestry narratives. An example from elsewhere in Northern Ireland illustrates the point:

> That's right, they moved from here to Legg. The Elliot's lived here first, then they moved to Legg. They bought . . . what they called Gandy Elliot. It was what they called big Gandy and wee Andy. The son was wee Andy. They were split up then and bought the place in Dooneen. That would be the same Elliot. George now would be the same Elliot that lived here (Dawson 1994: 64).[5]

According to the code, only when ancestral continuity is not a possibility can land be placed on the market. However, the market is not entirely open. Less exclusive group-land associations and a series of refinements of the code come into play. The code becomes fragmented. Thus, it makes sense then to speak about land transfer codes. These refer to wider concerns about social composition beyond the continued residence of family. In the rarest of cases people would not transfer outside the occupational community to a non-farmer, or outside the local community to, for example, an urbanite.[6] More commonly, people would not transfer outside the ethnic group to a Catholic. In the light of such refinements, the ways of expressing the basic family land transfer code are invested with new ambiguities. For example, the common dictum, 'together in adversity, apart in heredity,' is used variously to refer to non-family as opposed to family, non-farmer as opposed to farmer, urbanite as opposed to ruralite, and, above all, Catholic as opposed to Protestant.

Similarly, landscape is used to express wider fears about threats to the traditional social composition of the area wrought by infringement of the refined codes and by recent political and social transformations; by unresponsive government, by peri-urbanisation and by change in the ethnic balances of population and privilege. Dismal visions are symbolised by the imagery of the enclave. To the north and east is the sea which divides the area from Great Britain. To the west are the hills which barely hold back the city sprawl. To the south is the bogland beyond which lies the land that hosts what is a growing, increasingly prosperous and, in some eyes, hostile Catholic population.

The salience of ethnic considerations in fears about land and social composition may be regarded as surprising. With some considerable justification, Ards has been characterised as amongst the least sectarian areas in Northern Ireland (see, for example, Buckley 1982).[7] However, alongside this reality there has always been widespread potential for the periodic manifestation of sectarian fear and action.[8] Events in the early 1990s, during the period of this research, certainly provided conditions for the hardening of a sectarian land ownership transfer code. For some, operation of such a code constituted a political statement. This was the era of the aftermath of the Anglo-Irish accord. The accord had intensified the sense of Protestant political impotence and of the precariousness of the Union with Britain. For some, its operation constituted a response to fear of the ethnic 'other'. This was an era of escalating Republican paramilitary violence against specifically Protestant targets. Even in the Protestant heartlands, places like North Ards, feelings of vulnerability were high, and reports from other parts of the world enabled the apocalyptically inclined to represent land transfer outside of the ethnic group as a form of auto-ethnic cleansing. However, in most cases its operation reflected the fear of sanctions brought by one's own; the fear that transfer might bring retribution or, more usually, whispers of disapproval.

As stated, the target of growth is a quintessential feature of the kind of 'modern farm' that proliferates in North Ards. Recent policy, allied to increasing prices for local land, may have removed many of the economic imperatives for this model of farming. However, it is clear that many of the social imperatives remain intact. Land holding consolidation and expansion guarantee retention of land within the family, ethnic group and, providing that the heir will act as a successor by continuing to farm, the occupational group. Thus, they ensure fulfilment of the social imperatives of family provision and maintenance of social composition. In contrast, land holding reduction threatens infringement of the local land transfer codes, slippage of land outside of these groups and failure to fulfil the social imperatives. This situation might be regarded as adding weight to the argument that while the productionist years, an era of land holding expansion and consolidation, were suited to the typical local farmer, the post-productionist years, a land-

holding reductionist era in many respects, were not. This is, however, not necessarily the case.

Land holding consolidation and expansion: pluri-activity and the economic value of status

Given that land holding consolidation and expansion constitute the fulfilment of
an economic ideal and a set of social imperatives, it is not surprising that they
bring status. However, what is most important to note is that the acquisition of status through land holding is pursued for economic as well as social reasons.

While there is no consensus about the constitution of the North Ards farm
family core, specific names appear with regularity. These are usually the very
largest farmers. They dominate also in positions of seniority within the community and in the market for highly remunerative part-time agricultural related
employment. For example, two regular informants were church elders and agricultural insurance assessors, and another was a leading member of the Rotary
Club and director of a rendering company. His wife was also a figure of province-
wide importance in the Women's Institute. All three claimed explicitly that they
had been offered their positions within the community and in business because
they belonged to the set of core farm families. They are well-known and their
judgement, advice and opinions are trusted. These are key assets to a rendering
company wishing to offer its services locally and to insurance companies whose
reputation in cases of damage claims between farmers depends on the perception
of objectivity and fairness.

In areas like North Ards, where the majority of farms has rarely benefited
from recent agricultural policy's welfare measures, but have faced many of its
anti-productionist measures, the physical use of farming land has become increasingly uneconomic. Nevertheless, it is clear that it may still make economic sense
to consolidate or expand land holding. Declining returns are offset by increases in
production capacity, and, more interestingly, as the farmers referred to in this case
study show, land may be used as a form of cultural capital to exploit opportunities
for profit from alternative non-agricultural sources. As stated, there are a number
of reasons why 'modern' farming may not be out of place in the post-productionist era; for example, the high levels of modernisation and remuneration. In showing that land holding consolidation and expansion can serve to facilitate
development of the kind of pluri-active economic strategies encouraged by recent
policy, the cases described here offer an additional and locally specific reason to
substantiate the argument.

Land holding reduction: justification, incompatibility of social imperatives and creative manipulation of ideas of tradition and identity

Because land holding reduction may be regarded as failure to fulfil an economic
ideal and land transfer a set of social imperatives, both may attract social sanc-

tions. However, justification for engaging in these practices is found through a number of means.

Readings of the economic, political and social climate facilitate representations of a growing incompatibility between provision of land and maintenance of social composition. Such representations reflect concerns beyond the obvious problem of the increasing shortage of farm successors. In some cases provision of land is seen as dangerously counterproductive. One young farmer angrily explained how his father had split up a viable farm, retaining only a few acres of land, in order to finance a series of high risk business ventures. The father justified his actions by reference to ideas about the need for farmers to be economically innovative, by pointing out that ownership of the farm would be threatened by his son's alimony payments, the poor prospects of the agricultural industry and, perversely, the woeful lack of commitment to farming amongst the young. In his words:

> embracing change is always what's kept farms here ahead of those in the south and west.[9] A failure to embrace change will result in his [son's] birthright becoming a complete dead duck . . . He'll be in debt up to his eyeballs with family maintenance to pay and a repossession order over his head. [Without] the love of the land [and] the experience of coping with the bad times that my generation had, he'll be packing his bags to join the other failures with the Provis down at Disneyland.[10]

This may be an extreme example. Nevertheless, similar fears lie behind commonplace modifications of the provision imperative. Land transfer by sale or renting is increasingly considered as a means of financing the kind of educational and business opportunities needed for siblings to survive in a harsh local economic climate. Indeed, for some, it is only through the kind of peri-urban development which transfer facilitates that a more diverse and dynamic economic climate can be developed. Even amongst the majority who intend to pass on land to their children, there is a significant number who feel that some land transfer out of the family is necessary in order to finance investment in other forms of provision, or in order to offset the threat to farm ownership posed by declining farm incomes.

Reduction of land holding and the transfer of land are also justified by creatively manipulating ideas of tradition and identity. The process of cultural compression discussed earlier is central in this respect. At one level boundaries of identity are eroded. This enables refinement of the land transfer codes. Spatial and temporal compression serve to legitimate the use of more inclusive forms of identity, and in some instances more flexible interpretations of endogamy, as the primary bases for sociality. Some people argue that with accelerating peri-urbanisation everyone can claim to be ruralite, urbanite, both or neither. Others argue that if many of the offcomers were to trace their ancestry back far enough, they would find that their own descendants were North Ards farmers. Consequently, the right of farming people to remain the principal custodians and owners of the local land is often regarded as nonsense based on a false view of rural isolation or on a short term view of history. Almost anyone in Northern Ireland can claim the right to land custodianship and purchase. Conversely, boundaries of identity are restated and enriched. Again, the ideas of Protestant non-conformity and individualism are important here. Through their representation as being at odds with the prevailing economic and social imperatives of land use, expansionist and consolidationist land holding strategies are condemned. For some, the persistence of modern farming and its expansionist orientation smacks of a conformity typical of the Republic of Ireland's Catholic farmers (Beale 1986), and not of Protestant non-conformity. For others, the goal of maintaining the social composition of the area through the operation of restrictive land transfer codes smacks of a collectivism typical of the Catholic farmer, and not of Protestant individualism. Also, when glossed as 'Ulster canniness', the ideas are celebrated as lying at the root of a trend towards land holding reduction and the speculative development culture in general. Such celebration takes place usually through public story-telling, as the following illustrates:

The story of William Browne
In an attempt to earn a little extra cash Mr. Browne made use of the milking sheds that had been made redundant when the farm was modernised and the land that immediately surrounded them. Without seeking planning approval, he converted one of the sheds into workshops. These were let out on an informal 'rent now, buy later' agreement to a number of small-scale entrepreneurs. His actions were risky. However, he had calculated that the planning office, aware of concern for local economic growth and the current Thatcherite talk of an enterprise culture, would not want to be responsible for the eviction of fledgling businesses. As it turned out, the calculation was correct. When word of the development was brought to the planning office, the workshops were granted approval.

Flush from the success of the first development, Mr. Browne decided to convert another shed into workshops. Aware that he would not get away with the same trick twice, but aware also that, having set a precedent, the planning office could hardly backtrack, he applied for planning approval in advance. It was granted. However, restrictions were placed on the kind of enterprises that could set up shop. These did not include the car body repair business, run by a Mr. MacShane, that two of the new workshops were rented out to. Initial whispers of disapproval from local residents developed into vocal protest. Keeping to the words of the planning office, their main concern seemed to be that this type of business was entirely inappropriate for a rural area such as this.

Mr. Browne was aware that the protest would only sway the planning office into forcing him to evict the new business. So, inspired by the dramatic protests of French farmers that he had read about in the *Farmers News*, he sought recourse to fairly drastic measures. Over a number of weeks he scoured the scrap merchants of Northern Ireland to obtain several large and unsightly items of redundant agricultural machinery. These were placed strategically throughout the farm for maximum public visibility.

This is one of a number of similar stories that are told and re-told locally. Its resonance lies in the celebration of a local farmer's display of cherished cultural traits. His manipulation of officialdom is typical of Protestant non-conformity. His form of counter-protest is typical of Protestant individualism. It may not have shown the French farmers' flair for aesthetics, symbolism or irony. They demonstrated their power through the chaos-making release of pigs in the Champs Elyseés, and their centrality to French public life by constructing a mock-up of the Louvre pyramid out of vegetables. Mr Browne's actions did not need to remind the protesters of their hypocrisy. The argument that the business was inappropriate concealed other concerns; the fact that its owner was Catholic, and the worry that it may become an eyesore. These were conveyed in the story-tellers' knowing tones. Instead, his actions parodied the protesters' image of the rural idyll. Country life has always been made possible by the kind of semi-industrialised activity against which the protest was directed. Beyond this, his actions constituted little more than an act of brute blackmail; shut-up or put-up with an even bigger eyesore. However, for the story-tellers his actions have a special significance. They resonate with ideas of Protestant tradition and identity. In particular, in his looking to the French for inspiration, he showed a creative and individualistic flair for turning the erstwhile alien into one's own.

Conclusion

This chapter has highlighted a set of fundamental contrasts within the responses of North Ards farmers to agricultural restructuring in the post-productionist era. The key to understanding these contrasts lies in the conceptualisation of responses as strategies, in a recognition of the differing roles that ideas of tradition and identity play in strategising, and in an appreciation of the impact that recent social changes have had on processes of identity construction.

Representations and practices

Almost all the farmers in the case study represent post-productionism as an era in which their farms are out of place. However, while many still persist with a 'modern', productionist style of farming, many others are adapting to 'new', post-productionist styles. The contrast between representations and practices cannot be put down solely to the fact that local farming consists increasingly of a combination of the modern and the new where, at one extreme, few farmers are embracing diversification in preference to specialisation and, at the other extreme, many are moving from growth-oriented to reduction-oriented land holding strategies. The contrast is rooted also in local farmers' conceptualisations of the research encounter.

Political and economic strategies

Agriculture is arguably the most comprehensively researched and reported of contemporary policy issues, and Northern Ireland is undoubtedly amongst the most
comprehensively researched and reported of European contexts (Whyte 1990). In
recent years much of the media coverage has highlighted the potentially negative
impacts of research on farming interests. One much discussed farm newspaper
article illustrates the point:

> information collected on a sample of 55,000 European farmers, including 3,500
> in the UK, could be used to draw up a hit list aimed at taking support away from
> those with non farming income. Hardly a just reward for those with the acumen to
> diversify out of food production (Fry 1991: 3).

Given the way in which research on farming is reported in this article, it is not surprising that Northern Irish farmers are often acutely aware of the links between
research and policy outcomes, and thus of the politicisation and potential counter-
productivity of the research encounter. The contrast between practices and representations can be regarded as a consequence of this awareness. The former
constitute the everyday manifestations of individual economic strategies. The latter constitute part of a set of political strategies which coalesce around the theme
of the local farmer as policy victim, and which are articulated through a range of
actions and contexts, from the representation-making of local MPs in Westminster
to the face-to-face representation-making of local farmers in the research
encounter.[11]

Constraint and enablement

The uses of ideas of tradition and identity differ according to strategy. In political
strategising they are represented almost invariably as constraining and in economic strategising as enabling. The contrast shows through in the representations
and practices surrounding the economic diversity route to farm survival. The articulation of a self-deprecating experiential reasoning grounded in assimilationist
visions and cultural stereotypes serves to represent local farmers as ill-equipped
to diversify. However, in some cases the status attached to significant land holding which derives from the fulfilment of social imperatives, of family provision
and maintenance of the social composition of the area, is used in order to develop
pluri-active strategies. It shows through also in the representations and practices
surrounding the possibility for movement from growth- to reduction-oriented land
holding strategies. Farmers are quick to point out that land transfer must be negotiated against a background of pervasive social imperatives. However, in practice
such transfer is justified through the creative manipulation of ideas of tradition and
identity. Finally, it shows through in representations and practices concerning

change in general. Almost all the farmers in the case study represent production-ism as an era of the ruralite and Protestant and post-productionism as an era of the urbanite and Catholic. However, they draw on ideas of Protestant non-conformity and individualism to justify changing farm practice.

Village voice and village voices

By drawing attention to these contrasts, the chapter has highlighted the sense in which responses to restructuring and the ideas of collective tradition and identity which inform them are intra-locally diverse. In so doing it has tried to escape the kind of excessively structure-centred approach to much research on agriculture which imputes an erroneous uniformity and assumes a single 'village voice'. Nevertheless, it has sought also to retain an appreciation of structural issues. In their strategising in general, and their construction of traditions and identities in particular, people draw upon a range of cultural resources and identity options which, because of social, economic and political change, is ever widening. This lies at the heart of the ability of local farmers to sustain and represent as unpara-doxical their contrastive practices and representations, economic and political strategies, and representations of identity as constraining or enabling. In this con-text of farming change, peri-urbanisation and changing ethno-religious demogra-phy, people can represent themselves simultaneously as, new post-productionist or modern productionist farmers, as urban-oriented or steadfastly rural people, and as non-sectarian liberal minded or steadfastly Protestant people with a con-cern for maintaining the social composition of the area. However, beyond this, maintenance of such contrasts requires also the deployment of a suitably flexible idiom. The ideas of individualism and non-conformity perform such a role. In political strategising local farmers represent themselves as constrained by tradi-tions and identities which leave them locked into a post-productionist model of farming. In economic strategising they represent their traditions and identities as enabling adaptation to post-productionist models of farming. However, dualities of constraint and enablement, uniformity and diversity, and tradition and change are rendered irrelevant by the ideas of individualism and non-conformity. They serve to portray Protestantism as a collective identity of idiosyncrasy and as a tra-dition of anti-traditionalism.

Notes

1. Research for the chapter was carried out as part of the Economic and Social Research Council sponsored 'Changing Farm Economies' project. The ethnographic component of this multi-disciplinary project considered the social and cultural dimensions of eco-nomic decision-making on farm households in Northern Ireland.

2.   Similar approaches have been applied to the study of rural social life in Northern Ireland. For example, using Goffman's dramaturgical perspective and his distinction between 'front-stage' and 'back-stage' forms of behaviour, Larsen (1982) points to a process of identity manipulation whereby violence is avoided, but the construction of ethnic stereotypes is facilitated. This chapter does not share this widespread interest in the issue of violence avoidance. However, it does share the central idea of the resourceful and strategic use of identity.

3.   A reference to the Common Agricultural Policy.

4.   In the context of farming the reasons for purchase and sale are various. In most cases they are direct responses to declining incomes wrought by anti-productionist measures. Sometimes this fits the general pattern of the expansion of some farms at the expense of others. Land is purchased to facilitate expansion. Land is sold to meet debts or to facilitate partial or total departure from farming. Sometimes it does not fit the general pattern. Land is sold to finance the consolidation or expansion of existing farm enterprises. In a smaller number of cases the reasons are a direct response to the income opportunities brought by the promotion of economic diversity. Varied types of land are purchased in order to compete in a market place that demands greater product diversity, and to maximise absorption of the shifting range of subsidies. Also, land is sold to finance development of new farm or non-farm enterprises. This list of reasons is not exhaustive.

5.   This was recorded by Iain Macaulay, one of the project team members, in West Fermanagh and presented in a preliminary fieldwork report.

6.   One would expect further refinements of land ownership transfer codes with the increasing internationalisation of local land sale (Pepinster 1996).

7.   Indeed, North Ards has become something of a heartland for non-sectarian political party organisation. It is, by and large, regarded as the natural home for the Alliance Party and the fledgling Northern Irish Conservative Party.

8.   For example, 1974 saw the active participation of many local people in protest against the power-sharing Sunningdale Agreement. The images of otherwise law-abiding local farmers blocking the roads with their tractors loom large in local memory. Also, 1993 saw a significant rise in the local vote for the Democratic Unionist Party, perhaps the most sectarian of Protestant political parties.

9.   An oblique reference to Catholic farming, since the major concentrations of the Catholic population in Ireland are in the south and the west.

10.   A reference to the Disney World development which, at the time of research, was under construction in Paris. A large number of Irish workers was involved in its construction. Among the many stories which surrounded the construction was one claiming that the residential quarters for labourers on the site were being used as a refuge for Republican paramilitary fugitives, and a storage point for illegal ammunition from eastern Europe awaiting transportation to Ireland.

11.   The term representation is used here in its dual sense, meaning both interpretation and advocacy (James, Hockey and Dawson 1996).

References

Barth, F. 1969. Introduction. In F. Barth (ed.), *Ethnic Groups and Boundaries: the Social Organisation of Cultural Difference*. London: Allen and Unwin.

Beale, J. 1986. *Women in Ireland: Voices of Change*. London: Macmillan.

Buckley, A.D. 1982. *A Gentle People: A Study of a Peaceful Community in Ulster.* Cultra, Co. Down: Ulster Folk and Transport Museum.

Bufwack, M.F. 1982. *Village Without Violence: an Examination of a Northern Irish Community.* Cambridge Mass.: Schenkman.

Boon, J.A. 1982. *Other Tribes, Other Scribes: Symbolic Anthropology in the Comparative Study of Cultures. Histories, Religions and Texts.* Cambridge: Cambridge University Press.

Bowler, I.R. 1985. *Agriculture Under the Common Agricultural Policy.* Manchester: Manchester University Press.

Bruce, S. 1994. *The Edge of the Union: the Ulster Loyalist Political Vision.* Oxford: Oxford University Press.

Cockcroft, W.H. 1978. *Review of Rural Planning Policy: Report of the Committee under the Chairmanship of Dr. W. H. Cockcroft MA, DPhil, FIMA.* Belfast: HMSO.

Cohen, A. P. 1987. *Whalsay: Symbol, Segment and Boundary in a Shetland Island Community.* Manchester: Manchester University Press.

_____. 1989. *The Symbolic Construction of Community.* London: Routledge.

Cole, J. 1977. Anthropology comes part-way home: community studies in Europe. *Annual Review of Anthropology* 6, 349–78.

Crotty, R. 1986. *Ireland in Crisis: a Study in Capitalist Colonial Underdevelopment.* Dingle: Brandon.

DANI (Department of Agriculture Northern Ireland) 1990. *Annual Statistical Review.* Belfast: HMSO.

Dawson, A. 1994. Cultural identity and economic decision-making in three peripheral areas of rural Europe: a comparative ethnographic account. In J. Phelan, P. Bogue and M. Henchion (eds.), *Constraints and Competitiveness in EC Agriculture: a Comparative Analysis.* Dublin: University College Dublin.

Drummond, L. 1980. The cultural continuum: a theory of intersystems. *Man* 15, 352–374

Ennew, J. 1980. *The Western Isles Today.* Cambridge: Cambridge University Press.

European Society for Rural Sociology 1995. *XVI Congress,* 'From Productionism to Sustainable Rural Development? The Transformation of Rural Economy, Society and Space in the Late 20th Century'. Prague.

Fry, J. 1991. Diversify and loose grants. *Farm News* 15 November 1991, p. 3.

Fischer, M.J.M. 1986. Ethnicity and the Post-Modern Arts of Memory. In J. Clifford and G. Marcus (eds.), *Writing Culture: The Poetics and Politics of Ethnography: Experiments in Contemporary Anthropology.* Berkeley: University of California Press.

Gasson, R. and A. Errington 1993. *The Family Farm Business.* Wallingford: CAB International.

Haan, H. de 1994. *In the Shadow of the Tree: Kinship. Property and Inheritance Among Farm Families.* Amsterdam: Hetspinhuis.

Herzfeld, M. 1985. *The Poetics of Manhood: Contest and Identity in a Cretan Mountain Village.* Princeton: Princeton University Press.

Hobsbawm, P. and T. Ranger (eds.) 1983. *The Invention of Tradition.* Cambridge: Cambridge University Press.

James, A., J. Hockey and A. Dawson (eds.) 1996. *After Writing Culture: the Practice and Politics of Representation.* London: Routledge.

Larsen, S. 1982. Two sides of the house: identity and social organisation in Kilbroney, Northern Ireland. In A. P. Cohen (ed.), *Belonging: Identity and Social Organisation in British Rural Cultures.* Manchester: Manchester University Press.

Lowe, P., G. Cox, M. Macewen, T. O'Riordan and M. Winter 1986. *Countryside Conflicts: The Politics of Farming. Forestry and Conservation.* Hants: Temple Smith/Gower.

Mansvelt Beck, J. 1988. *The Rise of the Subsidized Periphery in Spain. A Geographical Study of State and Market Relations in the Eastern Montes Orientales of Granada.* Amsterdam: Netherlands Geographical Studies 69.

Milton, K. 1990. *Our Countryside Our Concern: the Policy and Practice of Conservation in Northern Ireland.* Antrim: Northern Ireland Environment Link.

Mormont, M. 1990. Who is rural?, or how to be rural. In T. Marsden, P. Lowe and S. Whatmore (eds.), *Rural Restructuring: Global Processes and their Responses.* London: David Fulton Publishers.

Paine, R. 1992. The Marabar Caves, 1920-2020. In S. Wallman (ed.), *Contemporary Futures.* London: Routledge.

Pepinster, C. 1996. If you meet a farmer who tells you he's poor, he's lying. *Independent on Sunday,* 3 March p. 5.

Phelan, J. and A. Markey (eds.) 1993. *Constraints and Competitiveness in EC Agriculture: a Comparative Analysis.* Dublin: University College Dublin.

Pile, S. 1990. *The Private Farmer.* Aldershot: Dartmouth Publishing Company.

Rapport, N. 1993. *Diverse World Views In an English Village.* Edinburgh: Edinburgh University Press.

Redclift, M. 1986. Survival strategies in rural Europe: continuity and change. *Sociologia Ruralis* 26 (3–4), 218–27.

Sahlins, M. 1968. *Tribesmen.* Englewood Cliffs, N. J.: Prentice-Hall.

Shortall, S. 1994. Farm women's groups and the concept of farming in Northern Ireland. Paper presented at American Anthropological Association conference, Atlanta.

Tarrow, S. 1977. *Between Center and Periphery.* Yale: Yale University Press.

van der Ploeg, J. D. and N. Long (eds.) 1994. *Born from Within: Practice and Perspectives of Endogenous Rural Development.* (European Perspectives on Rural Development). Assen: van Gorcum.

Whatmore, S. 1988. From women's roles to gender relations: developing perspectives in the analysis of farm women. *Sociologia Ruralis* 28 (4), 239–62.

Whyte, J. 1990. *Interpreting Northern Ireland.* Oxford: Oxford University Press.

Winter, M. 1991. The sociology of religion and rural society. A review article. *Sociologia Ruralis* 31 (2–3), 199–208.

4 Inside the citadel: rural development policy in practice

Iain Macaulay

This chapter is based on ethnographic fieldwork carried out in West Fermanagh as part of the Changing Farm Economies and CAMAR Projects. The Changing Farm Economies Project was conscientiously multi-disciplinary. It approached the condition of farming in Northern Ireland from several different theoretical and methodological angles with the aim of providing a comprehensive analysis of its social, cultural, economic, political and environmental aspects. This ecumenical approach created an opening for the ethnographic component to inform and draw inspiration from other disciplines. It created the conditions for the ethnography to comment on the culture of policy-making, as well as on the local impact of policy, which is, perhaps, more familiar territory for policy-oriented research in anthropology.

An ethnography of farming is intrinsically a grassroots investigation of the social and cultural complexion of farming communities and the farm household: an orientation that is a secure orthodoxy in rural sociology too. However, farming is circumscribed by a regime of support which is the antithesis of the local. In some ways, the pervasiveness and sheer immensity of the Common Agricultural Policy (CAP), which infiltrates the minutiae of local and household decision-making, invites a top down sociology and anthropology of farming. An economist and commentator on agricultural policy, Andy Conway, writes:

> That the international context conditions the development of rural areas is abundantly clear from the effects which GATT negotiations are having on the future options for farming and agricultural policy. The EC, having used the 'benefits of free trade' as an argument in favour of the single market, cannot reasonably argue that international free trade is not good on a wider international basis. The EC has agreed that agriculture should become more market-oriented and that there will be substantial progressive reductions in agricultural support and protection (Conway 1991: 10).

The political obliquity of the CAP would resurrect a Marxist approach to the ethnography of farming (see Bergmann 1990). So, the alternation of focus from the culture of the farm household to the culture of the policy-makers is not an indulgence. It is a necessary part of a full ethnography of farming.

The Changing Farm Economies Project was built around a questionnaire which sought to elicit information about the structure of the farm economy, farmers' responses to radical changes in the regime of supports which have buttressed the farm economy, and their attitudes and opinions about farming in a time of uncertainty and change. The ethnographic research was conducted alongside the questionnaire, with the intention that its findings would fill out and colour the statistical portrait of the farm economy generated by the questionnaire and perhaps provoke a higher level of interpretation of that data. At the same time, a qualitative study of the political culture of the policy-makers was undertaken.

Related projects were carried out simultaneously in England, Wales and Scotland. These promised to add a multi-national dimension to the Northern Ireland study, stimulating cross-regional comparisons of the farm economy, and revealing what is uniquely different about farming in Northern Ireland. The CAMAR project built on this methodology, but extended the geographic horizons of the research to encompass Greece and the Republic of Ireland. Both the Changing Farm Economies Project and the CAMAR Project were thus multi-disciplinary, multi-national and cross-cultural, and provided a secure foundation for anthropology to comment on public policy.

At the root of the ethnographic research were very practical questions about the economic activity and the social fabric of farm households in West Fermanagh; information which could be converted into an analysis of the social, cultural and economic orientation of farming communities. However, this chapter attempts a kind of binocular vision, seeking to isolate some of the fixed points in the farmers' world view, whilst also attempting to locate the essentials of the rural policy-makers' perspective. The common ground where farming communities and policy-makers meet is in rural development. Rural development is no longer on the periphery of the changing farm economy. It is at the heart of agricultural policy and support.

West Fermanagh

North Down and West Fermanagh were chosen as the ethnographic study areas. The choice was made to sample the Northern Ireland farm economy at opposite ends of a spectrum of production and opportunity. North Down is considered to be Northern Ireland's agricultural 'Garden of Eden'. It is the cradle of market gardening with an exceptionally good growing environment. Farmers are thought to enjoy ideal conditions for farming and to be amongst the vanguard of progressive farmers. North Down is also a peri-urban setting abutting Belfast. Farmers, therefore, neighbour the major produce markets. They can diversify production and land management with some prospect of a market demand.

In contrast, West Fermanagh is considered to be peripheral. Fermanagh is the westernmost county of Northern Ireland, removed from the political and economic engine house on the eastern seaboard of the province. The sense of belonging to a discrete political province—whatever interpretation is placed on that membership—dissipates along Northern Ireland's east/west axis. In Northern Ireland, the West is invested with the kind of mythic connotations of the American frontier. But it does not achieve the heroic proportions of that frontier. Instead, Northern Ireland's West is defined by its distance from the political and economic hegemony in the East and associated with a kind of primitivism, which can either be a demonstration of a lost or alternative lifestyle or can symbolise a menacing non-rational mentality. This very basic cultural caricature is extended to agriculture and often lodged in the farming community.

At the edge of West Fermanagh is the border with the Republic of Ireland— another actual and symbolic space. Though it has erected a political and economic wall between Fermanagh and the adjoining counties in the Republic of Ireland— Monaghan, Cavan, Leitrim and Donegal—many communities dispersed along the border in Fermanagh are still oriented to neighbouring settlements in the Republic. The preservation of these social ties, forged several generations ago, reinforces the county's isolation. Within the county, the pattern of settlement is dispersed, with townlands as the warp and weft which makes the local tapestry. Though Enniskillen, the county town, is the powerful commercial hub of the county, the rural townland communities seek a distinct social identity, based primarily on kinship, but also on a shared sense of belonging which is consolidated by something more than family ties— in many cases the solidarity of a community under threat.

That threat is of deprivation and disadvantage. The economic profile of Fermanagh encourages a downbeat appraisal of the prospects for its people. Agriculture is 'two to three times more important in the NI economy as a whole than it is to the UK' (Moss et al 1991: 39). In 1987 an estimated 7.9 per cent of Northern Ireland's population was employed in agriculture, forestry and fishing, with 'a further 3 per cent of civil employment . . . provided by the ancillary sectors' (Moss et al 1991: 39). The local Department of Agriculture Executive has shown that farming accounts for 42 per cent of Fermanagh's workforce (Morrow and O'Neill 1986: 2). Manufacturing was decimated during the 1980s. The service sector, which retains the same percentage of the working population, is heavily dependent on the fortunes of farming. It is a monolithic agricultural economy.

Yet, farming in the county is not remunerative. Low-lying land is blanketed by a ubiquitous, heavy glacial till and uplands are peat-covered. The land is wet— it rains two days out of every three and 10 per cent of the land is covered by lake or river—the soil unpliable, and farming is almost entirely restricted to grassland enterprises such as dairying, beef production and sheep. While that picture corresponds to the statistical profile of farming in Northern Ireland, the dependence on grassland enterprise is more extreme and ingrained in Fermanagh where it accounts for 98 per cent of the Total Gross Margin from farming. Because of its agricultural poverty, 92 per cent of Fermanagh is designated *Older* Less Favoured Area and 6 per cent *New* Less Favoured Area. Unemployment, largely structural unemployment in the county's towns, fluctuates around the 25 per cent mark. Endemic under-employment on farm holdings which do not constitute a labour unit is considered by economists an equal and perhaps more corrosive evil.

The farm economy, already elementally disadvantaged, is exhibiting signs of strain and decay. Dairying has traditionally been the mainstay of the full-time family farm in Northern Ireland's grassland economy. In Fermanagh it is also the most inherently profitable grassland enterprise; in 1991, dairying generated 41 per cent of the Total Gross Margin from only 15 per cent of the number of cattle kept in the county. That year, the average annual income from a dairy cow was £ 590 with the prospect of £ 250 for the sale of its progeny, a drop calf; a suckler cow and its calf could expect to earn their owner a little less than £ 350. As well as offering greater profit, dairying provides a regular monthly income against the customary annual cheque from the sale of cattle *stores* and lambs. Although there has been an increase in productivity in the dairying sector over the past five years, the number of dairy cattle has dropped by 15 per cent, betraying a widespread retreat from dairying. Despite the decline of the dairy herd in the county, the total number of cattle has increased, and this highlights an inexorable gravitation to beef production. Yet the contribution of beef production to the Total Gross Margin from farming has remained static, demonstrating the depressed state of the marketplace for beef, and the precarious position of farmers who have come to rely on that marketplace for their livelihood, something further exacerbated since the BSE crisis. Sheep numbers have increased dramatically in these five years and the Total Gross Margin from sheep production has doubled, something advocated strongly in the Maher Report (1986). However, the rising prominence of sheep in the farm enterprise has been brought about by the decision of many of the more prosperous dairy farmers, escaping from restrictive quotas and exacting milk standards, to divert partially to sheep production. This re-orientation of the dairy farm enterprise, encouraged by the attractive subsidies offered on breeding ewes in LFAs, has generated competition with traditional mountain sheep farmers and flooded the marketplace with lambs, depressing prices for all.

With respect to farming, West Fermanagh conforms to the axiomatic western slide to hyperbole: go west and the soil is poorer and the land more mountainous. It is the farmers in West Fermanagh, set down on the heavy clay soils of the lowlands or the bare rock and steep gradients of the limestone uplands, who have led this most recent retreat from dairying. In 1980 a team of agronomists from Loughry College carried out an audit of farming in the Knockninny district, which abuts the study area, and returned a decade later to repeat the study (Stevenson and Martin 1983; Loughry College 1990). Dairying had declined from a 54 per cent share of active farms to 35 per cent. Dairying had occupied 75 per cent of farms in 1970. On smaller farms—the majority of farm holdings on the lowlands of West Fermanagh are under 40 acres—the surrender of dairying to beef production, where it coincides with succession, usually means a shift from full-time to part-time farming. Beef farming in Fermanagh is at the dead end of an atrophying chain of production. It produces a low grade raw material—a store calf—which is finished elsewhere. The commodity price and surplus value are lost.

Symbolising deprivation

Reduced to its statistical essence, the West Fermanagh farm economy exhibits the traits of dissolution and an apparently terminal decline. Farming is corralled in a depressed grassland economy, and farms are retreating to the rump of that economy: farms are small; there is low income, high dependence on transfers, chronic unemployment, and under-employment; the population is ageing—in Knockninny 48 per cent of farmers were over 60; the young and old are abandoning the country for the county towns. The academic interest of the place is high. If the intention is to examine farming at the edge, this is surely the place to be. The study area was, correspondingly, drawn around some of West Fermanagh's most marginal mountain land.

The ethnographic work in West Fermanagh revealed a far more complex picture of farming there than a voyage around the statistics and the literature would suggest. Numerous quirks subverted expectations. For example, mountain sheep farming on the poorest bogland is one of the last strongholds of the full-time family farm. The discovery of detail behind a wash of statistics is both an experience of anthropologists and a vocation: indeed, both projects sought to use ethnography for this purpose. What made the given profile problematic was that it conscientiously illuminated—almost as an iconography—all the facets of decay in the farm economy.

Nevertheless, the statistical portrait remains unavoidably a genuine likeness of the farm economy. It corresponds to the experience of farmers and reveals the challenges they face. At the same time, the choice of West Fermanagh as a study site for the Changing Farm Economies and CAMAR Projects was being almost subliminally guided by the transfiguration of West Fermanagh from a locality to an incarnation of rural deprivation.

The academic journey to West Fermanagh made here retraces a route trailblazed by the policy-making community which pioneered rural development thinking and practice in Northern Ireland. My contention is that the transfiguration of West Fermanagh has been achieved by them, almost unconsciously. It is not that they have somehow misunderstood or miscast the conditions of existence for the farmers and the rural communities of West Fermanagh which they embody. It is that they have re-invented West Fermanagh as a fixture in conceptual space which is encompassed by the touchstones of rural development thought, and that their and our understanding of the area is then driven by the lexicon and grammar of that thinking. This inevitably opens a gap with what people who inhabit the place experience and articulate as everyday life.

This process of symbolising deprivation as a place and vice versa is akin to what Ardener (1987) describes for the ascription of remoteness. What the rural development thinkers and policy-makers have done with West Fermanagh can, without too great an intellectual caprice, be likened to an objectifying anthropology as Bourdieu (1977) conceives it. That contention lifts this examination of how rural development thought has impacted on the West Fermanagh study area out of the commonplace, which would be a functional analysis of the socio-political content of rural development thought and its operation, into a more anthropological discourse which treats policy-making as a cultural activity. A *cultural* approach, incidentally, offers some explanation for the conundrums which policy-makers have faced in enacting policy objectives.

The process of transfiguring West Fermanagh from place to symbol has been assisted by the location there of several landmark projects which have helped define the experience of rural deprivation and shape the discourse on rural development. This culminated in 1991 with the creation of a government-supported Rural Development Council and the arrival, considered long overdue, of a rural development policy for Northern Ireland: this is a significant event in latter day policy-making for Northern Ireland.

A classic landmark deprivation study for West Fermanagh is the *Roslea Housing Study* (NI Housing Executive 1987). The finding of this study were dramatic—43 per cent of rural houses were, using statutory criteria, *unfit,* in 1974 and, by 1984, 27 per cent were still unfit. But, the study's impact was deeper than the surface shock it delivered. It legitimised housing as an emblem of rural deprivation and a theme in rural development. Five years later the Housing Executive's radical re-draft of its rural housing policy, *The Way Ahead* (NI Housing Executive 1991a; see also 1991b), has embraced the bottom up—community development—philosophy, which anchors rural development thinking in Northern Ireland, and translated that philosophy into a policy initiative for rural housing. The ancestry of that initiative can be traced directly to the Roslea Housing Study. The assimilation of that study into the policy-making community where it assumed iconic proportions helped to objectify Roslea as a symbol, as well as a place, of rural deprivation, and that symbolisation extended comfortably to encompass West Fermanagh.

It was the arrival, in 1986, of the Rural Action Project (RAP) riding the crest of the European Community's Second Anti-Poverty Programme which confirmed West Fermanagh`s credentials as an incarnation of rural deprivation. Prior to the Rural Action Project, rural deprivation and rural development were in the blind spot of government and its policy makers. Reviewing the Rural Action Project's work at the end of its term in 1991, Kilmurray wrote:

The concept of a regional rural community development body was decidedly novel in the Northern Ireland context, while the realisation of the potential extent of poverty in rural areas was also a matter that had received little attention (Kilmurray 1991: 12).

The timing of the RAP initiative was propitious:

> What was generated in the late 80s, however, was a clear demand for governmental action to address the problems of disadvantaged rural communities across Northern Ireland . . . In addition to this, prevailing winds of change were also felt at an economic and EC policy level: the CAP had been under serious review for a number of years and an important policy document, 'The Future of Rural Society', had given rise to a re-evaluation of rural development. The latter was to emphasise such approaches as farm diversification, community involvement in forward planning and an 'integrated rural development' concept, which were all issues that related closely to RAP initiatives (Kilmurray 1991: 2).

RAP was to act as a conduit of embryonic EC and government policy for rural areas, which meant channelling information from Brussels and Belfast to local communities. At the same time, it was to imbibe grassroots experience of deprivation and to translate that into community action for change. Despite its origins in a directive of the European Community policy-making constituency, which is popularly represented as an hermetically sealed bureaucratic culture, RAP had adopted an exemplary community development approach to rural development. It chose to be rooted in the local community, and West Fermanagh became one of its four target communities in Northern Ireland. The community development approach which RAP pursued is analogous to an anthropology with a conscience, though the fixation with action and achieving change which the funders imposed, meant that RAP did not have the luxury of intellectual self-scrutiny. There was, however, an unmistakable academic pedigree in the RAP approach.

The Rural Action Project was established in Belcoo and drew a West Fermanagh study area around the village. The arrival of the Rural Action Project and its early publication of a West Fermanagh Study Area Report (Ditch 1987), which conscientiously identified the emblems of rural deprivation in the local area, confirmed the entry of West Fermanagh into the gallery of rural deprivation.

West Fermanagh had become a place where an ailment—rural deprivation—was acted on by an experiment in rural development. Though RAP applied borders to its West Fermanagh study area, within the policy-making community it is not a bounded geographic space. The title has been used to refer to all points on a 50 mile east-west stretch of Fermanagh from Roslea to Garrison. Locally, Roslea is south, or south-east Fermanagh but, because it has become associated with rural deprivation, it is assimilated into the rural development lexicon as West Fermanagh. This imprecision has been deliberately preserved in the work of the Rural Development Council, an offshoot of the Rural Action Project. The Council began by isolating and prioritising the areas of rural Northern Ireland where the

problems of multiple rural deprivation were deepest. The Chairman of the Council
wrote:

> In the late 80s, the Policy Planning and Research Unit (PPRU) defined the distrib-
> ution of disadvantaged areas in Northern Ireland to facilitate the resource alloca-
> tion decisions of the International Fund for Ireland. Using the 1981 population
> census results and levels of male unemployment as the primary indicator, 181 elec-
> toral wards were identified as disadvantaged. An attempt to broaden the index by
> including three other variables relating to housing standards and level of car own-
> ership brought in 19 new electoral wards. This spatial distribution of deprivation is
> perhaps easiest described as consisting of five regions: the Glens of Antrim, the
> Sperrins, Fermanagh, the Loughshore, and South Down and South Armagh (Smyth
> 1991: 5).

Though, contrarily, the title has become Fermanagh, the focus of the
Council's work continues to be in the real and symbolic West Fermanagh.
However, the bottom up edict which was carried through from the Rural Action
Project and enshrined in the Council's mission statements, has been conceived as
all-encompassing:

> The approach we have adopted to assist community groups in Northern Ireland is
> one where, if the group can demonstrate that their area is disadvantaged, then we
> would be more than happy to provide them with assistance (GARCDA and Rural
> Community Network 1992: 32).

Thus, it is less belonging to a geographic space which qualifies a rural community for assistance from the rural development initiatives, than its capacity to
become articulate in the discourse about rural deprivation. This is the logical conclusion of the symbolisation process.

Rural development and the rural community

The argument that West Fermanagh is no longer simply a rural place where people suffer from deprivation—and it should not be forgotten that the epithet of rural
is itself subject to constant scrutiny and re-definition—but a conceptual landmark
invested with the emblems of rural deprivation is persuasive. What makes West
Fermanagh a compelling case, both for the rural development community and
here in an analysis of that community at work, is that it possesses not only the hall-
marks of rural deprivation but the qualities of what policy-makers envisage as the
rural landscape of the future. West Fermanagh exists in the corners of the rural
development world view not just as an image of the problem of rural deprivation,
but as a representation of its resolution. This duality was encapsulated by
Fermanagh District Council's Principal Policy and Resources Officer in a speech
to the Irish Planning Institute's 1991 Annual General Meeting:

County Fermanagh . . . is at the extreme western periphery of the province bordered on by four of the six Republic of Ireland border counties. It reflects a general EC trend in that its main opportunities lie with its growing tourism industry and its main limitation is found in its dependence on its primary industry of agriculture. Therefore, while it is considered the 'jewel in the crown' of the Northern Ireland tourism industry for its superb quality of landscape and successful tourism product, at one and the same time, it is also recognised by the Department of Agriculture NI, the Rural Action Project, the Rural Development Council and the EC (98 per cent is of Less Favoured Area status) as an area of extreme rural deprivation.

Tourism in a conserved landscape is regarded as a mainstay of the rural economy of the future. As agriculture atrophies, tourism will enter and fill the economic void which the decline of farming creates. The go-west ordinance applies to the future farm economy. The green tourism exalted in the Northern Ireland Tourist Board's *Tourism in Northern Ireland: An Indicative Plan 1990-1995,* and placed at the heart of Fermanagh District Council's own *Tourism Strategic Development Initiative,* will occur in the county's most appealing landscapes. In this conceptual and policy framework which, in fact, has a forty-year ancestry, aesthetic appeal conventionally coincides with conservation value. The parts of Fermanagh with a high conservation value were identified by the Countryside and Wildlife Branch of the Department of the Environment in its study, *Fermanagh: Its Special Landscapes.* In this document two ecosystems of extraordinary conservation value were isolated and proposed for designation as Areas of Outstanding Natural Beauty (AONB): the Erne Lakeland AONB and the Caveland AONB.

The putative Caveland AONB lies over much of West Fermanagh. Already West Fermanagh is home to one of Northern Ireland's top tourist attractions, the Marble Arch showcaves. The showcaves are a local government venture, but they are hailed in both the Maher Report (1986) and the Northern Ireland Tourist Board's *Indicative Plan* (1990) as an archetype of green tourism. In the future rural economy, local people and local communities, including farmers, will exploit their cultural and natural heritage in the environment for tourism.

West Fermanagh is thus a crucible in which the contrary elements of deprivation and opportunity are fused in a rural development experiment. However, the indispensable flux for this experiment is people. West Fermanagh is once again perceived to be in a position of advantage. Fermanagh's Principal Policy and Resources Officer remarked:

However, despite such anomalies, Fermanagh's population increased . . . over the past ten years. The question we may ask is why? What is keeping the people here? The answer lies with the people themselves and the strong sustaining community identity and spirit that refuses to lie down, but instead faces up to and challenges adversity.

The West Fermanagh communities which became the laboratory for the Rural Action Project were tempered in the fire of this experiment to emerge as self-confident, award-winning local organisations. RAP had a twin focus in West Fermanagh. It worked with the people of Belcoo village and the surrounding district to establish organisations representative of local opinion and aspirations. These organisations partnered RAP in shaping a local development plan which was published as the *Belcoo and District Area Plan* (Quinn 1988). This was a classical exercise in community development. In the meantime, RAP had initiated a Farm Diversification Programme working, this time, on a one-to-one basis with local farmers (Rural Action Project 1991; see also Rural Action Project 1990). The Programme sought both to cultivate a set of diversification projects, conceived by local farmers, and to import new ideas and test these on local farms.

Visionary statements

Whether RAP succeeded in remaining cognisant of, and faithful to, its original aims, and was able to implement these grand designs in West Fermanagh, is not the province of this chapter. RAP was always conscientious about self scrutiny, and Kilmurray's analysis of RAP's work (Kilmurray 1991) and the Farm Diversification Programme Final Report (RAP 1991), as well as advertising the successes of the Project, admitted and agonised over the failures.

The pivot of a functional analysis of the impact of the rural development initiatives in West Fermanagh would be the meeting of the Project and the local community. It would look at how the community responded to the RAP message and offer of assistance. Such an analysis would likely uncover an indigenous re-modelling of community. In the last ten years community organisations have emerged from the grassroots throughout Fermanagh, with the most vigorous being in West Fermanagh. In a Community Services Strategy Document: 1991–1995, Fermanagh District Council was able to demonstrate a blossoming of community action. In 1976, when the community services function was inaugurated in the Council, community action was galvanised almost entirely by. external forces, such as the Church, sports associations and political organisations. In 1985, a classical pro-active and integrationist community development approach was adopted by the community services function in Council. Between 1985 and 1991 the number of community associations—which are mostly rural—more than tripled, rising from 15 to 52. Village associations doubled—from 11 to 22—and townland associations, a new phenomenon in 1985, numbered 16 at the time of research. There was a corresponding rise in the number of credit unions, senior citizens' clubs, playgroups and women's health groups, all of which are dispersed throughout rural Fermanagh. The Council added to its own stock of community centres, and eight new independent community centres were built to house these activities.

Alongside this modest but significant reorganisation of the social order in rural Fermanagh, there was a cultural revival. Historical societies sprang up across the county, the mummers' and rhymers' group, which performs a primitive play laden with elemental imagery, was reborn, and traditional music, song and dance thrived as the expression of an indigenous tradition and as a cultural export.

Sociologists and anthropologists treat a flowering of community spirit, especially when nurtured by formal community organisations, with extreme caution. In the literature of rural sociology, especially in the classic rural England community studies, incomers or professionals project the community voice to the outside world. That voice rarely matches the pitch of the people's voice. However, the Fermanagh experience is quite different. The community groups are all genuinely grassroots.

The other obstacle to the acceptance of the siren call of a community voice is the realisation that it can be manufactured by external agencies. Certainly, the remarkable blossoming of community organisation and action in Fermanagh would not have occurred without the intervention of a strong community services department in the Council. The Department's mission statement confirms its interventionist credo and could lead to a suspicion that the animation of community has been the result of a piece of social engineering:

> Community services in Fermanagh recognises and values the rich diversity of community life in the County. It is strategically placed to identify local needs and to promote an integrated approach to the effective targeting of resources from many sectors towards meeting those needs. The overall aim of the Department being that of enhancement, preservation and improvement in the quality of life for all socially, culturally, economically and intercommunally (Fermanagh District Council n.d.: frontispiece).

However, it is a plausible argument that the strength and clarity of the voice projected by Fermanagh's community groups springs from a rooted and independent collective will and, though it is often a voice raised in instinctive protest at the speed of social and economic change and its destination, it is equally often a voice calling policy-makers into an alliance and joint action.

The network of community groups provides a template which the rural development policy-makers and practitioners can engage. This is a synapse across which rural development policy passes, and which will, together with the CAP reform, re-shape the farm economy. The meeting of community groups and rural development policy-makers and practitioners is an interesting social event. It is also a challenge to the orthodoxy of rural sociology which has devolved its focus to the farm household. In West Fermanagh, the farm household is the building block of the farm economy, but the community groups are arbiters of change and in the vanguard of it. It has become customary to examine the socio-economic condition of farming from the threshold of the farm household. But to understand the direction and impact of policy in West Fermanagh, and the way in which the farmer and the farm household orient themselves to that policy, the view from the community must be considered.

LEADER and INTERREG, two of the principal funds for the European Community's rural development vision, percolate only as far as the local community level. The EC Structural Funds, mediated through Northern Ireland's Community Support Framework—Northern Ireland is an Objective 1 region— engage community groups. Farmers in West Fermanagh can tap the Agricultural Development Operational Programme (ADOP), which originates in the EAGGF Structural Fund, and the Farm and Conservation Grant Scheme, as well as the Rural Development Council's own Farm Diversification Scheme. But the kind of grassland farming which is ubiquitous in West Fermanagh is viewed as irredeemably dependent on supports, and these are gradually being removed from the tarnished ground of agricultural intensification and re-installed in the hallowed ground of diversification and rural development. In this way farmers' actions are being moulded to match the rural development vision.

A strictly functional analysis of the introduction of rural development policy into West Fermanagh does reveal a seismic movement in the embedded social structure, and also suggests that the orthodox vision which rural sociology carries to the farm economy and the farm household might need to be revised in this new policy scenario. But the negotiation of rural development policy is not purely a pragmatic introduction of new constraints and opportunities for the farm household and community groups. It involves the negotiation of a vision and, for anthropologists, this is an equally compelling and instructive exchange.

The Rural Development Council's vision for the rural communities of Northern Ireland is expressed as follows:

> Our vision is of a vibrant rural society with a rich quality of life, a sound, sustainable economy and a high quality environment with suitable housing reflecting the traditional settlement pattern. We will strive to play our part in providing employment through viable businesses, agricultural development and enterprise based on a firm foundation of local, decentralised community participation, underpinned by appropriate Government policies.

This vision is inherently interesting because it establishes not just a set of objectives but an iconography of the new farm economy and rural world. It is also interesting because it is a local expression of a wider vision which the European Community has composed for rural Europe (see Commission of the European Community 1988). It is regularly expressed by Eurocrats like Ray McSharry, the EC Agricultural Commissioner, who gave voice to it at 'Rural Europe `92: New Beginnings', a showcase conference to launch Britain's premiership of the European Community:

> I do not need to convince anyone here of the importance of rural development to Europe as a whole, or of the challenges which rural areas are facing. Let me remind you that rural areas account for 80 per cent of the territory of the European Community and nearly 50 per cent of its population. It used to be considered that their main purpose was to be the providers of food. Now, in addition to that role,

they have increasingly become the providers of a much wider range of goods and services to the rest of the population. Agriculture, which in 1950 involved 21 per cent of the economically active population, now involves only about 7 per cent—a loss of two thirds; between 1970 and 1987 some 800,000 farms disappeared. In many rural areas this trend has led to the abandonment of the land and a serious deterioration in the quality of the environment. The drift of population away from many of our rural areas is a cause of serious and urgent concern; it is a concern not just for those people who find they cannot maintain a livelihood in rural areas, but for all our people, including those who live in increasingly congested urban areas. A healthy rural economy and environment is an important part of our common heritage and of the quality of life in Europe.

The Rural Action Project and its successor the Rural Development Council are on a proselytising mission for the rural development community. The encounter between the rural development practitioners and policy-makers, and West Fermanagh's rural community groups, is not built simply on an exchange of information and some social engineering: it involve—in the same way as the symbolisation of deprivation—a cultural discourse. This discourse negotiates a vision of the present and the future of the rural community of which the farm economy is the backbone.

Conclusion

Examining the canons of rural development thought and practice through the lens of anthropology allows us to work on their cultural context and content. This can immensely enhance our understanding of the impact of rural development policy on the farm economy and the farm household.

The encounter between the rural development policy-makers and practitioners and the community groups in West Fermanagh is built on a community development experiment which has become enshrined in the bottom up ordinance of the Rural Development Council. Funds for community-led development will flow across that gap between a policy-making community and the local community.

The outcome of this encounter will rest on the capacity of the community groups to project a collective voice and to become articulate in the cultural discourse about rural development. However, this task is surrounded by contradiction. The *raison d'être* of the community groups is that they are a mouthpiece of the community, able to distil and articulate its collective concerns. At the same time, they are involved in a negotiation which generates pressure to uproot from these indigenous collective concerns and spiral off into the policy-making vortex, entering a new world view. The leaders of these community groups are in a particularly interesting and perilous position. They must constantly shift identity, stepping between the West Fermanagh which is their social and cultural landmark to the symbolic and symbolised West Fermanagh of the policy-making community. They are fitting the template of their own experience to the world view of the policy-making community.

The union of rural development policy and community action has had success in West Fermanagh because rural community development is of long-standing there—originating in the District Council's exemplary work—and community animateurs have become adept at shifting between cultural discourses. The Rural Action Project and its successor, the Rural Development Council, have themselves strived to tap grassroots opinion and understand something of the indigenous world view. They have rooted rural development in practical work. They are linked by an umbilical cord, created by action research, to the social and cultural world which they impact upon. This has enabled the community animateurs and leaders to present rural development policy as benevolent and optional: apart, that is, from those elements of rural policy—especially planning—which are regarded as inappropriate and intrusive (see Maginnis 1991). Perhaps the key to success here lies in a convergence of focus. Common ground and common objectives are reached as the rural development community concentrates on the grassroots and as the indigenous community looks towards policy and the rural development initiatives. This convergence is achievable because the community movement has always been a child of opportunism, emerging and growing in response to the widening sphere of grant aid for indigenous community projects. Community leaders thus operate with a mandate which is both an invocation to present the community view, and to deliver injections of grant aid.

The community development experiment succeeds because the rooted community can open and sustain a discourse with the rural development policy-makers and practitioners, even if the cultural content of that discourse does not entirely gel. However, the Farm Diversification Programme which brings the rural development community into contact with the occupational community of farmers has not achieved a convergence of focus, although it has been used and applauded by many farmers in West Fermanagh. The reluctance of the farming community to embrace the diversification message—throughout Northern Ireland 5 per cent of farmers have diversified against 15 per cent for the United Kingdom—is something of a conundrum for policy-makers. Their message to farmers is that the monolithic grassland economy, which Fermanagh so neatly symbolises, is inexorably in decline, and that diversification is salvation. The message is reinforced with a sea-change in agricultural policy and supports.

The ethnographic work in West Fermanagh for the Changing Farm Economies and CAMAR projects revealed a profound distance between the occupational community of farmers and the prevailing policy for agriculture and rural development. Amongst farmers in the study area, diversification and environmentally sensitive farming are noises off stage. Their drama is a struggle for survival in the aftermath of a velvet revolution, for that is what diversification is. Few farmers have engaged the ideology of diversification. Fewer still have the financial wherewithal or the confidence in the notion to diversify. None of the exhilaration of novelty has travelled with this revolution. Above all, it has been felt as the disappearance of the mainstay of established farm practice—grants for intensification and specialisation of production.

Most farmers in West Fermanagh are condemned to farm in the tram lines of beef production and sheep, which are leading to a dead end. While these farmers are unconvinced that diversification offers them opportunity or can sustain a new farm economy, they realise that the pursuit of intensification and specialisation, the ethics of the post-war 'production' years, is no longer viable. So they are caught somewhere in a limbo between a crumbling old order and the promised land. Meanwhile, ominous sounds are emanating from the GATT talks, presaging a gradual decline over a decade in supports for intensive farming and their eventual elimination.

The first Farm Diversification Programme, begun by the Rural Action Project, was purposely experimental. It targeted the small-scale farmers of the RAP West Fermanagh study area—most of them part-timers—who were thought to be at most risk of atrophy in farming and deprivation. The Final Report set out the lessons learnt from that experimental Programme and charted the way ahead for a second Farm Diversification Programme which was more extensive—pushing out the geographic boundaries of the first Programme—and which sought to embrace a broader cross-section of the farming community.

There is no doubt that the Farm Diversification Programme, especially in its second stage, has conveyed the notion of diversification and advertised its potential with far more vigour, and that it has made a greater impact than the Department of Agriculture's various diversification grants. In the Rural Development Council's own view:

> The RDC programme had a high uptake, possibly due to a combination of realistic rates of grant aid and hands-on guidance and support from field officers in the two areas (Hobson and Patterson 1992).

However, the reluctance to embrace diversification remains, as does the cynicism about its ability to engender change or improve the prospects of farmers.

This cynicism is evident at both grassroots and institutional levels, among ordinary farmers as well as in their organisations such as the Farmers' Unions. Within the policy-making community, farmers' disavowal of diversification is sometimes treated as symptomatic of an ingrained conservatism which fears and denigrates the new, whilst irrationally preserving an old and spent order. This view is, itself, imprinted by a deeper vein of cultural stereotyping.

However, if we return to the earlier representation of rural development policy as a cultural message conveyed in visionary statements, it becomes possible to explain the farmers' withdrawal from diversification without having to resort to cultural stereotypes. The vision which the rural development policy-makers have of the new model farm economy has been engaged by West Fermanagh's community groups, but it has not travelled beyond these to the farm household. The occupational world view of an older generation of farmers, who continue to control the majority of holdings and to constitute the social and cultural orthodoxy in West Fermanagh, remains that of the cradle. Loyalty to the twin props of the farm economy of the post-war years—intensification and specialisation—remains widespread. Faith in the production ethic is not purely the result of a vague desire to preserve the dogmas of an ancien regime. It is the revolutionary's faith in his creed. Lord James Douglas Hamilton, speaking to rural development policy-makers and practitioners at 'Rural Europe '92: New Beginnings', stated:.

> We have been through two major revolutions affecting rural live. The first transformed our landscape from one dominated by forests and wildlife into one where the land was shaped by agriculture. That took many hundreds of years. The second [was when] our industrial nations attracted people away from the land into the cities. Today, there are signs that we are on the brink of a third, an exciting opportunity to establish thriving rural economies, to enable people to live full and satisfying lives in the countryside whilst at the same time caring for our priceless natural heritage.

The careers of the older generation of farmers reveal that a third revolution already occurred during the Second World War, and in the immediate post-war years. Buchanan has argued:

> . . . in 1941, the Province's rural communities had yet to experience the full affects of the wartime drive for increased food production; in many respects, the scale and techniques of farming and farm technology were closer to those of the 1850s than those of the present day (Buchanan 1989: 28).

The farm economy was driven from tradition—a mixed cash and subsistence economy with diversified cropping and animal husbandry—to modernity a highly mechanised, intensive and specialist economy—within two decades. This older generation was the harbinger of that change. What makes their experience arresting is that they were exhorted to abandon the mixed farm economy and to follow the production ethic. Many argue as if farm diversification is a rejection of that experience.

Rural development policy and practice proceeds both from a set of prescriptions for change and from an accumulation of visionary statements which are crafted in the European Community and by national government and then carried to the rural communities in Northern Ireland, and to their backbone, the farm household. The remarkable success of community action in Fermanagh, and in West Fermanagh particularly, is both the happy outcome of social engineering and a testimony to the strong collective will and unity of these small, dispersed rural communities.

The evolution of rural development policy and practice is generally talked about in purely functional terms: the logistics of achieving a measurable change in the morphology of the farm economy. The obstructions which that policy and practice encounter in its descent from the community to the farm household are often located in the failure of farmers to recognise the need for change and to act on that need. Re-creating the cultural context for rural development policy and practice, and talking about the sought for changes in the farm economy as a process of acculturation, better represents the farmers' viewpoint and reveals the distance which rural development must travel before it can become accepted as an orthodoxy.

References

Ardener, E. 1987. Remote areas: some theoretical considerations. In A. Jackson (ed.), *Anthropology at Home.* London: Tavistock.

Bergmann, T. 1990. Socioeconomic situation and perspectives of the individual peasant. *Sociologica Ruralis* 30.

Bourdieu, P. 1977. *Outline of a Theory of Practice.* Cambridge: Cambridge University Press.

Commission of the European Community 1988. *The Future of Rural Society.* Luxembourg: EC Commission.

Conway, A. 1991. Taking the EC way out. In D. Smyth (ed.), *Opening the Field: Rural Perspectives.* Belfast: Fortnight Educational Trust.

Countryside and Wildlife Branch (DoE NI) 1990. *Fermanagh: Its Special Landscapes.* Belfast: HMSO.

Ditch, P. 1987. *West Fermanagh Study Area Report.* Derry: Rural Action project.

Fermanagh District Council n.d. Community Services Strategy Document: 1991–1995. Unpublished report.

_____. 1990. *Tourism Strategic Development Initiative.* Enniskillen: Fermanagh District Council.

Hobson, T. and D. Patterson 1992. The Impact of CAP Reforms on Rural Development. *Network News,* November 1992.

Loughry College 1990. *Knockninny: Ten Years On: a follow-up rural development report.* Loughry College.

Kilmurray, A. 1991. *Rural Action Project Anti-Poverty Initiative.* Derry: Rural Action Project.

Maher, T.J. 1986. *On an Integrated Rural Development Programme for Less Favoured Areas in Northern Ireland.* Brussels: EC Parliament (A 2–105/86).

Maginnis, K. 1991. No child of the new afforestation. In D. Smyth (ed.), *Opening the Field: Rural Perspectives.* Belfast: Fortnight Educational Trust.

Morrow, S. and J. O'Neill 1986. The biological potential of land resources in Fermanagh. DANI: Fermanagh Executive.

Moss, J., H.L. McHenry, D.P. Caskie, A.P. Markey and J.F. Phelan 1991. *Study of Farm Incomes in Northern Ireland and the Republic of Ireland.* Belfast: Co-operation North, UFU and IFA.

Northern Ireland Housing Executive (NIHE) 1987. *Roslea Housing Study.* Belfast: NIHE.

_____. 1991a. *The Way Ahead.* Belfast: NIHE.

_____. 1991b. Rural Housing Policy: Leading the Way. Belfast: NIHE.

Northern Ireland Tourist Board 1990. *Tourism in Northern Ireland: An Indicative Plan, 1990-1995.* Belfast: NITB.

Glens of Antrim Rural and Community Development Association (GARCDA) & Rural
    Community Network 1992. *Community Tourism in the Glens.* Rural Community
    Network.

Quinn, B. 1988. *Belcoo and District Area Plan: the community perspective.* Derry: Rural
    Action Project.

Rural Action Project (RAP) 1990. *Rural Development: A Challenge for the 1990s.* Derry:
    Rural Action Project.

_____. 1991. *Farm Diversification Programme: Final Report.* Derry: Rural Action Project.

Select Committee on the European Community (House of Lords) 1990. *The Future of Rural
    Society.* London: HMSO.

Smyth, D. (ed.) 1991. *Opening the Field: Rural Perspectives.* Belfast: Fortnight Educational
    Trust.

Stevenson, R. and L. Martin 1983. *An Analysis of the Potential Development in Agriculture in
    the Knockninny Area.* Loughry College.

5   The green conundrum: translating principles into policy in the Green Party

Jude Stephens

This chapter examines how the Northern Ireland Green Party (NIGP) is attempting to 'green' Northern Irish politics, in other words how it is making green politics relevant to the Northern Irish context without abandoning its green credentials. The Party faces the challenge of reflecting central ecological themes whilst attempting to produce relevant and credible policies for specific problems in Northern Ireland. I consider if and how the NIGP has attempted to avoid incorporation into one of the two main political blocs in Northern Irish politics. There are two related questions here. The first considers whether the NIGP has found it necessary to compromise its ecological values in order to render its policies more palatable to both the nationalist and the unionist communities. Are there, for example, occasions when the NIGP is unable to voice its true political feelings for fear that its intentions will be misinterpreted? The second question concerns the degree to which any policy born of green principles can be considered appropriate for a wide and varied range of socio-political contexts.

What makes this study of the NIGP particularly interesting from an anthropological perspective is the process by which the Greens set about defining their green, global responsibilities within the Northern Irish political context without losing sight of Northern Ireland's special needs. This process of localising the universal has received a good deal of anthropological attention. It is not easy to define the boundaries between the 'global' and the 'local'. As Fardon (1995: 2) points out, these terms 'work off one another in mutual provocation'. Cultural variability is typical of contemporary complex societies where there is no uniformity of experience. The NIGP's task of presenting a coherent green understanding of the world is fraught with difficulties. Hannerz (1992: 44) has argued that,

> As each individual engages in his own continuous interpreting of the forms surrounding him, how can we take for granted that he comes to the same result as the next fellow? There is nothing automatic about culture sharing. Its accomplishment must rather be seen as problematic.

In this chapter I shall argue that the NIGP has sometimes found it necessary to compromise its ecological values in order to render its policies more palatable to both the nationalist and the unionist communities. I shall present four case studies which illustrate that there are occasions when the NIGP is unable to voice its true political feelings for fear that its intentions will be misinterpreted. At such times the Party's concerns are silenced by the dominant hegemony.

Bailey (1969: 7) claims that each culture 'has its own idiomatic set of rules which summarises its own political wisdom'. The NIGP is attempting to establish such a set of rules. In the meantime, however, Party members must make decisions for which there is no satisfactory green 'guiding structure' (what Bailey refers to as 'private wisdom'), or where there is a number of possible choices. While Party members desire to avoid the partisan-oriented private wisdom of Unionist and Nationalist parties, they do, nevertheless, have access to it. Thus they can fairly confidently assess the effects of possible political decisions upon their own green political credibility. The NIGP also desires to make sound ecological choices based on global green principles. The conundrum lies in bringing 'those abstract, general principles forcefully to bear upon particular cases, when people are uncertain of their application or infirm in their resolve' (Goodin 1992b: 157).

The green political agenda

> What, at root, makes the green political agenda form a particularly tight package is the fact that all the elements within it are informed by a single moral vision (Goodin 1992a: 14).

Green politics is utopian in its thrust, setting forth a vision for an alternative, qualitatively better future society. Green policy is informed by the basic precepts of ecology, such as stability in diversity and the holistic interdependence of all things. Greens use the term 'holism' to suggest a kind of 'earth politics' which embraces the whole planet rather than isolated parts of it. Holism is characteristically found throughout green politics. In matters regarding health, for example, the individual is seen as a whole being rather than a sum of parts which can be treated separately from each other. This principle holds that each action has a consequence somewhere else. Hence the local and the global are inextricably linked. The holistic structure of green politics embraces three major tenets: grass roots politics, economic sustainability, and social justice and responsibility. Green politics therefore means more than just electoral politics: it is about new economics, new values and new lifestyles. In the words of one green author, 'Green politics will have to turn our present systems upside down' (Wall 1990: 6).

How can ecological principles advance a new kind of politics? One of the most important means of achieving social and environmental stability is thought to be through diversity. The German Green Party's (*Die Grünen*) motto of '*Einheit in der Vielfalt*' (unity in diversity) suggests collective strength in every aspect of life through diversity. The motto expresses an ideology in which diversity of culture, practice and lifestyle is highly valued. Cultural diversity enriches society and the desired green implementation of, for example, strong anti-racist policy reflects this aspiration. Green parties envisage a new form of politics which, unlike that which Greens condemn as contemporary grey[1] male-dominated, ego-centred, aggressive and patriarchal politics is neither hierarchical nor anti-feminist. However, one might ask to what extent such universal green objectives apply to particular localities.

An important question which presents itself when considering the universal thrust of green philosophy is that once an aim or an objective has been agreed on by a particular green party, can it be generalised to apply to other green parties on a global level; in other words, should green principles (and the policies which stem from them) apply 'across the board'? If so, how do particular aspects of greenness come to be defined and accepted? What, if any, degree of cultural adaptation is necessary before a general green principle can be implemented in a 'specific' context?

The Northern Ireland Green Party

The Northern Ireland Green Party has been active since the early 1980s. It began life as the Ecology Party which was formed in Northern Ireland in 1982 by a few committed individuals who sporadically stood as candidates in local elections in subsequent years. The Party in Northern Ireland functioned as a branch of the United Kingdom Ecology Party.[2] The NIGP's profile in Northern Ireland was generally low and those interested in ecological politics often joined the United Kingdom Green Party without realising that a regional green party, in which they might take an active part, had been established in the province. In February 1989, the Green Party of Northern Ireland was launched in Belfast: it was to replace the old branch of the United Kingdom Ecology Party.

Since its foundation, the NIGP has had a somewhat ambiguous relationship with the parent party in the United Kingdom. Following the relaunch of the NIGP, details of those who joined the England, Wales and Northern Ireland (EWNI) Green Party were forwarded to the NIGP office in Belfast, whose responsibility it was to inform these new members of Party events and meetings in Northern Ireland. EWNI Green Party members resident in Northern Ireland had the same voting rights at EWNI Green Party conferences as members in England or Wales. Individuals who joined the NIGP through the Belfast office, however, could only acquire voting rights by subscribing to the London Green Party office to become full EWNI members. A proportion of the NIGP membership fees is paid to the London EWNI Green Party office and this capitation ensures that the NIGP receives any new publications, discussion papers and policy documents which emerge from the EWNI Greens. Membership of the EWNI Green Party thus results in automatic membership of the NIGP and the subscription rate is consequently somewhat higher than that of the NIGP.

Yet the NIGP has in many ways felt itself to be 'a party apart' and at its AGM in 1993 NIGP members opted for a greater degree of regional autonomy. This was ratified at the EWNI Green Party conference in 1994. The NIGP is now, in effect, fully autonomous, although its Constitution states that formal links with the green parties of England, Ireland, Scotland and Wales continue. The exact nature of these 'formal links' is somewhat unclear but green parties throughout Great Britain and Ireland are generally content to entertain (although not to confer voting rights on) members of other green parties at party conferences.

The Green Party in the Republic of Ireland was formed in 1981 as the Ecology Party. In 1988 the name was changed to *Comhaontas Glas*/Green Party. Relations between the NIGP and *Comhaontas Glas* have always been cordial. Representatives from Northern Ireland attend the *Comhaontas Glas* annual convention and visits to Northern Ireland from Irish Greens, including the *Comhaontas Glas* TD[3] and one of its two MEPs, have been frequent.

The NIGP has not, as yet, had any measurable effects on regional policy making. Nor does it have a well-defined electoral clientele. Its political relevance can therefore be seen as marginal. Political culture in Northern Ireland revolves around the constitutional future of the province and this is reflected in the NIGP's primary concerns of democracy, security and devolved government with appropriate forms of power-sharing.

The Greens in Northern Ireland are aware that without some degree of political representation the Party does not have even symbolic relevance; hence they are keen to contest elections when funding allows. Between 1989 and 1994 the NIGP has contested a number of elections, at the local, parliamentary and European levels: they were successful in none.

A major problem for the Greens in contesting Northern Ireland elections is that the province's voters are usually unwilling or unable to set aside long-standing political allegiances. There is a saying in Northern Ireland that 'you get your politics in the maternity ward', in other words, that voting patterns remain much the same with each successive generation. NIGP members understand only too well the importance of embracing the constitutional question, and of adopting a position on 'the border', if they hope to be considered a credible force in Northern Ireland's political arena. What has proved to be so time-consuming and contentious for the NIGP has been its effort to formulate a policy which addresses the fears both of unionists and of nationalists. While the Greens may have enjoyed some of the benefits of raised environmental awareness, polling what many Party members term a 'reasonable' percentage of the vote in view of the difficult political context in which they operate, they have remained an 'also ran' party within the intense sectarian polarisation of Northern Ireland politics.

The NIGP has not attracted political refugees in the way that the Greens elsewhere in the United Kingdom have done. At its height in 1992, membership of the Party was around one hundred and sixty individuals, only some twenty of whom were active at any one time. Activists periodically came and went, leaving a core of about a dozen committed individuals to continue dealing with the Party's administration, elections and campaigns. Male activists have always hugely out-numbered their female counterparts, although the number of women members is relatively high. Green Party candidates for elections contested in Northern Ireland during the period of my research (1990-92) were all male, despite the Party's com-mitment to equal representation of the sexes. Women members in Northern Ireland have shown little interest in standing as candidates, a matter which has troubled members of the EWNI and Irish Green Parties, whose higher proportion of female speakers, election candidates, Party officers and, in the case of *Comhaontas Glas*, elected politicians, reflect those parties' aims to ensure gender balance.[4]

In contrast to Great Britain, where the political scene is dominated by two political parties, one might expect the NIGP to be advantaged by competing in a multi-party system through proportional representation. Indeed, this has been the case in the Republic of Ireland where *Comhaontas Glas* is represented at the local, national and European levels. On the other hand, the constitutional political par-ties of Northern Ireland (the Alliance Party excepted) are more or less concen-trated into two large blocs representing unionist and nationalist voters.

No political party in Northern Ireland can afford to overlook the issue which is uppermost in the minds of many voters, that of the province's constitutional future. During the initial launch of the NIGP in Belfast, the question of Northern Ireland's constitutional status was introduced and it soon became evident to Party members that, without a credible policy to address this issue, they were battling against the odds. Although Greens in Britain and the Republic of Ireland have held a shared policy on Northern Ireland's constitutional matters since 1983, NIGP members were growing concerned that this was now somewhat outdated and inap-propriate. The formulation of a new policy would have to include more than bland, neutral statements. It had to be relevant to unionist and nationalist alike in order for NIGP support to be drawn from both those camps and to avoid any possibility of Greens in Northern Ireland being branded as yet another partisan element in the dispute. In addition to the non-partisan status of any policy which the NIGP might produce, it was also essential to ensure that party policy was ecologically sound, encompassing green philosophy and aims. Certain fundamental tenets of green politics, such as demilitarisation and the diminution of borders, are also part of the ideology of Sinn Féin in Northern Ireland; hence the complexities of formulating a new policy quickly became clear. NIGP members were aware that any tendency to skimp on the ecological emphasis might cost them the support of Greens in Britain, the Republic of Ireland and even farther afield. Given the international nature of green politics, members considered that such links were to be preserved rather than jeopardised.

The problems did not stop there. NIGP members do not share a coherent green ideology. Many hail from sectarian backgrounds (some have made a deliberate attempt to escape the confines of an inherited partisan ideology) and such individuals are inevitably accompanied by a certain amount of 'cultural baggage' of a kind which impedes the neutral stance sought by the NIGP. Thus the Party has to deal not only with divergent emphases between green parties in Great Britain and the Republic of Ireland, but also to accommodate differences of opinion within its own ranks.

Greens share a common frame of reference in subscribing to a single (if incomplete and evolving) cosmology. Although NIGP members adopt the same eco-principles that are held by members of other green parties, there are often competing ideologies at work in their attempts to reach an understanding of certain aspects of green philosophy. This is most clearly visible in their attempts to formulate suitable policies for Northern Ireland. NIGP members choose to frame their political arguments carefully in order to avoid being branded as partisan. The NIGP may, for example, favour demilitarisation, yet the Party acknowledges that any decision to replace British troops with an alternative peace-keeping presence must fulfil green principles, i.e. any such decision must be (and be seen to be) the result of a green, democratic process, rather than the result of Anglo-Irish dictat. The decision must not be perceived as a British withdrawal from Northern Ireland or the Party will be labelled as part of a pan-nationalist front.

If the NIGP is to formulate policies which are ecologically sound by the standards of other green parties, it must condemn all forms of violence, whether it is violence performed by the state, the violence of terrorism, or that which NIGP members perceive to be enshrined in voting systems, such as majoritarianism. To question the wisdom of majoritarianism in Northern Ireland, however, is to threaten the unionist position and to risk association with the nationalist cause.

When an organisation aspiring to neutrality attempts to bridge the gap between two mutually antagonistic communities, it may be almost impossible to avoid offending one or the other. Thus virtually any social, economic or political recommendation which the NIGP may make must be a balanced one which does not explicitly favour one or other community. Greens undoubtedly desire the best and most ecologically sound solution to problems, but any proposed solution will have to be couched in terms which will not cost them their neutrality or alienate potential voters. The promotion of political and economic self-determination and self-reliance for both the nationalist and unionist communities has been a useful means of addressing this problem.

Policy formulation in the NIGP

In 1990 the NIGP set up a policy working group to rewrite its Northern Ireland Policy.[5] The term 'Northern Ireland Policy' refers to a package of policies. All the green parties involved in the Northern Ireland Policy formulation emphasise the importance of a holistic approach in addressing Northern Ireland's problems. This holistic approach requires an integrated set of policies which will deal with all aspects of the situation. The aim of the protracted Northern Ireland Policy process[6] was to formulate a shared policy which was acceptable to all the green parties in Britain and Ireland. The NIGP's suggestions therefore had to be recognisably green in order to satisfy the 'international' criteria of the green parties in England, Wales, Scotland and the Republic of Ireland. As far as the NIGP was concerned, however, compromise was called for if the ecological content of their policy was in danger of being perceived by the Northern Irish people as succumbing to sectarian loyalties. Elements of compromise—such as the NIGP's decision not to include within its policy an immediate recommendation for talks with paramilitaries or a definite date for the withdrawal of British troops—were a perpetual source of resentment amongst the EWNI Green Party's English 'romantic republican element'.[7]

The case studies which follow illustrate the debate which took place in four areas of policy-making; the issue of talks with paramilitary bodies, the integration of political prisoners, democratic electoral systems, and education. These case studies illustrate the process whereby NIGP members negotiate greenness both within their own ranks and with other green parties. This negotiation is conducted within the context of the search for an appropriately 'green' Northern Ireland Policy. It illustrates how, through dialogue, NIGP members reach (or fail to reach) agreement about what greenness constitutes for them by contesting fundamental components of green ideology. The philosophy to which Greens aim to adhere is introduced briefly in each example.

Pacifism is a major principle within green ideology. In spite of anti nuclear proclamations, defence remains a somewhat confused area within green thought. Although some Greens are fully pacifist, most favour, in principle, a non-nuclear, non-aggressive defence policy with sufficient weaponry to deter an aggressor. Goodin (1992a) comments on a 'curious anomaly' in green defence policy, noting how, on the one hand, Greens advocate demilitarisation, whilst on the other hand they recognise the right of individuals to social resistance and self-defence. For the NIGP, issues of defence, security strategies and demilitarisation within its own troubled community have proven consistently contentious in policy formulation, especially given their need to address problems which are specific to the province such as anti-terrorist legislation, internal exile and the citizen's right to protection. Thus the question of a military presence has been problematic for the NIGP, which stresses that armed forces must be linked to community, and be peace-makers rather than war-mongers.

Case studies 1 and 2 consider the principle of pacifism within ecological thought and examine how green philosophy is tempered by local concerns. Case Study 1 illustrates how the adoption of a pacifist principle in response to a particular matter may elicit conflict in the form of opposing views from NIGP members while, in Case Study 2, I show how the principle may be unconditionally upheld by the whole group.

Case study 1: talks with paramilitary groups

The following exchange occurred during a NIGP working group[8] meeting in 1992 in Belfast when four members—Paul, Brian, Justin and Nick—discussed whether they should advocate talks with paramilitaries if such groups were to be incorporated in the political process.

> Paul: Are we advocating that we talk to terrorists at the minute as they murder people . . . ?[9]

> Brian: ANC were doing it and the British talked to them.

> Justin: If we look at it from a green perspective we accept we are all one community and we should talk to them . . .

> Paul: And we bring in the Shankill butchers and talk to them about the rights and wrongs of cutting people up? To be honest there are green things I can accept and some I can't and I wouldn't want to be in the same room as them. I certainly couldn't talk to them until they told me they weren't going to kill anyone else.

> Brian: If you have unionists whose families have been murdered, do you expect them to sit and talk to the murderers?

> Nick: If tomorrow it were widely known in the press that the Northern Ireland Green Party was engaged in talks with Sinn Féin . . . or are we advocating that, for example, Unionists should be doing it?

> Brian: In our position at the minute it would be strategically disastrous. I think there are plenty of groups that are not political parties that could be doing it.

> Nick: There's no point us talking to them 'cause we don't have any power anyway. The British government should.

> Justin: There is good reason for us to talk to them. It gives you a good insight into the strength of some of their feelings.

> Nick: That's not denied but as pacifists do we talk?

> Justin: The pacifist is bound to use of minimum force. Quite likely they'll turn on the pacifist and continue fighting with each other. But the principle suggests that our job is to listen to them anyway.

The topic of talks with paramilitaries was a contentious one which was broached on numerous occasions. No decision was ever taken to advocate openly that the NIGP desired talks with any paramilitary organisations. The pacifist argument in favour of peaceful dealings with paramilitaries was played down in view of the possible repercussions, i.e. that the Northern Irish press would interpret such an act as evidence of empathy with the republican cause. Labov (1990: 155) suggests that:

> An ideological conflict would seem to involve a competition between simultaneously held but conflicting beliefs. Such a conflict would be resolved on the basis of which ideals were more strongly held, or perhaps even which were considered more expedient at a particular moment.

The kind of expediency to which Labov refers is apparent in the above exchange. The issue of talks with paramilitaries was never satisfactorily resolved within the NIGP. Most members admitted to having doubts as to how the media would interpret such an action even if it were pacifist in principle and thus carrying a green stamp of approval. We can see how a basic component of green thought was being moderated by other concerns and how constraints on choice outweighed the generalised incentive to follow the pacifist principle of dialogue. In case study 2, in contrast, we can see how the pacifist principle may be vigorously upheld.

Case study 2: forced integration in prisons

It is a green principle to advance human rights. Yet in the Northern Irish context, the advancement of human rights necessitates that the NIGP adopts an anti-internment position which members anticipate may be perceived by certain sections of the public as condoning republican paramilitary activity. Prior to the following exchange, the NIGP secretary received a draft paper from Springhill Community Centre in Belfast. The paper was entitled 'Integration in Northern Irish prisons'. NIGP members were asked to study the paper and to respond with comments. The meeting was attended by Tim, Paul, Sandra, Alf and Gerry. Alf articulated the main thrust of the document, which stated that prisoners should not be forced to integrate against their will.

> Tim: Is there a principle here as well? If I have to work with someone I can't stand, I can get out of the situation but in the prison I can't. Integration should be by consent rather than force.

> Paul: Are they integrated in blocks or cells? You should include the point that they are willing to cooperate in drug dealing.

> Sandra: No, that's looking at it very clinically.

Alf: Some people in paramilitary organisations feel committed to their politics as we may feel committed to green politics. We shouldn't trivialise them.

Sandra: Some are not convicted, they're on remand.

Gerry: Do both sides want to be segregated?

Tim: As pacifists, shouldn't we be against forcing people to do anything?

Alf: When you allow things to happen on a voluntary basis you get more co-operation. Look at the UVF man who started learning Gaelic.

Tim: So we say 'encourage' integration if people want it and accept that prisoners are fellow human beings.

Sandra: Yes. If they are forced, then that constitutes state violence.

The principle of pacifism received unambiguous support in this exchange. Sandra defended the green theme of non-violence with regard to the behaviour of the state as an important element within NIGP policy. In some cases it would appear that a principle is upheld and in others it becomes expedient to overlook it. Here the principle was upheld.

The integration of paramilitary prisoners is an issue which involves individuals from both unionist and nationalist communities. To adopt a position on this matter does not necessarily require a response which may be interpreted by the public as partisan. If forced integration is opposed, it may be done so on the grounds that it is unreasonable for all paramilitary prisoners. NIGP members proposed a statement to oppose forced integration of prisoners from the ranks of both loyalist and nationalist paramilitary groups. Thus a green ideological commitment was able to override concerns of neutrality, in this instance by playing down the Catholic/Protestant issue and focusing on what members of the two communities had in common.

A grass-roots political approach means a bottom up structure which seeks to incorporate all views. Grassroots democracy guarantees that every individual has his or her say, or at the very least, has an opportunity to participate. This kind of grassroots politics should occur at all levels of decision-making, whether within the local political party (in order to avoid power-heavy centralised decision-making), or within the general community (in order to avoid the imposition of unsolicited or unsuitable policies from a central body). Participatory democracy of the kind favoured by the NIGP for Party decisions can be a slow process. Each member must be consulted in any decision, as opposed to the more effective system of representative democracy which is advocated by the England and Wales Green Party (see note 2). All members agree that power in the Party should, at least theoretically, reside in its base and this should be reflected in social arrangements.

The principle of decentralisation is closely related to that of democracy and green politics seeks to decentralise power in society to the lowest possible level. Decentralisation means giving the grassroots level priority and granting powers of autonomy and self-administration to regional and local levels. Greens argue for a decentralised structure in the social, political and economic spheres, which is essentially a 'bottom up' affair, with all possible decisions taken at grass-roots level, and only matters of regional or national interest dealt with at a higher band.

One might expect similar policies for the same problem to emerge from different green parties. Yet the various green parties concerned to formulate a joint policy did not always agree on policy recommendations and there were distinct difficulties experienced by each party in committing green principles to specific acts in particular cases. Greens in Northern Ireland, Great Britain and the Republic of Ireland are broadly subscribing to the same goals and principles, but clearly it is more difficult for them all to agree on the same means to achieving those goals.

Any policies which are formulated for Northern Ireland should, argue some NIGP members, be credited with the same validity in other socio-political contexts. If, for example, a policy in Northern Ireland is born of green principles which comprise a globally relevant value system, then that policy should be perfectly legitimate in England, Bosnia or beyond. Yet many members of the EWNI Green Party and of *Comhaontas Glas* were reluctant to accept certain policy recommendations which emerged from the NIGP's policy working group.

The following case study highlights this problem. In general, green demands and proposals are shaped by fairly broad ideological considerations although these may be tempered in emphasis. Scottish Greens, for example, stress the need for a regional Scottish Assembly as part of a wider green decentralisation programme. Yet their Northern Ireland counterparts must go a stage further than issuing a simple demand for regional government. They must additionally advocate structures and mechanisms which will accommodate power-sharing between Unionists and Nationalists.

The England and Wales Green Party has formulated general policies which are in keeping with a broad understanding of green philosophy. However, if their demands are extended to include the needs of Northern Ireland, then elements of these policies may be compromised. An example of this occurs within the EWNI Party's policy for demilitarisation. In demanding a reduction in the number of armed forces which the British Government maintains, any green argument for continued military presence in Northern Ireland becomes untenable. Yet the consequences of an immediate and total withdrawal of troops from Northern Ireland (as has been proposed by a small section of the EWNI Party) is one which the Northern Ireland Greens refuse to accept. Their refusal is based not only on the grounds that they will forfeit their impartial anti-sectarian status, but also that human life will be put at risk. Neither of these scenarios, they argue, is green.

In responding to the Northern Ireland situation and in recognising the need to become a credible Northern Irish political party, the NIGP is stating its demands within a specific politically and culturally acceptable discourse. NIGP members simultaneously maintain that the degree of greenness in their policies is sufficient that other green parties should unquestionably adopt them. This fusion of the local and the global levels begs the question of what occurs when cultural norms set the agenda for appropriate political issues and whether each green party considers its own culturally specific solutions to be applicable on a universal scale. If each green party has the potential to consider its policies to be relevant universally, and if the green movement in general attempts to be a global one, a clash of interests is likely.

NIGP members had discussed at length amongst themselves the most appropriate form of power-sharing arrangements for Northern Ireland and had drafted various papers on consensus voting systems. These systems included the preferendum (see below) and forms of proportional representation. A green objective is to achieve self-determination on the basis of consensus; that is, to encompass the views of all participants by selecting a compromise which is the most suitable to the majority and the least suitable to only a very few. NIGP members have taken democratic decision-making a step further than many Greens in Great Britain and the Irish Republic with the adoption of the preferendum as a decision-making tool. The preferendum is a form of multi-option referendum which, NIGP members declare, 'offers an ingenuous method for making a collective choice out of a range of possibilities' (NIGP draft Northern Ireland Policy 1992). Any number of options may be selected to deal with the question in hand. These choices are then voted upon in order of preference. Voting papers contain a list of all options and the option which receives the greatest number of points is considered to have achieved the greatest degree of consensus. The preferendum does not exclude the pursuit of individual interests but makes it possible for diverse views of people to be accommodated in a process which can arrive fairly at a valid and binding decision. It also encourages compromise; this is denied in a referendum, which only offers the voter two choices. Consensus politics rejects the notion of fixed or permanent majorities which may crystallise at any level in society. It is a voting system which allows dissenters to be heard, and their opinions to be reflected in a final decision which embraces the sentiments of the entire community. What makes consensus politics ecologically sound, claimed one NIGP member, is its relation to pacifism; and its ability to encourage compromise and a creative (rather than a competitive) process.

Case study 3: adopting the preferendum

During a policy workshop held in Belfast in 1993, NIGP member Justin argued that any form of democratic voting system which was suitable for Northern

Ireland should be perfectly adequate for other contexts. Max, the EWNI Green Party Policy Co-ordinator, was not convinced of the value of applying proportional representation and the preferendum in every case.

Nick: Would the English Greens agree that Northern Ireland should have PRSTV? [Proportional representation, standard transferable vote.]

Max: If a lot of general provisions for Northern Ireland appear in this policy, I can't see England and Wales saying no, even if you want it and we think you shouldn't. The problem comes when you say that we should all adopt it as a general principle.

Victor: But the English will include the definite idea of the preferendum, surely?

Justin: It sounds very much as if the English are in the mode of Lloyd George, imposing power on Northern Ireland and not on themselves. I feel strongly that a green solution would come here if people outside Northern Ireland asked how they could help, and if Belfast decided to share power, then they should do it too.

Max: Conference won't see it that way. We don't want precise wording and precise models for the preferendum.

Alf: Surely we are just having a dig at the English here?

Justin: Well, why tell us to share power when they don't?

Max: You are trying to foist extremely vague policies on us.

Nick: If it's good for Ireland then it's good for England. The only argument the Unionists have for majoritarianism is that it's over there, and if it wasn't over there, then it wouldn't be over here.

Justin later suggested that, should the EWNI Green Party fail to accommodate the NIGP's wishes to include a detailed section on consensus voting, then the NIGP, which was already progressing towards full autonomous status, *Comhaontas Glas* and the Scottish Green Party might ratify the new policy without EWNI Green Party support. In this way Justin effectively presented Max with an ultimatum. Max finally agreed to include references to consensus politics, although he insisted that the NIGP must formulate its own detailed policies on consensus voting to accompany the briefer Northern Ireland Policy which would eventually be included in the EWNI Green Party's Manifesto for a Sustainable Society. Although Justin was aware that the EWNI Green Party would not favour his decision, he tried to ensure that the advantages gained for his Party were equal to the disadvantages, i.e. he modified his behaviour in the direction of the optimum gain. Max had two choices: on the one hand, he could refuse to accommodate the policy demands of the NIGP and risk his own Party being isolated from the policy process altogether. On the other hand, he could partially concede to the wishes of the NIGP and accept the unfavourable repercussions from the EWNI Green Party. In assessing the advantages to be gained, he decided that, in view of the time and effort already invested in the policy-making endeavour and the alienation likely to be experienced from the other three green parties, the latter decision would be the less damaging of the two.

Case study 4: education policy

Greens agree that one of the most important steps to creating an ecologically sustainable society is education. Greens criticise the existing educational structure for its essentially antagonistic nature. NIGP members stress that, in their struggle against the grey educational establishment, they face the added problem of tackling the institutionalised segregation of Protestant and Catholic children in schools. Many Greens suggest that, throughout society generally, the rewards for conventional success are too high and the penalties of failure too severe. A new green culture of education would put content and meaning above teaching methods. Education as a resource should enable individuals to 'create' themselves, to explore and learn to relate to one another and to understand the inner person. In this way a teaching environment which fostered a reflective rather than a competitive mode would pave the way for participation in a community which encouraged similar relationships and which was not based on the authoritarianism characteristic of existing educational, commercial and professional institutions. Greens stress the essential interplay between school and community, since only if a person's perception of an alternative way of life is grounded in reality, in other words confirmed by actions and deeds within the community, can that person be expected to gravitate towards 'living green'. Yet some argue that, no matter how green the education system is, a simultaneous push from governments is a necessary corollary to self-education.

The NIGP's Northern Ireland Policy includes a section on education which advocates the introduction of integrated schools and the phasing out of subsidies to segregated educational establishments. On one of his visits to Northern Ireland, the EWNI Green Party Policy Co-ordinator stated that, if he were to insert the amendments for education which had emerged from NIGP discussions recommending the provision of integrated schooling for all children as a human right, there would be immediate repercussions from the EWNI Green Party Education Policy working group, whose recommendations had been supported by the EWNI Green Party's Spirituality working group.[10] The EWNI Green Party's Education Policy working group supports local cross-community initiatives in the field of Northern Irish education, offering specific support for the concept of non-denominational education. Yet as NIGP members point out, the relatively small number of integrated schools which are operative in Northern Ireland, such as Belfast's Lagan College, have a specifically Christian ethos. One section of the EWNI Green Party wished to go a step further and recommend a complete separation of church and state, suggesting that, while inter-denominational schools cater for named denominations, non-denominational establishments cater additionally for Muslims, Jews, atheists and other minority religions in the United Kingdom. The term 'non-denominational' is therefore preferable to 'integrated', since the latter effectively excludes certain religious groups.

The following conversation illustrates the dilemma faced by the NIGP in its attempt to apply green principles across different cultural contexts, in this case, Great Britain, Northern Ireland and the Irish Republic. The discussion took place at a Northern Ireland Policy fringe meeting in April 1993 at the EWNI Green Party's spring conference. During the meeting Alison, a member of the EWNI Green Party Education working group, expressed concern that, in keeping with green principles of diversity, the element of choice within education must not be overlooked. While integrated education is a human right, it is only one of a number of possible options and should be viewed as a privilege rather than the rule. Absolute implementation of an integrated system would, she claimed, be disastrous. Echoing the sentiments of a number of NIGP members, Alison argued that any withdrawal of funding to Catholic schools would result in 'exacerbating what is at the root of the trouble'. Greens would have more influence if they provided educational resources and joint projects designed to bring students together. To implement non-segregated education was, she stated, 'using Northern Ireland as an experiment—like the poll tax in Scotland—and treating them like second class citizens'.

Other participants in the discussion claimed that Alison's analogy was 'rubbish' and that, if the EWNI Greens were planning to adopt an approach in Northern Ireland different to the 'mainland green approach', it was simply because Northern Ireland was a different place. Alison's reaction was one of amazement. There was no reason, she argued hotly, why green principles, which she understood to have universal application, should apply in Great Britain but not in Northern Ireland. Contrary to her understanding of green philosophy, she continued, the Northern Ireland education system was clearly being designated by certain EWNI Greens as being in need of 'special' legislation in some way. Thus the basic problem for Alison was the concern of her fellow Greens that the application of EWNI legislation in Northern Ireland would only be effective if it was tampered with in some way to render it appropriate to a different and 'special' context.

The following exchange took place at a Belfast Workshop in 1991 between Max of the EWNI Green Party, Victor of *Comhaontas Glas*, and members of the NIGP Northern Ireland Policy working group, Gerry and Tim, regarding education in Northern Ireland.

Max: We'd like to take education a stage further than 'integrated' to 'secular'.

Gerry: 'Secular ' is a bad word in Northern Ireland.

Victor: Integrated education discriminates against people who want their kids educated in one religion. You have to cater for all or you are approving of something that actually discriminates because of the Northern Ireland problem.

Tim: Integration is a basic human right. If Paisley [leader of the Democratic Unionist Party] wants a special school, then he funds it himself.

Max: We have adopted a watered down version of this.

Victor: If only non-religious schools are subsidised, then others will pay more so they are discriminated against—private will become elite.

Tim: There's no Jewish way to teach French, or Muslim way to teach Maths.

Victor: No, but there is an ethos in schools. The point is that you'll be discriminating against some people because you want a particular policy which is going to suit Northern Ireland. It won't work everywhere.

In this exchange we can see that NIGP members desired a green education policy which neither the EWNI Green Party nor *Comhaontas Glas* considered to be appropriate to its own context. EWNI Green Party members were split between advocating secular schooling or free choice, while members of *Comhaontas Glas* were fully aware of the electoral repercussions should they recommend a secular programme in the Irish Republic. Another difficulty of encouraging integrated education at the cost of segregated schooling is considered to lie in establishing the means by which it would be enforced. Even integrated schools have an ethos which caters for the majority of pupils. It would be necessary rigorously to impose policy and some doubted whether this could, or should, be achieved.

Max outlined the difficulties which he anticipated the Catholic Church would have with the concept. The Catholic Church distinguishes between 'religious education' and 'religious formation'. Religious education is the Protestant concept whereby one has education and as part of that receives religious education. Religious formation is the concept that one has to be educated within a Catholic context because the Catholic faith is universal and therefore applicable to everything. It was in essence, Max claimed, 'the Christian holistic equivalent of Islam'.

The broad discourse within which any political party sets its demands is based on cultural norms which promote certain issues and inhibit others. In Northern Ireland, cultural norms within the political arena frequently force issues to be interpreted within a sectarian framework, hence the Greens must convert their demands by translating general principles into specific policy demands which override sectarian concerns of patriotic affiliation.

This discussion of education offers an example of the way in which the cultural norms of a political system affect matters considered appropriate for party demands. In this case, all three green parties held different views about the wisdom of each others' proposals and some members were clearly reticent about advocating anything which might be culturally inappropriate. Easton (1965: 101) suggests that:

> It is commonplace to observe that systems vary with respect to the subject matters that are incorporated into binding decisions. What may be considered an appropriate topic for political action in one system will be completely excluded from political consideration in another.

Each green party therefore found it necessary to structure its needs according to its own political system's cultural norms. It was of primary importance to the NIGP to integrate the schooling of Protestant and Catholic children as one move within a wider holistic vision for the whole community and, in so doing, to transcend the religious division in education. The EWNI Party's education working group was formulating policy with quite a different emphasis in order to deal with a different set of criteria befitting its own cultural norms. EWNI Greens were concerned to cater for multicultural, multi-religious and non-religious situations. Finally, members of *Comhaontas Glas* felt that they would, in the words of one individual, be 'putting themselves on the line' by demanding secular schooling in a Catholic state.

Conclusion

The political issue of the day in Northern Ireland is that of the constitutional question. Thus in many ways the Party has been obliged to focus its scarce resources on responding to culturally specific needs at the expense of what the public perceives to constitute recognisably 'green' issues such as conservation, energy, transport or pollution. The business of conforming to an acceptable image of a Northern Irish political party has had its price, hampering the Greens' ability to muster wider support in areas which the public associates with greenness. In other words, the NIGP's main challenge of creating a credible image through the formulation of a relevant policy for Northern Ireland has been a challenge which has not dogged the progress of green parties in Ireland and Great Britain in quite the same way. For the NIGP, 'environmental' issues have taken second place to more narrowly defined political struggles. This has occurred at the expense of the kind of campaigning routinely undertaken by green parties.

Pacifism, human rights and democracy are all major modes in which green cosmological ideas are expressed. If NIGP members choose to express an understanding of a particular phenomenon which deviates from that held by green parties elsewhere, then the wider general stock of ecological values to which all members undoubtedly aim to subscribe may not always fit neatly into sets of ideas held by a particular community. Certain circumstances may result in ambiguity and misunderstanding and, as Hannerz (1992: 45) notes, 'People who make active use of certain cultural forms may intend them differently than they are understood by observers; different observers may not understand them in the same way either'. Hence certain cultural values may be adopted, transformed, or selected for inclusion or omission by the communities to whom they are passed. It is important, therefore, to 'provide the empirical evidence of what is in fact the process whereby cultural expression is constructed in the particular societies and domains we are treating' (Barth 1987: 9).

In view of the context in which the NIGP is operating, the Party has rationalised its position on numerous occasions although not, I would argue, to the detriment of ecological principles, but as a result of a slightly different understanding of those principles. Perhaps it is more apt to argue that, rather than recommending a crude application of green philosophy to a volatile situation, the NIGP has attempted to incorporate ecology into its Northern Ireland Policy by employing a degree of subtlety born of cultural understanding. The case studies in this chapter thus reflect a common area of interest in anthropology, that of the interface between the local and the global. There is a two way process at work. On the one hand, key elements of global ecological philosophy are being reinterpreted at the local level and sometimes transformed in keeping with local values. On the other hand, local tradition plays a part in shaping green universal values.

In assessing the comparative value of research undertaken in Northern Ireland, I would suggest that the nature of the dilemmas experienced by Greens there may be common to other green parties striving to formulate an ecological agenda which can be mapped onto a particular political context. The NIGP follows the pattern of green parties in Great Britain and Ireland (and farther afield) in challenging modern capitalism. This challenge should, theoretically speaking, present neither more nor less difficulty to the NIGP than it presents to other green parties. It seems reasonable to suggest that the NIGP has been somewhat less successful than its counterparts in Great Britain and the Republic of Ireland in this respect in that its somewhat limited resources have been geared towards dealing with issues which reflect the sectarian dimension of Northern Irish politics. The application of green values to the problems of democracy, security or power-sharing in Northern Ireland was straightforward for the NIGP. The problems which arose during policy-making were to be found less in principles than in pragmatics; in other words in translating those principles into action or, put simply, in 'getting there'. Green principles which might not prove troublesome in other parts of the United Kingdom or Ireland have called for extra consideration in the Northern Irish context.

Notes

1. Greens view traditional politics of every kind as grey politics, hence 'grey' is a broad term which encompasses political philosophies of all colours, e.g. blue (Conservative/capitalist) or red (labour/socialist/Marxist). Some scholars have also drawn on this general contrast between green and grey. Goodin refers to 'parties that are "green" (bright, lively) and ones that are "grey" (dull, drab, flat, boring)' (1992a: viii). Goodin includes a third category of 'brown' to allude to parties which strongly favour industrialism and thus contribute to pollution. For Greens, the grey also encompasses philosophies of nationalism, fascism, patriarchy, imperialism, injustice and oligarchy. Each of these is (in varying degrees) opposed by green parties. Thus for Greens, what constitutes the 'grey' is composed of that which is not green.

2. The United Kingdom Ecology Party was successor to the People Party in 1973, changing its name first to the United Kingdom Ecology Party and then to the United Kingdom Green Party (see Parkin 1989). In 1990, The Scottish Green Party became independent and the United Kingdom Greens became known as the Green Party of England, Wales and Northern Ireland (EWNI). In 1994, following the Northern Ireland Green Party's successful bid for full autonomy, the former EWNI Greens became simply the England and Wales Green Party (EW).

3. *Teachta Dáil*, a member of the Irish Parliament.

4. In 1994, two women candidates from *Comhaontas Glas* were elected to the European Parliament.

5. The period of my research between 1989 and 1993 corresponded with the efforts of the Greens to produce 'specific' policies for Northern Ireland. Policy working groups were regularly established to discuss how policies in the EWNI Green Party's manifesto might be tempered to suit Northern Ireland's different economic and natural resources.

6. The policy-making process began in earnest in December 1990 and continued until January 1993.

7. The term 'romantic republicanism' was coined by some members of the EW Green Party International Co-ordinating Committee and refers to those English and Welsh Greens who adopt a nationalist position on the future of Northern Ireland.

8. The NIGP Northern Ireland working group consisted of some dozen individuals who met regularly to discuss the formulation of new policies on a range of issues.

9. The meeting took place prior to the 1994–1995 cease-fire.

10. The EW Green Party's Spirituality working group seeks to express and accommodate the views both of world religions and of minority religious and spiritual groups in society.

References

Bailey, F.G. 1969. *Strategems and Spoils.* Oxford: Oxford University Press.

Barth, F. 1987. *Cosmologies in the Making.* Cambridge: Cambridge University Press.

Easton, D. 1965. *A Systems Analysis of Political Life.* Chicago: Chicago University Press.

Fardon, R. 1995. Introduction. In R. Fardon (ed.), *Counterworks: Managing the Diversity of Knowledge.* London: Routledge.

Goodin, R.E. 1992a. *Green Political Theory.* Cambridge: Polity Press.

____. 1992b. *Motivating Political Morality.* Oxford: Basil Blackwell.

Hannerz, U. 1992. *Cultural Complexity: Studies in the Social Organisation of Meaning.* New York: Columbia University Press.

Labov, T. 1990. Ideological themes in reports of interracial conflict. In A.D. Grimshaw (ed.), *Conflict Talk.* Cambridge: Cambridge University Press.

Parkin, S. 1989. *Green Parties: an international guide.* London: Heretic Books.

Wall, D. 1990. *Getting There: steps to a green society.* London: Green Print.

6 Social conflict and the failure of education policies in two deeply divided societies: Northern Ireland and Israel

Colin Irwin

One of the major characteristics of Northern Ireland is the existence of a strongly segregated society (Boal et al 1976; Boal 1982; Keane 1990; Boyle and Hadden 1994) in which political, social and economic divisions persistently separate the Catholic and Protestant populations. It has often been suggested that segregation and social injustice represented by, for example, differentials in access to resources and employment, continue to aggravate high levels of inter-community hostility (Compton 1981).

In his comparative study of the divided societies of New Brunswick (French and English Canadians) and Northern Ireland (Catholics and Protestants), Aunger (1981) uses the theory developed by Lijphart (1968) to explain the differences in the levels of political stability and instability that exist in these two societies. In this comparison he describes how structural divisions in New Brunswick do not consistently fall along the English-French divide, while in Northern Ireland these divisions do fall along, and so reinforce, the Protestant-Catholic divide. If this analysis is correct, then other deeply divided societies might be expected to share with Northern Ireland many of the social characteristics that contribute to the polarisation of their constituent communities.

In his study of the mechanisms used to maintain social boundaries in Northern Ireland—mechanisms which include the Churches, the Orange Order, social ranking, residential segregation, separate education and endogamy—Whyte (1986: 230) concludes that 'Education divides the population into two communities more precisely than any other marke[r] which we have so far examined'. Given the importance of education (both formal and informal) to the processes of enculturation and group formation (Irwin 1992; 1993), this finding is far from unexpected, and similar processes of childhood segregation and socialisation would predictably be at work elsewhere in places like Israel.

With such points in mind I began a programme of comparative research in 1987 to describe the education policies and practices of both Northern Ireland and Israel.[1] In this chapter I review my principal findings in the hope that by documenting the parallel social failures of these education systems, the respective governments might be prompted to institute the reforms needed to build on the flagging peace processes underway in their separate states. Such an objective necessitates a certain degree of political optimism, but some progress has been made. I also hope that others might take note of the education policies and practices to be found in these two societies and consider themselves to be fairly warned.

Education and Social Justice

Discrimination in Israel

I will not attempt to give a detailed account of all the instances of discrimination in education directed by the State of Israel against the Palestinians in the Occupied Territories. A few examples from a review by Johnson and Taylor (1990) will suffice. Before the Intifada, Bethlehem University was closed when a student was killed by the Israeli Defence Force in October 1987. This was followed by collective closures of West Bank universities and, on 3 February 1988, 1,194 schools, excluding east Jerusalem, were also closed. These closures were repeated in 1989. Closures in Gaza were not collectively organised, but between 35 and 50 per cent of school days were lost through individual closures and curfews. Attempts by the United Nations Relief and Works Agency controlled schools to distribute home study packs in 1989 were blocked by the authorities. Schools were also defaced, vandalised and commandeered for use as temporary detention centres and military posts. Student prisoners have been denied tertiary education since 1981 and Palestinian institutions have been subject to taxes and customs duties for which Israeli universities receive refunds or subsidies. Students and faculty have been subject to detention, interrogation and denied access to libraries, bookshops and international conferences.

Few would question the long term individual and social value of a good education. Conversely, the harm that has been done to the youth and future society of Palestine cannot easily be undone. In drawing parallels with South Africa, Afif Safieh (Safieh 1994), the Head of the PLO Delegation to the United Kingdom, pointed out that the struggle against Israeli rule had sacrificed the creative potential of a generation and that this loss would make the implementation of a stable peace more difficult to realise and sustain.

Discrimination in Northern Ireland

Since the formation of Northern Ireland after the partition of Ireland in 1922, government schools, which are *de facto* Protestant, have always received more funding than their Catholic counterparts. The classification and financing of schools in Northern Ireland is complex, but a few statistics taken from Dunn (1990) will help to illustrate the point. While Protestant schools have always been fully funded, Catholic schools have received between 0 per cent of their capital costs in 1923 rising to 65 per cent in 1947, as much as 85 per cent in 1976 and finally 100 per cent in 1994, subject to changes in the structure of their governing boards. Like the Catholic schools in 1923, integrated schools, which seek to enrol equal numbers of Catholics and Protestants, did not receive any funding when they started in 1981. However, this was raised to 85 per cent in 1984 and to 100 per cent in 1989.

Discrimination in the Northern Ireland education system has not been limited to simple percentages of capital and operating grants. Differences in the sizes of the schools, provision for teaching science and access to grammar school places have also favoured Protestants over Catholics (Cormack et al 1992). In their Seventeenth Report, the Northern Ireland Standing Advisory Commission on Human Rights made a number of specific administrative recommendations to monitor and rectify these discrepancies (SACHR 1992) and government policy is now shaped by the principle of equality of provision in education (Smith 1994).

In addition to this kind of institutional discrimination, children can also fall victim to individual acts of prejudice and bigotry perpetrated against them by other children, by parents, and by teachers associated with Northern Ireland's segregated schools. For example, rates of mixed marriage in Northern Ireland have steadily increased from 1.3 per cent in 1943–47 to 9.7 per cent in 1978–82 (Compton and Coward 1989). However, there are only places for approximately 2 per cent of children to attend integrated schools in Northern Ireland, so it must necessarily follow that literally thousands of children from mixed marriages are obliged to go to segregated schools where they may be subject to violent discrimination.[2]

Boy, aged 13, from a mixed marriage
I came to Lagan College on the ninth of September from Bally High School [pseudonym]. I left Bally High School because my Dad was a Catholic and my Mum is a Protestant, and as Bally was a Protestant school I didn't seem to be liked by quite a lot of the people. They found out that I was half and half because they knew my Dad because he refereed in the local football league.

I never stood up and told any of the teachers about what sort of problem I was having. Sometimes in class they would call me a Taig [i.e. a Catholic] but the teachers let on they never heard them. But there was one day when I went to the toilet and six or seven fourth years followed me and gave me a kicking in the toilets and then I went and told a teacher. He understood the matter as he knew me and my family very well. He tried his hardest to get the matter stopped but it backfired, it started to get worse. He tried to give them detentions, but still it didn't stop, it started to get more worse, the crowd got bigger.

I didn't go back to the school on the last three days as I was so shaken that they were going to get me and kick my head in. So it was the last week of the summer holidays when my Dad phoned Lagan College and it was the ninth of September before I got in.

Additionally, those who choose to promote peace-building through integration are often thought of as a threat to the *status quo* of their divided communities and systems of separate education.

Catholic girl aged 12
I went to a Catholic Primary school. Across the road was a Protestant school. It did not matter to me about Catholics and Protestants. When I was in P 6 we were told all about religion. My P 6 teacher did not agree on having a school for both Catholics and Protestants. It was coming time for me to do the eleven plus. The teacher asked me what school I would like to go to. I said 'Lagan College'. Then the teacher started asking me all these questions. The teacher said 'Why do you not want to go to a Catholic school'. I replied 'just because that's where I want to go and my parents want me to go'. When my results came out I had passed my eleven plus. My teacher asked our class again what school do you want to go to. There was me and 3 others that had said they were going to Lagan College. Then the teacher took us out of the room. He said to us 'What are you going to Lagan College for?' When I was in P 6 and P 7 I always got chased because I was Catholic and called Fenian. So our teacher would say it would be worse at Lagan College because it was mainly Protestant.

Protestant girl aged 13
The area in which I live is mostly Protestant. There are very few Catholics, maybe 2 or 3, and it is not well known. If Catholics come to the estate they would get chased and a group of Protestants would start a fight. Even if you are Protestant and are suspected of being Catholic a fight may be started. This is not all the time. Sometimes if a Catholic came to visit a Protestant friend nothing would be said. If I brought a Catholic friend to visit I would maybe change their name, because even though nothing might not be said I wouldn't like to take a chance. It can annoy me because I would like to bring people from school without changing their names.

As I go to Lagan College some people think that I am Catholic and taunt me. It doesn't really worry me. People say I should change schools and not to mix.

Education and peace-building

A failure to promote tolerance and understanding in Israel

As a response to Jewish and Arab riots in Palestine in the 1930s and 1940s, the British Government would like to have introduced a system of integrated secondary education, since they felt that:

> It would be natural to suppose that in the field of education, more easily and effec-
> tively perhaps than anywhere else, something could be done to bring the two dis-
> cordant races of Palestine nearer together. But, in so far as any policy of that kind
> would tend to moderate the full-blooded nationalism of both races, it would be
> vehemently opposed by the spokesmen of both . . . The existing Arab and Jewish
> school systems are definitely widening and will continue to widen the gulf between
> the races (Secretary of State for the Colonies 1937: 248).

But such a policy was impossible to implement, since Article 15 of the 1923
British Mandate had conferred 'The right of each community to maintain its own
schools for the education of its own members', with the result that public institutions and opinion had already been shaped along lines of social division in matters of education (Secretary of State for the Colonies 1937; 1946).

In an effort to counter this unfortunate and continuing state of affairs in post-
independent Israel a Dominican, Father Bruno, founded the Neve Shalom: Wahat
Al-Salam community and School for Peace in 1971. It does not receive the full
support of the state as enjoyed by other new communities and schools. However,
it does receive the support of the Church. It has been established on 100 acres of
Church land leased to Father Bruno for this purpose from the adjacent Latrun
Monastery. Promotional materials for the Neve Shalom nursery, kindergarten and
primary school state that:

> The principles of coexistence and equality are our guide at all-times. Here, in the
> only bi-national, bi-lingual school of its kind to date, the children absorb these val-
> ues naturally and are taught about their national and cultural differences, whilst
> stressing their own individual identities (Neve Shalom: Wahat Al-Salam n.d.).

As might be expected, Father Bruno has been criticised by some members of
his Church. However, questioning and discussion are both natural and healthy pre-
requisites for constructive action. The point is, Father Bruno was able to gain the
support of his Church, and perhaps this is one of the reasons why he has also
received nominations for the Nobel Peace Prize. When the President of Israel,
who was born in Belfast and grew up in Dublin, visited Neve Shalom, he suggested that if Israel did not adopt the educational policies practised there, Israel
would end up like Northern Ireland. President Hertzog made these comments
before the Palestinian uprising, the Intifada.

Neve Shalom: Wahat Al-Salam has set a standard for peace education in
Israel against which all other efforts can be judged. It provides a wide variety of
services that, in addition to the ecumenical community itself and their integrated
school, includes a hostel and seminar facilities. These are used extensively for
encounter groups made up from both sides of the Jewish/Arab divide. Contact
schemes for Jewish and Palestinian school children at the Peace School have been
refined and perfected through an ongoing programme of research undertaken by
the Israel Institute of Applied Social Research in Jerusalem and funded by the
Ford Foundation.

By way of contrast, programmes for peace education instituted by the state of Israel are token and ineffectual. They are limited to informing each group about the culture of the other and about how this kind of knowledge is used in the establishment of group relations. Research on this programme, conducted by the Bar-Ilan University, was reported to the *First International Congress on Prejudice, Discrimination and Conflict* in Jerusalem in 1991 (Ben-Ari et al 1991). At that time one token Palestinian was working on the project and research was limited to studies amongst the Jewish Israeli population. In spite of these limitations, the programme seems to have flourished. The Department for Democracy and Coexistence in Israel now 'acknowledges the need for the nurturing of the cultural identity of both Arab-Israeli students and Jewish-Israeli students toward promoting a multi-cultural society' (information booklet of the Department quoted in UNESCO 1994a: 24). Since most 'Arab-Israelis' consider themselves to be 'Palestinians', the expressed objectives of the Department for Democracy and Coexistence appear to be contradictory, incompatible and self-defeating.

The reality behind this tokenism are systems of segregated education which teach the superiority of Islam and Judaism alongside a denial of a right to existence for the state of Israel and the validity of a 'Greater Israel' respectively. These polarised visions of the Middle East are taught with greatest conviction in the fundamentalist schools such as those operated by Hamas and Shas (Helm 1993). In the most extreme of these schools, such as the ones run by settlers in the Occupied Territories, the relationship between inhuman attitudes and inhuman behaviour correlate with deathly clarity. After thirty worshippers were killed in the Hebron massacre, a follower of Rabbi Kahane expressed the view that 'There are no innocent Arabs. These deaths are necessary and it is necessary to kill a lot more. Baruch was a hero, a hero of all the Jews. He was a perfect man, a kind man and a sweet man'. This opinion was echoed by a child of 13 who observed that 'The killing was very good. It shows the Arabs we have the power' (Helm 1994a). Dr. Baruch Goldstein, who shot the Palestinians at prayer, considered the Arabs to be 'like an epidemic—the pathogens that infect us' (Helm 1994a). In this context we should not be surprised to discover that the Israeli Defence Forces deployed in Hebron were under orders not to shoot settlers because, according to Major-General Shaul Mofaz, 'We do not shoot Jews, they are not the enemy' (Helm 1994b). Conversely, outside Israel and the Occupied Territories, in south Lebanon, extremist Muslim groups like Hizbollah believe it is their religious duty to destroy the state of Israel and they teach and practise their violent philosophy with similar vigour and determination (BBC 1994).

A failure to promote tolerance and understanding in Northern Ireland

Successive governments have believed that integrated education could do much to improve inter-community relations and promote peace in Northern Ireland. The first national system of education established in Dublin in 1831 was intentionally created to be non-denominational with the expressed 'hope that by learning to live together as children they would at least tolerate each other as adults' (Akenson 1970: 158). Unfortunately, this early effort to produce a united or mixed system of education was strongly opposed by the Churches, with the result that it became denominational or segregated within less than twenty years of its foundation. Sectarian interests also prevented the formation of an integrated school system in Northern Ireland in 1922 (for reviews of the history and politics of education in Ireland, see Akenson 1970 and 1973). Again, during the brief life of the power-sharing Executive in Northern Ireland, the Minister of Community Relations attempted to put integrated education on to the agenda. But this effort failed with the collapse of the Executive in 1974 (Parliamentary Debates 1974).

In a similar fashion to the efforts of Father Bruno in Israel, the 'All Children Together' movement (ACT) and Lagan College have set a standard for peace education against which all other efforts can be judged in Northern Ireland. Indeed, I believe that these kinds of institutions set standards for the world. After the resumption of 'the Troubles', as the sectarian conflict in Northern Ireland is known, a group of concerned parents formed ACT (in 1972) with the expressed goal of seeking 'changes in the educational system of Northern Ireland that will make it possible for parents who so wish to secure for their children, an education in shared schools acceptable to all religious denominations and cultures' (ACT 1974; and for a review, see ACT-LETT 1994: 1–5). In the absence of effective government initiatives on these objectives, ACT stimulated public debate and founded the first integrated school, Lagan College, in 1981 in a scout hut with 28 students and 2 full-time and 5 part-time teachers. During its first three years, the College received no government funding and had to raise over 1.5 million pounds from the international community to cover its building and operating costs. Ten years later, in 1994, Lagan College had a student population of nearly one thousand and another 23 integrated schools had been established in the province. The intense lobbying of ACT also led to significant changes to education legislation in Northern Ireland. Most importantly, the Education Reform (NI) Order 1989 requires the government to promote integrated schools and make Education for Mutual Understanding (EMU) a part of the cross-community curriculum throughout the province. Unfortunately, resistance from local politicians (BBC 1991), the churches (Gallagher and Worrall 1982), and school boards (White 1992) have prevented these programmes from developing to their full potential (Pollack 1993) and, in spite of much popular support, the government is reluctant to oppose this resistance, since they require the co-operation of the church and community leaders in other areas of policy development (Morrow 1992). As always, such decisions are driven by short-term political interests (Guelke 1994).

Resistance to integrated education has also come from those in the academic community who tried to predict the inevitable institutional or social failure of such an enterprise. For the most part these critiques have been made by scholars from Northern Ireland: for example, Salters (1970), Russell (1974), Darby et al (1977),

Loughran (1987), McEwen (1990), Hughes (1994) and for reviews see Gallagher and Worrall (1982) and Irwin (1991; 1992; 1994). Although these criticisms and reservations have become more tempered in recent years, they were probably taken seriously by many officials in the Northern Ireland Office, providing them with excuses for a lack of effective action. Perhaps research on conflict in deeply divided societies should only be undertaken in collaboration with 'outside' scholars, who might be less inclined to dismiss new social opportunities and possibilities out of hand. Local experience is invaluable, but local opinion needs to be challenged.

My own studies suggest that the children coming to Lagan College from throughout the Greater Belfast area are not so very different from their peers in the segregated schools (Irwin 1991; 1993). Although there is a great deal of variation between individual children, many find it difficult to make friends across the sectarian divide when they first arrive. For some children, it takes several years to cross this barrier, and it is therefore not surprising that Hughes (1994) discovered children in her study who found such friendships difficult, and who avoided discussion of sensitive political issues. However, there would be many more of these children in first year than there would be in fifth year, by which time all the children at Lagan College had made at least one friend in the other community (Irwin 1991; 1993), and for most of the children at the school questions of denomination became substantially unimportant. Unfortunately, out of school, some children could only meet their friends from the other community in the neutral shopping centre 'down town' or take them to their home by masking their identity with, for example, a temporary change of name.

But friendships are not everything, values are also important. A study completed by Montgomery (1993) compares the inter-community attitudes of fifth year children at both integrated and segregated schools in Belfast. As might be expected, the values of the integrated students were consistently more pro-social than their counterparts in the other schools. However, when the sample was broken down, Montgomery also found evidence to suggest that integrated education was more important than a mixed marriage background in the development of these positive social attitudes. Perhaps the importance of peer groups has been greatly underestimated by some researchers.

In this context it may be important not only to consider the benefits of integrated education but also the social harm done by segregated schools. A study by Douglas (1983) of children who transferred from an integrated primary school to a segregated secondary school suggests that their positive social attitudes may not have been well enough developed to be entirely secure.

> The change in attitudes at the intergroup level found in pupils at an integrated school appear to be lost within 3 months of attending a segregated Secondary school. One reason that could be given to account for this change of attitudes in such a short period of time is that it is due to social conformity. The children who go to the segregated Secondary school from an integrated Primary school may have to conform to a different set of social norms (Douglas 1983: 61).

Fortunately, as children mature through puberty and gain the self confidence of young adults, they become more independent minded and less susceptible to transient social pressures (Irwin 1991; 1992). Montgomery is drawn to the conclusion 'that integrated schools are the best forum in which to address . . . [the curricular demands of Education for Mutual Understanding and Cultural Heritage]; these schools do make a difference to the pupils who attend them and they must be taken more seriously as an alternative to the segregated/sectarian schools' (1993: 52). The following essays written by children from Lagan College may help to further illustrate this dichotomy of segregation and integration and of social harm and social good.

Protestant boy aged 13
I have lived all my life in a small coastal village in County Down. It is a very quiet place, the police can walk the streets unarmed and in ordinary clothing and the army never patrol. There are no shootings and the last bomb exploded in Main Street by accident in 1972 before I was born. I am Methodist but five houses away Father O'Brian, the local Catholic Priest, lives. I grew up with boys who went to his church so I could not understand why they had to go to the Catholic school and the rest of us to the local school. It is hard for a child to understand why people should hate each other when they live in a quiet area. I was nine before I learned of the madness that gripped the Province. It was then that I learned words like 'Dirty Fenian', 'Filthy Taig' and to yell 'Mick'. At Lagan none of this matters. Who you are is more important than what you are. I have regained the innocence of the child who played with anyone.

My friend David grew up in Belfast on the Ormeau Road where daily army patrols are common place. He has only to lift two pencils and he is beating out the rhythm of 'The Sash'. Yet he sits beside Mathew, a Catholic from a part of Belfast which David wouldn't be seen dead in. One day they will both be men. Will they meet on a building site? Will they use the same Café or Pub? Maybe. One thing I do know even now is that they won't teach their children to hate.

We have nothing to fear but the unknown. Lagan College has seen to it that some of us will know each other very well. We may only be a few when we grow up . . . But we will be a start.

Catholic girl aged 15
I really couldn't say that there is both Catholics and Protestants in the area where I live simply because there is a road that divides us, which is sad really. I never really thought about this before, I suppose I was just like the rest, I thought about them as everything else except real people. Lagan College changed all my feelings towards this and having friends which are the opposite religion to mine made me feel against politicians who are confusing the people and probably the cause of the troubles today.

When I see my friends fighting with Protestants I become mad and give off to them all. Lagan College has made me feel a kind of duty to pull us together and has shown me that we are all the same inside.

I know that if I had of went to an all Catholic school I would be against Protestants by following the example of people around me. But after this experience I would be sure to send any children of my own to integrated schools.

A failure to provide freedom of choice in Israel

Shortly after the 1967 war, Meron Benvenisti, the then Deputy Mayor of Jerusalem, briefly promoted the idea of Arab and Jewish integrated education in an effort to unite the separate communities of that divided city (Benvenisti 1989). In mid-1968 the Jerusalem Municipality conducted a survey of Jewish attitudes in the city which revealed that 55 per cent would not allow their children to attend a mixed Jewish-Arab school (Benvenisti 1983). As a matter of simple arithmetic it follows that as many as 45 per cent would not have strong objections, although, in practice, experience in Northern Ireland suggests that the percentage who would freely send their children to an integrated school would be considerably less.

After the 'First International Congress on Prejudice, Discrimination and Conflict' was held in Jerusalem in July 1991, the delegation from Northern Ireland went on a tour of Israel and the Occupied Territories organised by Peter Lemish of the International Centre for Peace in the Middle East, Tel Aviv. In the northern city of Accro, we met with Palestinian municipal leaders and discussed a wide range of issues including efforts to start an integrated school in their community after the '67 War. As in Jerusalem, a significant percentage of parents desired access to such a school, but they were a minority, and thus, through a simple ballot, their wishes were denied. To my knowledge the kindergarten and primary school at Neve Shalom: Wahat Al-Salam continues to be the only integrated school in Israel. At first they only made their facilities available to members of their own community. However, in 1991, they were erecting new school buildings with a view to taking children from outside their village in response to requests for integrated education from non-residents. Unfortunately, as an ecumenical community they were not given equal access to monies that are normally available to new Jewish settlements in Israel and they had to finance much of their construction costs through contributions from international donations. In any society where those who wish to make peace are a minority, their efforts at peace-building are frequently frustrated by the 'tyranny of the majority'. Additionally, in Israel and the Occupied Territories, where schools and universities are forcibly closed, freedom of choice in education, integrated schools and peace-building understandably become matters of secondary concern. As a peace settlement is slowly implemented in the Middle East, the human rights of peace makers should become a policy issue of primary importance if the peace is to be progressively strengthened in the long term.

A failure to provide freedom of choice in Northern Ireland

Although limited access was provided to a small number of historically integrated 'Mill' schools (for a study of these schools see Douglas 1983), general access to integrated education in Northern Ireland has never been a reality, since the alternative to the optional Catholic schools were the government 'Controlled Schools', which are *de facto* Protestant as already mentioned. In 1968, a National Opinion Polls survey conducted for the *Belfast Telegraph* recorded as many as 65 per cent of young people between seventeen and twenty-four years of age as being in favour of integration at the primary school level, and 70 per cent as supporting integration at the secondary level (*Belfast Telegraph* 1968a). A similar majority of parents also expressed their desire for integration in another survey conducted a year earlier (*Belfast Telegraph* 1968b).

From its humble beginnings in the 1970s, the integrated schools movement has now established itself as a legitimate third sector through the efforts of ACT, the Belfast Charitable Trust for Integrated Education, the Northern Ireland Council for Integrated Education and several other organisations. This growth in the integrated sector has been assisted by the Education Reform (NI) Order of 1989 which allows integrated schools to receive full public funding (subject to government approval) and existing segregated schools to become integrated if more then 50 per cent of the parents vote for change. Unfortunately, the costs of establishing new schools, particularly secondary schools, is prohibitive and the political difficulties of changing the status of a segregated school to integrated is subject to numerous social pressures that can range from simple obstruction to blatant intimidation (BBC 1991; White 1992). As a consequence of these failures, this legislation continues to deny the rights of substantial minorities who may wish an integrated education for their child, and acts as a serious impediment to the natural growth of the integrated sector.

Many of those who apply for admission to an integrated school are turned away for lack of places. For example, 252 parents chose Lagan College as the first preference on their 1991 'Transfer Procedure' forms, although only 150 places were available. Some parents do not apply because an integrated school does not exist in their area. The integrated sector can only accommodate about 2 per cent of the student population of Northern Ireland, while recent research suggests that approximately 30 per cent of parents would like to send their children to such schools (Dunn and Cairns 1992). This research also notes that a much higher proportion of parents, approximately 80 per cent, believes it is important for children to be educated together. Students representing the schools of Northern Ireland at a 'Schools Assembly' meeting held in 1993 voted 68 to 16 in favour of complete integration of the education system with 7 abstentions and 81 to 9 in favour of non-compulsory integration with only 2 abstentions (Opsahl Commission 1993). This desire for integrated education amongst the young is also reflected in comments made by some of the children who chose to attend Lagan College.[3]

Protestant boy aged 13
Now people want to be friendly with people of other religions and not always fighting over stupid things like religion. Sometimes it is the child who sees and under-
stands and he wants to go to Lagan College. These children tell their friends how
good and how much fun it is at Lagan College. So friends want to go to Lagan
College.

Catholic girl aged 13
I came to Lagan College because I wanted to see what it would be like working
with Protestants. I thought that there would be a lot of fighting. But my friend told
me there was not a lot of fighting and that both Protestants and Catholics get on
well.

Protestant girl aged 11
I am eleven years old. My Mum and Dad wanted me to go to Ulster High but I did
not want to go so I told them that I wanted to go to Lagan College.

The system of segregated education in Northern Ireland contributes to the
perpetuation of prejudice and social conflict in the province, while integrated education increases cross-community understanding and friendship. Unfortunately,
in the face of local opposition, the Northern Ireland Office and Department of
Education have failed to provide every child with a real option of attending an
integrated school. This failure represents a breach of the human rights and fundamental freedoms of the children of Northern Ireland. Some of the parents who
have not been able to secure a place for their child at Lagan College have
expressed their disappointment in the following terms:[4]

Being denied the right to attend an integrated school, my daughter has been denied
the right to mix and find out more about her Catholic peers in a safe environment
that hopefully would have helped her form lasting relationships that is the only way
forward for this country of ours.

My child was not successful in receiving a place at her choice of school (i.e. Lagan
College). There is no integrated school in the immediate area, and we were prepared to have her travel to Belfast to be educated at an integrated school.

I think it is a disgrace that my children have been denied the opportunity to be educated in an integrated school due to the limited number of places available. If more
spaces were available it would allow my children to work and learn with children
of different religion and backgrounds, thus understanding the problems faced in
Northern Ireland and playing their part in easing them.

We are a mixed (Catholic/Protestant) marriage, and an integrated school is the only
place where our children, whom we wish to have an Irish and British cultural background can feel completely comfortable. This is also the only system which will
ease Ulster's sectarian troubles.

> Due to the situation in Northern Ireland and the area in which my family are living, integrated education would have given my son a chance to mix with others from different social and educational backgrounds. I feel bitter that this right has been taken from him. I have brought my children up to be peace-loving and to realise we are all equal, yet my choice for his future education was taken from me.

The Northern Ireland Standing Advisory Commission on Human Rights has long felt that the provision of integrated education was a proper subject for their attention (see SACHR 1988; 1989; 1990a; 1991; 1992). In the context of the *First Protocol of the European Convention on Human Rights and Fundamental Freedoms*, SACHR (1989) recognised the rights of parental choice in education and initiated a programme of research to investigate the desire of parents to send their children to integrated schools (Dunn and Cairns 1992). SACHR (1989) also anticipated the failure of government policies to meet the needs of these parents, observing that 'The proposed policies lacked the element of official planning which was necessary to ensure that the provision of places in the integrated sector in Northern Ireland was in accordance with parents' wishes' (SACHR 1990a: 4). Additionally, in their Second Report on *Religious and Political Discrimination and Equality of Opportunity in Northern Ireland*, SACHR 'concluded that the possibility of making more explicit provision in the education legislation for parents to have their children educated in denominationally controlled schools and in integrated schools and for equal funding for such schools should be regarded as a serious option' (SACHR 1990b: 95). It is also interesting to note that in the same report, in the context of seeking to improve community relations, SACHR concluded that 'There may therefore be some advantage in granting formal constitutional or statutory guarantees to both Catholic and Protestant schools that they will be treated equally and without discrimination, while also guaranteeing in some way the right of parents to choose integrated schooling if they so wish' (SACHR 1990b: 94). Finally, in the introduction to her book *Education Together for a Change*, Moffat (1993: 13–14) points out that:

> A further difficulty is that while the 1989 Order imposes a duty on the Department of Education to encourage and facilitate integrated education, it imposes no corresponding duty on area boards. Nor does it impose any specific requirement that the Department or area boards should ensure adequate provision of integrated schools, both primary and secondary, throughout Northern Ireland for those who want it, or even that they should take steps to ascertain the wishes of parents.

Clearly a very great deal still needs to be done to make integrated education as accessible as segregated education in Northern Ireland.

The role of the international community

In a divided society (and most societies are to various degrees) educational resources are rarely allocated equitably amongst the society's constituent groups (e.g. South Africa, see Oakley-Smith 1992) and standards are rarely monitored for consistency (e.g. Native Canadians, see Irwin 1989). As a consequence, equitability in employment, social success and political influence all become increasingly differentiated along lines of group division. Beyond simple equitability, the problems of integration need to be addressed (e.g. Northern Ireland, see Moffat 1993) and at a more basic level the very existence, recognition and rights of minorities should not be denied (e.g. Israel and the Occupied Territories, see Lemish et al 1991). Finally, and most seriously, no state should be allowed to use their system of education to actively promote fear and hatred with a view to the prosecution of war and genocide (e.g. the former Yugoslavia, see Pajic 1994). But all these educational failings and needs are subject to the pressures of numerous political forces and interests, as all the examples I have mentioned above illustrate.

In an effort to reduce conflict between societies, the Member States of the United Nations drew up the *Universal Declaration of Human Rights*. With reference to education, Article 26 of the Declaration contains three clauses to promote justice, peace and freedom through education by making it a universal right that is directed to the establishment of good relations between racial, ethnic and religious groups while remaining subject to parental choice. Those who worked so hard to include these provisions in the *Universal Declaration of Human Rights* would view with frustration the many deeply divided societies which continue to violate these fundamental principles of education established to promote equality of opportunity, mutual understanding and tolerance. If UNESCO's new programme for a 'Culture of Peace' is to meet with success, then these violations of educational rights must be addressed by the international community.

Some of the human rights abuses, as they relate to education in Israel and Northern Ireland, have been brought to the attention of the international community. For example, UNESCO sent a 'Mission' to the Occupied Territories in an effort to appraise the extent of human rights violations there. Subsequently, in his report to a meeting of the Executive Committee held on 25 August 1989, the Director General noted that:

> Neither in terms of the reasons invoked, nor in the context of legislation or international law, does the generalized and permanent closing of schools and universities and the paralysing of the entire educational system appear to be justified. Given the other measures of an obstructive nature applied for the past twenty years in the Occupied Territories, the consultant finds it impossible to dismiss outright the interpretation offered by the very many people, not only Palestinians but also foreigners, with whom he spoke during his mission, that it is the deliberate intention of the occupying power to oppose the development of a Palestinian elite, or even to destroy the Palestinian identity (quoted from Johnson and Taylor 1990: 98).

Through the efforts of an international campaign the schools on the West Bank were reopened, temporarily, in July 1989, and sanctions from the European Union directed at the suspension of scientific agreements with Israel helped to improve the circumstances of the Palestinian universities. Hopefully, the current peace process will bring an end to these systematic abuses of human rights in the Occupied Territories.

With regard to Northern Ireland, the UN Committee on the Rights of the Child did give careful consideration to the question of integrated education, when they examined the first report of the United Kingdom (HMSO 1994) in January 1995 (Nations Unies 1995). The Chairman of the UN Committee on the Rights of the Child questioned the United Kingdom government on the lack of provision for integrated education in Northern Ireland, and in their concluding observations the Committee suggested that the state provide further support to integrated education (UN 1995). Hopefully, the public discussion of these issues in relation to Northern Ireland will help to create opportunities for similar complaints to be brought against other states in the future, for example Israel.

Perhaps it was with such thoughts in mind that the head of the Israeli delegation to the 44th Session of the International Conference on Education (UNESCO 1994b) publicly made a commitment to the assembled international community that a greater effort would be made to increase contacts between Jewish and Arab students in his country. More recently, as part of the activities for the 1995 UN Year of Tolerance, the German Commission to UNESCO organised an international symposium (UNESCO 1995) at which teachers from both Lagan College and Neve Shalom: Wahat Al-Salam were able to share the lessons of their experiences with those who had to come to terms with similar problems in other parts of the world. All this international attention is to be welcomed. However, in the end such scrutiny, comment and exchange of views must be translated into domestic policy changes.

Education policy and public opinion

The way forward in Northern Ireland?

I believe that the comparisons drawn between Israel and Northern Ireland show little difference in the kinds of educational abuses reviewed here. The differences only seem to be a matter of degree. Peace-making is a political act that frequently requires a degree of bravery in deeply divided societies, and peace-makers must be given every possible advantage that public policy can offer if peace-building is to be effective. Unfortunately, peace, tolerance and understanding are not always in the best interests of the political leaders who claim to speak on behalf of the groups they say they represent. In large measure their political futures are contingent on the continuation of social divisions. Opinion polls in Northern Ireland have repeatedly shown that the people there want their political leaders to make greater efforts in their pursuit of peace (for reviews see Whyte 1990; Boyle and

Hadden 1994; Stringer and Robinson 1991; 1992; 1993). Unfortunately, the voices of moderation are, for the most part, ignored and disproportionate attention is given to those minorities who are willing to use violence to achieve their political ends. Peace cannot be built in this way. If individuals—teachers, parents and children—are willing to use education as a means to peace-making, then public policy must provide them with every possible opportunity to do so.

Deeply divided societies seem to fall victim to two forms of majoritarianism. The tyranny of the larger political majority over the smaller political minority and the tyranny of the politically intransigent in all groups over those who are willing to accept compromise and accommodation in all groups. It is this latter class of individuals which societies must seek to empower with all the means at its disposal to undertake the social tasks of peace-building. If this cannot be done through conventional majoritarian political processes, then perhaps it is time to look to less conventional methods that are consensual in character.

With regard to education policy, human rights have a role to play in setting appropriate minimum standards. The international community can, and has, assisted in this activity. In the past, public opinion surveys have only been used to identify the willingness of the electorate to accept general peace-building measures using questions that lacked real choice and focus (for example, the *Social Attitudes in Northern Ireland* surveys, Stringer and Robinson 1991; 1992; 1993). The results of these surveys are regularly dismissed by local politicians and bureaucrats alike as irrelevant (Boyle and Hadden 1994). But these difficulties could be overcome by designing surveys which include choices that meet human rights standards.[5] Even more could be achieved by giving such choices democratic authority through the use of public referenda or preferenda.

Notes

1. This research was supported by a Post Doctoral Fellowship from the Social Science and Humanities Research Council of Canada between 1987 and 1989 and by a grant from the Policy Planning and Research Unit of the Northern Ireland Office between 1990 and 1991.
2. The following essays, like those cited later in the chapter, were collected from children at Lagan College (an integrated school) in 1991. The names of individuals, other schools and places have been changed to protect the identity of the informants. However, these essays have not been edited in any other way.
3. These are extracts from the Lagan College essays referred to in Note 2 above.
4. These quotations are taken from forms completed by parents who were unable to secure a place for their child at Lagan College in 1993 and who voluntarily participated in the lodging of a human rights complaint with the UN Committee on the Rights of the Child.
5. In collaboration with Tom Hadden and Fred Boal of the Queen's University departments of law and geography respectively, I am presently piloting such a project with funding from the Rowntree Charitable Trust. In addition to education, the areas of public policy being researched include employment, housing, political development and policing, i.e. many of the social markers referred to by Whyte (1986).

References

Akenson, D. 1970. *The Irish Education Experiment: The National System of Education in the Nineteenth Century.* London: Routledge and Kegan Paul.

_____. 1973. *Education and Enmity: the Control of Schooling in Northern Ireland, 1920-1950.* Newton Abbott: David and Charles.

All Children Together (ACT) 1974. *Interdenominational Schools. How, Why and the Way Ahead?* Presbyterian Community Centre. Queen's University of Belfast.

ACT-LETT 1994. *ACT-LETT News From All Children Together.* IV (4).

Aunger, E. A. 1981. *In Search of Political Stability: A Comparative Study of New Brunswick and Northern Ireland.* Montreal: McGill-Queen's University Press.

Belfast Telegraph. 1968a. Clear Call for End to Religious Separation in Schools. In *Belfast Telegraph,* 22 October.

_____. 1968b. Poll Favours Integration of Education. In *Belfast Telegraph,* 22 October.

Ben-Ari, Riad Nasser, Aharon Bizman and Hadas Smadar 1991. Changing Attitudes and Perceptions in Intergroup Relations. *First International Congress on Prejudice, Discrimination and Conflict.* Jerusalem. July 1–4.

Benvenisti, M. 1983. *Jerusalem: Study of a Polarized City.* Research Paper No. 3, The West Bank Data Base Project, Jerusalem, P. O. Box 14319, Israel.

_____. 1989. Conversation with Meron Benvenisti. Jerusalem, 29 March.

Boal, F. 1982. Segregating and Mixing: Space and Residence in Belfast. In F. Boal and J. Douglas (eds.), *Integration and Division: Geographical Perspectives on the Northern Ireland Problem.* London: Academic Press.

_____. et al 1976. *Religious Residential Segregation and Residential Decision Making in the Belfast Urban Area.* Final Report to the Social Science Research Council.

Boyle, K. and T. Hadden 1994. *Northern Ireland—The Choice.* Harmondsworth: Penguin.

British Broadcasting Corporation 1991. Schools Out. *Heart of the Matter.* London, 7 July.

_____. 1994. Allah's Army. *Assignment.* London. 10 May.

Compton, P. A. 1981. Demographic and Geographical Aspects of the Unemployment Differential Between Protestants and Roman Catholics. In P. Compton (ed.), *The Contemporary Population of Northern Ireland and Population-Related Issues.* Belfast: Institute of Irish Studies.

_____. and J. Coward 1989. *Fertility and Family Planning in Northern Ireland.* Aldershot: Avebury.

Cormack, R., A. Gallagher, D. Murray and R. Osborne 1992. Curriculum, Access to Grammar Schools and the Financing of Schools: An Overview Paper. In *Seventeenth Report of the Standing Advisory Commission on Human Rights.* Report for 1991–92. London: HMSO.

Darby, J., D. Murray, D. Batts, S. Dunn, S. Farren and J. Harris 1977. *Education and Community in Northern Ireland: Schools Apart?* New University of Ulster.

Douglas, S. E. 1983. Differences in Group Identity and Intergroup Attitudes in Children Attending Integrated or Segregated Schools in Northern Ireland. Unpublished thesis, Department of Psychology, Queen's University of Belfast.

Dunn, S. 1990. A Short History of Education in Northern Ireland 1920-1990. In *Fifteenth Report of the Standing Advisory Commission on Human Rights.* Report for 1989–90. London: HMSO.

_____. and E. Cairns 1992. A Survey of Parental Opinion on Education in Northern Ireland. In the *Seventeenth Report of the Standing Advisory Commission on Human Rights.* London: HMSO.

Gallagher, E. and S. Worrall 1982. *Christians in Ulster 1968–1980.* Oxford: Oxford University Press.

Guelke, A. 1994. Promoting Peace in Deeply Divided Societies. *Frank Wright Memorial Lecture.* Queen's University of Belfast.

Helm, S. 1993. Divided at Birth. *The Independent on Sunday.* London, 22 August.

———. 1994a. Hebron settlers shed no tears after slaughter. *The Independent.* London, 28 February.

———. 1994b. Israeli troops 'under orders' not to shoot Jewish settlers. *The Independent.* London, 11 March.

HMSO. 1994. *The UK's First Report to the UN Committee on the Rights of the Child.* London: HMSO.

Hughes, J. 1994. Prejudice and identity in a mixed environment. In A. Guelke (ed.), *New Perspectives on the Northern Ireland Conflict.* Aldershot: Avebury Press.

Irwin, C. J. 1989. Lords of the Arctic: Wards of the State. *Northern Perspectives.* Vol. 17 (1).

———. 1991. *Education and the Development of Social Integration in Divided Societies.* Belfast: Northern Ireland Council For Integrated Education.

———. 1992. Integrated Education: From Theory to Practice in Divided Societies, *Prospects, UNESCO Quarterly Review of Education* XXII (1).

———. 1993. How Integrated Education Works. In C. Moffat (ed.), *Education Together for a Change: Integrated Education and Community Relations in Northern Ireland.* Belfast: Fortnight Educational Trust.

———. 1994. The Myths of Segregation. In A. Guelke (ed.), *New Perspectives on the Northern Ireland Conflict.* Aldershot: Avebury Press.

Johnson, P. and M. Taylor 1990. The Israel Occupied Territories (Palestine). In Laksiri Fernando et al (eds.), *Academic Freedom 1990: A Human Rights Report.* London: Zed Books.

Keane, M. C. 1990. Segregation Processes in Public Sector Housing. In P. Doherty (ed.), *Geographical Perspectives on the Belfast Region,* Geographical Society of Ireland Special Publications No. 5.

Lemish, P., W. Mula, H. Gur Ziv and E. Zaretzki 1991. Power Relations in Divided Societies: The Case of Education for Co-Existence. *First International Congress on Prejudice, Discrimination and Conflict.* Jerusalem, July 1–4.

Lijphart, A. 1968. *The Politics of Accommodation: Pluralism and Democracy in the Netherlands.* Berkeley and Los Angeles: University of California Press.

Loughran, G. 1987. The Rational of Catholic Education. In R.D. Osborne, R.J. Cormack and R.L. Miller (eds.), *Education and Policy in Northern Ireland.* Belfast: Policy Research Institute.

McEwen, A. 1990. Segregation and Integration in Northern Ireland's Education System. In L. Caul (ed.), *Schools Under Scrutiny: The Case of Northern Ireland.* London: Macmillan.

Moffat, C. 1993. Introduction. In C. Moffat (ed.), *Education Together for a Change: Integrated Education and Community Relations in Northern Ireland.* Belfast: Fortnight Educational Trust.

Montgomery, M.G. 1993. Integration by Chance or Design? Queen's University of Belfast: unpublished Master of Education Dissertation.

Morrow, D. 1992. Political Parties in Community Politics: Means or Ends? *Annual Conference of the Political Studies Association of the United Kingdom.* The Queen's University of Belfast, 7–9 April.

Nations Unies, Convention relative aux droits de l'enfant. 1995. *Comité Des Droits De L'Enfant, Huitième session, Compte Rendu Analytique de la 206ème Seance.* CRC/C/SR. 206 - 3 Février.

Neve Shalom: Wahat al-Salam (n.d.). published by the Coordinators and Representatives of Neve Shalom/Wahat al-Salam at Neve Shalom/Wahat al-Salam, Doar-Na Shimshon, 99761 Israel.

Oakley-Smith, T. 1992. Education and Transformation: The Challenge for South Africa. Paper presented at 'Conflict and Change: First International Conference of the Ethnic Studies Network'. Portrush, 8–10 June.

Opsahl Commission. 1993. Evidence given to the Opsahl Commission by Initiative 92: 'Schools Assembly'. Belfast, Queen's University, 25 February.

Pajic, Z. 1994. The Former Yugoslavia. In H. Miall (ed.), *Minority Rights in Europe,* The Royal Institute of International Affairs, Chatham House Papers. London: Pinter Publishers.

Parliamentary Debates 1974. Northern Ireland. 30 April.

Pollack, A. (ed.) 1993. *A Citizens' Inquiry: The Opsahl Report on Northern Ireland.* Dublin: The Lilliput Press.

Russell, J. 1974. Sources of Conflict. *The Northern Teacher* 11 (3).

SACHR 1988. *Thirteenth Report of the Standing Advisory Commission on Human Rights.* London: HMSO.

_____. 1989. *Fourteenth Report of the Standing Advisory Commission on Human Rights.* London: HMSO.

_____. 1990a. *Fifteenth Report of the Standing Advisory Commission on Human Rights.* London: HMSO.

_____. 1990b. *Religious and Political Discrimination and Equality of Opportunity in Northern Ireland, Second Report.* London: HMSO.

_____. 1991. *Sixteenth Report of the Standing Advisory Commission on Human Rights.* London: HMSO.

_____. 1992. *Seventeenth Report of the Standing Advisory Commission on Human Rights.* London: HMSO.

Salters, J. 1970. Attitudes Towards Society in Protestant and Roman Catholic Schoolchildren in Belfast. Queen's University of Belfast: unpublished Master of Education Thesis.

Safieh, A. 1994. The Palestinian-Israel Peace Process. Middle East Seminar Group, Public Lecture, Queen's University of Belfast, 10 March.

Secretary of State for the Colonies. 1937. *Palestine Royal Commission Report.* Presented to Parliament by Command of His Majesty, July 1937. Cmd. 5479. London: His Majesty's Stationery Office.

_____. 1946. *The System of Education of the Jewish Community in Palestine.* Report of the Commission of Enquiry appointed by the Secretary of State for the Colonies in 1945. London: His Majesty's Stationery Office.

Smith, A. 1994 The Management and Control of Schools in Northern Ireland. ESRC Seminar Series. Schools and inter-group relations. University of Ulster at Coleraine.

Stringer, P. and G. Robinson (eds.) 1991. *Social Attitudes in Northern Ireland, 1990-91 Edition.* Belfast: The Blackstaff Press.

_____. 1992. *Social Attitudes in Northern Ireland, The Second Report 1991–92.* Belfast: The Blackstaff Press.

_____. 1993. *Social Attitudes in Northern Ireland, The Third Report 1992–93.* Belfast: The Blackstaff Press.

UN Committee on the Rights of the Child 1995. Eighth Session, Consideration of Reports Submitted by States Parties Under Article 44 of the Convention. Concluding observations of the Committee on the Rights of the Child: United Kingdom of Great Britain and Northern Ireland. CRC/C/15/Add.34. 27 January.

UNESCO 1994a. Tolerance: the Threshold of Peace. A Teaching/Learning Guide for Education for Peace, Human Rights and Democracy (Preliminary version). UNESCO ED-94/WS/8. Paris.

____. 1994b. Forty Fourth Session of the International Conference on Education (ICE), organised by UNESCO and the International Bureau of Education (IBE), 3–8 October. Geneva.

____. 1995. German Commission and the Institute of Political Science. Tolerance in Transition. Magdeburg: University of Magdeburg Symposium, 14–16 October.

White, B. 1992. Testing time for Brownlow College. *Belfast Telegraph*, 28 January.

Whyte, J. H. 1986. How is the Boundary Maintained Between the Two Communities in Northern Ireland? *Ethnic and Racial Studies* 9 (2), 219–34.

____. 1990. *Interpreting Northern Ireland.* Oxford: Oxford University Press.

7 Rhetoric and realpolitik: the Irish language movement and the British government

Gordon McCoy

The Irish language revival in Northern Ireland is an extremely emotive issue, as it touches on Nationalist and Unionist self-concepts of identity, as well as on state intervention in the cultural arena.[1] The issue is often simplified in media debates, which have taken place between the most vociferous of opponents, often to the exasperation of Irish-speakers who for various reasons are reluctant or unwilling to express their views in public. An anthropological approach can contribute to an understanding of the Irish language issue by treating seriously all voices in the debate, especially those which are not often heard in the public domain. Thus the anthropologist can deconstruct naturalised and essentialist interpretations of the language which dominate much of the literature. Furthermore, such an approach sets the language issue in context, by relating it to other political and social issues in Northern Ireland.

This chapter draws on the ethnographic literature on language and identity in order to understand the public discourses generated by the interaction of the British Government and the Irish language movement. The Irish language movement consists of groups of Irish speakers who are actively engaged in promoting the language as well as in defining its ideological significance. Almost all members of this movement are Nationalist in outlook, but they differ in their views as to the ideological significance of the Irish language and the measures that would be most effective to ensure its survival. The British Government's response to the movement reflects the former's declared overall policy direction, which is to respect equally 'the two communities' in Northern Ireland.[2] The politics of the language at the local level therefore reflect macro-level socio-political concerns.

Within a social arena a language may symbolise a counter-ideology which resists a dominant social ethos, becoming an anti-language (Halliday 1978: 164–82). Subordinate languages may be powerful in their own domains, offering alternative versions of reality that have an appearance of autonomy (Grillo 1989: 228). A language may also retain its value as an emblem of ethnicity in the absence of a communicative function; therefore groups or individuals may maintain a strong symbolic and emotional attachment to a language in which they have little or no competence (Eastman 1984). In this way, a language may come to symbolise a 'culture'.

Social science has demonstrated how ethnic groups construct their identities vis-à-vis other groups. Although it is true that ethnic identity often involves the elaboration of real or perceived boundary-markers by groups in order to distinguish them from others, Cohen (1994: 120) insists that ethnicity entails positive self-evaluations as well as negative and oppositional forms of self-ascription. In fact, we could say that folk concepts of culture and identity mirror the early anthropological emphasis on boundary maintenance in identity construction; in ethnic conflicts opponents may accuse one another of having identifications based simply upon a rejection of others.

Anthropologists have long recognised that a language, like a symbol, can have multiple semantic associations at individual and societal levels. In Ireland the Irish language has become the symbolic language for some of the Nationalist population. However, the language is a polysemic symbol whose meaning has been contested. The language has been incorporated into competing discourses of cultural resistance and reconciliation, the latter discourse being utilised in language planning, or state involvement in the linguistic affairs of its citizens. When examining symbolic conflict and the Irish language in Northern Ireland, it is necessary to take into account the views and influence of the four main groupings involved; the Nationalist and Unionist populations, and the British and Irish Governments.

The Irish language in historical perspective

The dominant ideology embracing the Irish language was informed by the German Romantic form of nationalism, which objectified language as containing and transmitting the essential qualities of nations. Advocates of this form of linguistic determinism believed that each language expressed and created a distinct and autonomous system of thought. This ethnic form of nationalism claimed communal solidarity on the basis of a distinctive culture, which was to be defended and protected by a separate political administration; the state was the 'protective shell' of the nation (Smith 1971: 178). Thus the nation was conceived of as a large, politicised ethnic group, united by a common culture (Smith 1971: 176).

For much of the twentieth century Nationalism posited the binary opposition of the Gaelic and English worlds into that of the piously Catholic and Irish-speaking rural *Gael* and that of the secular, morally corrupt and urban, English speaking *Gall*. The interaction of the two was interpreted as one of oppressor and oppressed, and revivalists attributed the decline of the Irish language to a deliberate and systematic policy of Anglicisation by the British administration.[3] Learning Irish was believed to be important in de-colonising the Irish mind. Thus the language became part of a system of 'national parallelism', dichotomising Ireland from Britain, and isolating the country from the evils of the outside world (Tovey et al 1989: 16). Since it was believed that the British were antipathetic to the language, it was assumed that anyone interested in the revival of the language would support the movement to separate Ireland from Britain. Thus cultural protectionism and the struggle for political independence largely converged.

Following the campaign for independence, Ireland was partitioned, with separate legislatures in the south and north of the island. The southern state was initially a dominion of the British Empire, known as the Irish Free State. In 1949, the Free State declared complete independence from Britain and became the Republic of Ireland. Six counties of the north-east of the island, known as Northern Ireland, remained within the United Kingdom and were governed by the Unionist majority at the Stormont parliament near Belfast. The British Government interfered little in Northern Ireland's affairs for the fifty years following partition.

Since it was believed that the British administration had 'murdered' the language, it followed that state promotion of Irish at an institutional level would be sufficient to revive it. The Irish Free State embarked on an ambitious programme of Gaelicisation, which involved the acquisition of Irish in the educational system and its institutionalisation within the formal and administrative strata of society; the attainment of a pass in the language was required for the secondary school Leaving Certificate, as well as entry into the police force and civil service. Voluntarist Irish language activities waned as enthusiasts viewed restoration efforts to be the responsibility of the new state. State-sponsored bilingualism largely failed in its objectives, but Irish became a symbol for many citizens, leaving their daily pattern of communication in English unaltered (Edwards 1985: 111).

The partition of Ireland proved to be cultural as well as political. Compulsory Irish in the South proved a real boon to Unionist politicians and ideologues in the North, who used it as a further justification for partition; in the early years of the fledgling Northern Irish state, the Irish language issue occupied more space in Unionist newspapers than concern over Catholic domination of an Irish parliament (Kennedy 1988: 182). Irish revivalism was seen as increasing the impoverishment of the near-bankrupt southern state, and further evidence of its essentially autocratic nature. English was described as the 'mother tongue of the Ulster people', the 'foreignness' of Irish being accentuated by the promotion of the language by a hostile state (Kennedy 1988: 183). Unionist attitudes to the Irish language reflected the manner in which dominant elites elsewhere associate their language with literature, bureaucracy and science, while they conceive of minority vernaculars as backward and barbarous (Grillo 1989: 173–8 *passim*).

The dominant Northern ethos was utilitarian and modernistic, in contrast to the southern 'dreamers and idealists, impractical to the point of foolishness'

(Kennedy 1988: 183). Unionists felt little need to validate Northern Ireland by promoting a distinctive culture to justify partition; rather, they were content to emphasise the similarities between the 'province' and 'mainland' British culture. The culture of the public domain was to be thoroughly British, though 'Britishness' was an arbitrary quality to be interpreted differently by its adherents. Despite Unionists' self-idealisations of themselves as progressive and democratic, Nationalists were regarded as treacherous to the Northern state and their wishes were ignored; discrimination against the Nationalist population was widespread in many sectors of Northern Irish society (see Whyte 1990: 61–4 *passim*).

Nationalists asserted that the Irish language was part of the indigenous culture of Northern Ireland, but to no avail. During fifty years of Ulster Unionist Party (UUP) hegemony, Irish was to have no part in public life, a principle which was enacted in legislation in 1948, when street signs in languages other than English were banned by the Public Health and Local Government (Miscellaneous Provisions) Act. Though many Unionists regarded Irish-speakers as seditious, the Northern parliament's lack of support for the language was defended publicly on utilitarian grounds, which appeared to be less politically partisan. The BBC followed this approach, refusing requests to transmit programmes in Irish on the grounds that they would have limited appeal (Cathcart 1984: 47). The Irish language became the preserve of Catholic schools and a small voluntarist movement, located mostly within the Catholic population and often consisting of clerics, schoolteachers and other middle-class educated individuals. Support for the language tended to increase among Nationalists in periods of strong anti-British feeling (O'Reilly 1992: 41).

Irish language movement developments, 1960s-1980s

In the late 1960s Nationalists campaigned for the reform of Northern Ireland, and in 1969 serious conflict broke out between large sections of the Nationalist and Unionist populations. In 1972 the British Government prorogued the Stormont Government and introduced direct rule from London. Thereafter the Northern Ireland Office assumed the ultimate responsibility for governing Northern Ireland. The British Government represented itself as a neutral arbiter in the conflict, unlike its Stormont predecessor, though Nationalists and Unionists rarely believed this. From the 1970s onwards the Nationalist population was largely divided between supporters of the Constitutional Nationalist Social Democratic and Labour Party (SDLP) and supporters of the Irish Republican Army (IRA), which embarked on a military campaign to end British rule. Republicans believed that British Government policy aimed to weaken northern Nationalism, in particular support for the IRA. Many Nationalists did not believe Britain's claims to a neutral stance, believing that it wished to shore up partition. In 1994 the IRA and the Protestant paramilitaries called a cease-fire and negotiations to bring about a settlement to the conflict intensified. Nationalists claimed that they should be granted 'parity of esteem' for their political aspirations and cultural beliefs in a reformed Northern Ireland.

From the 1970s most of the Unionist vote has been divided between the UUP and the Democratic Unionist Party (DUP), which took a much stronger right-wing line than its rival. The DUP interpreted Northern Irish politics as a 'zero-sum' game; any gain for Nationalists was perceived to constitute a loss for Unionists and vice-versa. Loyalist paramilitary groups began a military campaign to maintain Northern Ireland's position within the United Kingdom. Since the introduction of direct rule many Unionists have feared that the British Government wished to disengage from Northern Ireland. This fear grew in 1985, when the British and Irish Governments signed the Anglo-Irish Agreement, giving Dublin a consultative role in the affairs of Northern Ireland. The publication of the joint London-Dublin 'Frameworks of the Future' documents in 1995 did little to allay these fears, as they proposed greater institutional co-operation between the two parts of Ireland. Therefore the period of 'the Troubles' was characterised by deep Unionist and Nationalist suspicion of the British Government's intentions.

The civil rights campaign of the 1960s generally ignored cultural issues, which socialist elements regarded as epiphenomenal mystifications obscuring class politics, which they considered to be the true basis of social organisation. Nevertheless, important developments took place in the Irish language scene in Belfast during this period. In 1969 a small group of language activists set up a neo-Gaeltacht in the Shaw's Road district of West Belfast. In 1971, they opened a *bun-scoil* (Irish-medium primary school) for their children, which expanded its intake by admitting children from English-speaking homes in 1978, for whom a *naíscoil* (Irish-medium nursery school) was established.

These developments occurred separately from the growth of Republicanism, which tended to view interest in the Irish language as a distraction from armed insurrection. This view changed dramatically in 1981 when some Republican prisoners went on hunger strike as a protest to achieve political (prisoner of war) status; the British Government regarded paramilitary prisoners as common criminals. The hunger strikes focused Nationalist attention on the prisoners, many of whom had learned Irish despite official disapproval. The language became a symbol of cultural resistance in the prisons, and released prisoners de-mystified Irish for working-class Nationalists, for whom Irish had represented a middle-class intellectual activity. Sinn Féin, the political wing of the IRA, formed a cultural department in 1982 to propagate the use of the Irish language as a form of cultural resistance that complemented the armed struggle. This potent mixture of language and politics had a wide appeal in Republican areas and the demand for Irish classes mushroomed, until by 1984 there were 60 in West Belfast alone (Ó hAdhmaill 1985: 2).

Irish was stripped of its rural and pious associations and given a modern urban image, though the discourse of Government oppression was maintained and reiterated. Sinn Féin also attempted to integrate Irish into a world-wide opposition to Anglo-American mass culture, reflecting the tendency for adherents of sub-cultures to reinforce their arguments by drawing on other counter-hegemonic discourses (Chapman 1992: 228; McDonald 1989: 116). The use of Irish in Republican wall murals and street signs gave physical representation to the ideological boundary between Unionist and Nationalist districts and allowed radical language enthusiasts to flout the law against Irish language street signs in acts of symbolic militancy. They also signified an attempt to imbue Nationalist neighbourhoods with an Irish language ethos, which would persuade their residents to support the language revival. Bilingual signs and murals were thus part of an internal and external dialogue on the Irish language. Sinn Féin and radical language activists transformed what had been a private-domain activity into a public one, thereby mirroring the increased self-confidence and assertiveness of northern Nationalists.

The revival mirrored a world-wide ethnic resurgence which transformed minority ethnicity from a social liability to a desirable identity to be achieved (Fitzgerald 1991: 97). The adoption of ethno-cultural activities compensated for the waning influence of religion and occupational specialisation as sources of self-categorisation; in Northern Ireland republicanism combined with secularisation to weaken the influence of the Catholic Church, leaving the way open for definitions of Nationalist identity that were non-religious in form. These were particularly welcome in working-class Nationalist areas, where many community organisations were resentful of the way in which state funding for community projects was channelled through the Catholic Church.

Sinn Féin's decision to contest the Northern Ireland elections in the 1980s brought the Irish language issue into the realm of local government, where the party recommended the implementation of bilingual policies, including the erection of Irish language signs. The Social Democratic and Labour Party adopted an Irish language policy, though in some areas with substantial Unionist populations individual councillors were reluctant to endorse bilingual measures that would offend large sections of the population. Nationalist promotion of Irish in local councils exacerbated the hostility of Unionist councillors to the language. When Nationalist-controlled councils erected bilingual signs at ethnic interfaces they were vandalised by Unionists who regarded them as marking out Nationalist territory. Local council debates on language gave both Unionist and Nationalist politicians a new means to demarcate their identities and distinctiveness vis-à-vis each other. Many Unionists believed that the Irish language revival was based on a rejection of Britain's political and cultural influence in Ireland. The DUP and the UUP bitterly fought the promotion of Irish at local government level, regarding bilingual policies as a form of institutional Nationalism. Sinn Féin and Unionist parties often quoted one another's more vitriolic statements in an atmosphere of complementary opposition; Sinn Féin often referred to a DUP councillor's memorable description of Irish as a 'leprechaun language' (Ó Muilleoir 1990: 127);

Unionists quoted a Sinn Féin councillor who described every phrase in Irish as 'a bullet in a freedom struggle' (Sinn Féin 1985: 4). Whereas Unionists accused Sinn Féin of politicising the Irish language by promoting it, Republicans maintained that Unionists and the British Government were responsible for the initial politicisation of the language by suppressing it. Unionist opposition to the language reinforced Sinn Féin's representation of Irish as a symbol of collective pride and victimisation.

The linking of the Irish language and Republicanism alarmed Constitutional Nationalist speakers of Irish who viewed the language as a peaceful cultural means of expressing their national identity. Some of them viewed the symbolic promotion of Irish language by means of street signs as gimmicks that do more harm than good, since they antagonised Unionists and inspired few Nationalists to learn the language. They also feared loyalist paramilitaries would target Irish speakers and that the close association between Irish and a political ideology would narrow its appeal; some cynics have suggested that in the event of a political settlement of the Northern Ireland conflict the language revival would vanish (Hindley 1990: 159–60). However, these 'culturalists' were often reluctant to express their opposition to Sinn Féin openly; they did not wish to be ostracised by Republican Irish speakers, and feared being stigmatised as Catholic 'Uncle Toms' who attempted to ingratiate themselves with the British Government and with Unionists. Furthermore, members of subcultures often feel that they must present a united front in public, to prevent their opponents from capitalising on their divisions (Scott 1990: 55–6). Disputes within the language movement were often conducted in the Irish language; the movement maintained a united front in the English language media.

As the 1980s progressed, interest in Irish spread beyond the earlier movement and those influenced by the ideology of Sinn Féin. The academic success of the Shaw's Road *bunscoil* generated a demand in West Belfast for Irish-medium education, which surpassed appeals to learn Irish based on the Nationalist/Republican tradition (Maguire 1991: 100). Parents were inspired to learn Irish by their children and they in turn aroused an interest in their friends and relatives (Maguire 1991: 143). The success of the Shaw's Road *bunscoil* provided a prototype for the development of other Irish-medium primary schools in Northern Ireland. The revival expanded to include social activities and entertainment, as well as Irish-language media, including a newspaper and pirate radio station. The Irish language movement eventually hoped to create an infrastructure in which Irish speakers would be catered for from the cradle to the grave, including educational, recreational and work facilities, taking the language out of the realm of part-time voluntarism and academia into day-to-day community life.

The revival provides a means for socially and economically marginalised Nationalists to find a sense of self-worth and purpose. Nationalist Irish speakers also draw on the revival to assert their cultural capital; West Belfast prides itself as being the centre of revivalist activities in Ireland. The movement is also proud of the fact that most of what it has achieved has been accomplished without government funding, drawing on a long tradition of community action and self-help (Maguire 1991: 18). Nevertheless, some projects, such as Irish-medium education, were expensive, and fund-raising proved to be difficult in areas that suffered from widespread social deprivation and unemployment. Therefore, it became necessary for the Irish language movement to cultivate a relationship with the Government that was not entirely negative and conflictual, in the hope that funding would be made available to alleviate some of the financial pressures involved.

Government language planning

Though many Irish speakers were hostile to the British Government, it did not follow that the state would attempt to thwart the language revival in Northern Ireland. Dominant elites may perceive counter-cultures as 'safety-valves' that release harmless aggression, thus reducing the tendency for subordinate groups to resort to violence and rebellion (Scott 1990: 187). Dominant groups may also choose not to interfere with linguistic counter-cultures if they do not challenge existing relationships of power (Grillo 1989: 228).

Furthermore, by the 1980s the British Government was in theory better disposed to the Irish language than its Stormont predecessor. London was more willing to address Nationalist grievances than northern Unionists. Post-war immigration had transformed Britain into a multi-lingual and multi-ethnic state and language movements agitated and received funding for the protection of Scottish Gaelic and Welsh (Edwards 1984). Gradually the British Government abandoned an assimilationist monocultural policy and embraced one of cultural pluralism, though this tended to apply more to indigenous (Celtic) language communities than immigrant ones. Overall, in examining state language planning the following factors must be taken into account: existing legislation and regulations; limitations resulting from previous policies; financial possibilities; and pressure for and resistance to change.

In Northern Ireland cultural pluralism, as articulated by Government sources and the intelligentsia, entails the development of progressive and non-triumphalist elements of both traditions in order that they may negotiate with one another from a position of cultural confidence. The cross-community potential of cultural resources is also promoted. Adherents of cultural pluralism view the Irish language as part of the common heritage of both communities in Northern Ireland, thus weakening its links to the ideology of traditional Nationalism. The language is thus viewed as contributing towards reconciling the two communities in Northern Ireland. The BBC, which began broadcasting programmes in the Irish language in 1981, has also adopted the 'common heritage' approach.

Cultural pluralism of a different kind is also reflected in the wording of the Anglo-Irish Agreement, which states that the British and Irish Governments would consider measures to 'foster the cultural heritage of both traditions' (Hadden and Boyle 1989: 30). The 1989 Official Review of the Agreement recognises the importance of the Irish language in the context of improving community relations (Hadden and Boyle 1989: 84–5). The Government approach to the Irish language has been described as contradictory in that its 'two traditions' discour identifies the language with the Nationalist tradition, yet its 'common heritage' approach interprets it as the property of both Unionists and Nationalists (Cadogan Group 1992: 14).

Cultural pluralism is part of the British Government's overall policy of the development of equality and equity of treatment for both communities in Northern Ireland. An important part of this process entails the alleviation of high levels of unemployment in deprived Nationalist areas. Therefore Irish language projects are funded, with the twin results of satisfying local demand and expanding work opportunities in these areas. The Training and Employment Agency provides employment in Irish language activities through Action for Community Employment (ACE) schemes, which provide temporary employment of up to one year's duration for the long-term unemployed. Funding is also provided by Making Belfast Work, an employment scheme which provides financial help for community organisations and small businesses in deprived areas of the city. The Arts Council for Northern Ireland provides grants for activities involving Irish in the fields of drama and literature. During the 1980s, the ban on learning and speaking Irish in Northern Ireland's prisons was gradually removed, successfully resolving one of the major sources of friction between the Government and the Irish language movement.

Community relations policy and the Irish language

In 1987 the Central Community Relations Unit (CCRU) was established to improve community relations and to advise the Secretary of State on the nature of the conflict in Northern Ireland. The CCRU became a major source of Government funding for Irish language projects, and also a channel for grants from the European Union. An Irish Language Advisory Group comprising eight members was appointed to advise the CCRU on the viability of funding applications. Early projects to be funded included an origin of place names project at the Celtic Department of Queen's University and the appointment of writers in residence at the Celtic and Irish Departments of Northern Ireland's two universities.

These projects were politically uncontroversial but gave the impression that funding was being diverted from revival activities 'on the ground'. Therefore, in 1989 a member of the Advisory Committee formed a charitable trust with the aim of attracting Government funding to Irish language projects through a central body with sufficient expertise to consider the merits of grant applications. The ULTACH Trust (ULTACH is an acronym for Ulster Language, Traditions and

Cultural Heritage) aims at achieving a mutually beneficial and consensual relationship with the Government, which was invited to nominate one of its own
trustees. The Trust aims to create a social network for existing Irish speakers,
encourage the growth of Irish-medium education, and develop the language on a
cross-community basis; to this end, trustees are drawn in equal proportion from
the Catholic and Protestant communities. The CCRU provided a seeding grant to
the Trust and also contributed towards a capital fund, which was established to
ensure the Trust's eventual economic independence from Government sources;
the interest from the fund would be used to cover day-to-day costs and to fund projects.

The ULTACH Trust hopes to interest Protestants in the Irish language, while
at the same time recognising that they may wish to remain Unionist, an approach
which challenged the common Nationalist belief that Unionist learners of Irish
would become Nationalist in outlook as they learned the language. The Trust
hopes to encourage Protestant interest in the language through the re-discovery of
a Protestant Gaelic past, the provision of lectures in English on Irish language topics, the funding of self-instruction packages, and the provision of Irish language
classes in 'neutral' and Protestant areas.

Although the Trust is partly funded by the CCRU, it considers itself to be part
of the Irish language movement, and largely independent of Government control.
Nevertheless, it will not become publicly involved in campaigns that may damage
its cross-community potential, such as issues involving prisons, local
Government, or state-sponsored bilingualism. Rather, the Trust has lobbied for an
all-Ireland television service in Irish, increased Department of Education spending on Irish-medium education, and greater Arts Council funding for Irish-language projects. The Trust has effectively replaced the Irish Language Advisory
Group in advising the CCRU on its Irish language policy.

Unionist reaction

Since politics is concerned with the allocation of scarce resources, and the Irish
language is often perceived as the preserve of the Nationalist community,
Unionists have tended to assume that the increased allocation of funding to Irish
language projects leads to a reduction in the resources available to them.
Consequently, some Unionists equated the Government decision to fund the
Shaw's Road *bunscoil* in 1984 with the closure of state schools, in which the
majority of Protestant schoolchildren were educated (*Irish News* 7 April 1984,
p.3). However, on the whole, Unionist reaction to the funding of Irish-medium
education has been muted.

The DUP maintained and continues to maintain that state support for Irish
language projects represents an attempt to appease Republicanism which will ultimately fail, further de-stabilising Northern Ireland. The DUP also draws on utili-

tarian discourses, arguing that public spending on the Irish language is a waste of money. Unionists often perceive Nationalists to be discriminating against themselves by learning a language which they think is of no practical function; this reflects a tendency for Unionists to blame the disadvantages of the Nationalist population on its inherent cultural distinctiveness, rather than on Unionist or British discrimination. Dominant groups often blame the inferior status of subordinate groups on the distinctive characteristics of those groups, rather than the unequal distribution of power (Scott 1990: 35–6).

Some elements within the UUP preferred to view the language revival as one that had benefits for an enlightened Unionist perspective. In 1984, the UUP recommended some proposals for the alleviation of Nationalist grievances, including state funding for Irish cultural activities in proportion to the degree of public interest or participation in them (Ulster Unionist Party 1984: 5). Unionists remained opposed to state-sponsored bilingualism, which they regarded as incompatible with their conception of Irish as a private-domain cultural resource.

However, UUP support for state funding of Irish language projects vanished in the wake of the Anglo-Irish Agreement, all concessions to the Irish language lobby being thereafter attributed to the machinations of Dublin. Fears of British disengagement from Northern Ireland has fuelled rumours that the increase in BBC Irish language broadcasts is part of an attempt to culturally condition Unionists to accept an eventual United Ireland. State-sponsored cultural pluralism therefore appears to Unionists to involve the implementation of a Nationalist agenda.

As the campaign against the Anglo-Irish Agreement wound down, some moderate Unionists began to look more favourably on the language, particularly in the light of attempts to promote it on a cross-community basis. The *Belfast Telegraph* praised the ULTACH Trust, describing it as funding 'lovers of the language rather than republican activists' (*Belfast Telegraph* 4 April 1991, p.10), revealing the common Unionist belief that Republicans were only interested in the Irish language as a source of political capital. Since 1993 the Unionist-controlled Belfast City Council has supported Irish language activities, even permitting Irish language events in the City Hall itself. The funding of private domain language activities does not diminish the public domain British ethos of Northern Ireland. The Cadogan Group, a Unionist 'think tank', has expressed the view that the promotion of Irish culture can be used to accommodate Nationalists within Northern Ireland. The group has proposed that Irish culture be promoted as a substitute for an institutional role for the Irish Government in the affairs of Northern Ireland. This 'non-political sense of Irishness' would provide the 'Irish dimension' essential to any settlement of the northern conflict (Cadogan Group 1995: 19). Thus some Unionists believe that cultural Nationalism could be used to obviate political Nationalism, whereas many Nationalists regard both forms of Nationalism as compatible. Unionist opposition to state or local government sponsored bilingualism remains implacable, this being viewed as a Nationalist 'political' issue rather than a language lobby 'cultural' issue.

Some Unionists who have an active interest in the Irish language attempt to divorce it from Nationalist ideology. Two prominent individuals involved in this exercise are Ulster Unionist councillors Ian Adamson and Chris McGimpsey. Adamson has incorporated the northern dialect of the Irish language, or Ulster Gaelic as he prefers to call it, within his concept of a unitary Ulster culture that would unite northern Catholics and Protestants, thus laying the cultural foundation for an independent Ulster (Adamson 1985: 73–81).[4] McGimpsey describes himself as Irish in nationality and British in citizenship; thus he asserts that the Irish nation need not be coterminous with the Irish state. McGimpsey claims that political separatists usurped the Irish language movement, which was originally devoted to cultural, rather than political issues (McGimpsey 1994: 10). The Irish language movement could facilitate the 'depoliticisation' of the language by concentrating solely on cultural and linguistic issues (McGimpsey 1994: 12).

Other Unionists have found difficulty in disassociating the Irish language from Nationalism. However, the association between cultural and political confidence has become such an influential discourse that some unionists feel they must justify their political beliefs in terms of indigenous cultural and historical experiences. One organisation which attempts to give Unionism a cultural aspect is the Ulster Society, which is opposed to the Gaelic revival's attempts 'to dye Ulster's cultural tartan a solid emerald green' (*New Ulster* 1993: 26). Some Unionists have responded to the Irish language revival by calling for a revival of Ulster-Scots, a distinctive speech variety which they claim is a separate language, though their detractors claim that it is merely a dialect of English.

The language movement and Nationalist reaction

Members of dominant groups who display a benevolent attitude towards the revivals of subcultures may be ignored, or credited instead with malicious denigration by oppressed groups in order to maintain the groups' conceptual relationship as one of oppressor and oppressed (McDonald 1989: 85). Thus Republicans have denied that the British Government has reduced its hostility to the Irish language, and often claim that Government language policies which sparked off major Nationalist protests revealed continuing state hostility to the language.[5] Republican cynics also believe that state funding for the Irish language stems from an attempt to undermine Sinn Féin, rather than an enlightened pluralist approach. They suggest that the British Government is attempting to promote the role of Constitutional Nationalists in Irish language activities while marginalising the Republican contribution to the revival; the eventual aim is to divide and weaken the language movement and by extension Nationalism. Sinn Féin (1989: 1) claims that the British Government is attempting to control Irish culture, neutralising its 'revolutionary potential'.

Social domination is also asserted within subcultures, which are internally patrolled for signs of disaffection (Scott 1990: 130). Anyone who attempts to curry favour with the elites will be punished through slander, shunning or even physical violence. Thus some Republicans have attempted to exclude ULTACH from the Irish language movement by representing the organisation as an agency of the state which vetoes funding to projects which involve Republican Irish-speakers.[6] The Government is also accused of 'window-dressing', by funding unimportant and 'bogus' projects while ignoring important ones; Republicans often make financial contributions to Irish language activities that are not grant-aided. Sinn Féin's aim of uniting the Nationalist community is expressed in its approach to Irish language campaigns, the successes of which are attributed to concerted Nationalist support, forcing a reluctant Government to make 'U-turns'.

More generous critics accuse the state of adopting an ad hoc, reactive approach, rather than a co-ordinated pro-active policy involving all Government departments. Despite fears of being co-opted, most Irish language groups accept state funding. They justify this approach in four ways: firstly, they claim that state support is necessary for minority languages to survive; secondly, they welcome funding for language projects from any source; thirdly, they claim that the Irish language revival has a right to Government recognition; and lastly, they assert that the British Government is morally compelled to facilitate the revival of Irish, since it was largely responsible for the decline of the language in the first place.

State-sponsored pluralism is seen by some Nationalists as having a Unionist agenda, divorcing the Irish language from Nationalism and undermining its role as a symbol of cultural resistance. Nevertheless, some Irish language activists have appropriated the pluralist discourse to justify their activities. The Nationalist-controlled Queen's University Students' Union justifies its bilingual policy in terms of cultural pluralism, an explanation refuted by Unionist students who view the policy as exclusively Nationalist in origin and orientation.

Many Constitutional Nationalists welcome attempts to encourage Irish on a cross-community basis, which they support as a counter to the Republican associations of the language. Partly as a response to Government policy, and in an attempt to widen the appeal of Irish, many Irish language projects are no longer 'political' in ethos, but are broadly 'cultural' in character.

In the early 1990s, two main discourses characterised the Irish language movement's negotiations with the Government. One interprets Irish as the symbolic language of Nationalism and the other, more recent approach, represents the language as a minority language within the United Kingdom. In the following section I consider each discourse and then outline their weaknesses.

The discourse of 'nation'

According to this discourse, the northern minority do not comprise an ethnic group, but are part of the majority population of Ireland, of which Irish is the national language. Therefore the degree of incorporation of the language into the public domain is indicative of the acceptance of the Nationalist position in Northern Ireland. This entails formal recognition of the language as a co-official language involving the following: the right to use Irish in court; permission to use Irish in the conduct of official business with Government and local-government authorities, involving the provision of bilingual or Irish language forms and documents, and translators; and the erection of bilingual street signs in Irish. The British administration should make Northern Ireland a bilingual region to make amends for its attempts to wipe out the Irish language over many centuries.

Calls for the institutionalisation of the Irish language have increased in recent years, often utilising the government principle of recognising the equality of the 'two traditions' in Northern Ireland. Since the paramilitary cease-fire of 1994, Nationalists in Northern Ireland have demanded 'parity of esteem' with the Unionist community, and the language movement has proposed that state recognition of the Irish language would facilitate this process. The Irish Government is viewed as the sponsor of the Irish language movement in Northern Ireland, a role that was enhanced after the signing of the Anglo-Irish Agreement. Dublin ministers have been invited to Irish language events in Northern Ireland. Considering the symbolic importance of the Irish language to northern Nationalists, an improved status for the language may be beneficial in reaching an overall settlement of the conflict. This discourse is especially favoured by Republican language activists.

However, the Government has announced that it has no plans for the creation of a bilingual society in Northern Ireland (Mayhew 1992: 17). A Government decision to revoke the law forbidding Irish language street signs was rejected as tokenism by many in the language movement. The experience of the Irish Republic has demonstrated how the institutionalisation of Irish has failed to halt its decline; in circumstances of limited resources, funding may be diverted from community-level projects better equipped to ensure the survival of the language. The possibility of this occurring is increased by the fact that state-sponsored bilingualism is expensive. Furthermore, the British Government does not have the authority to force local councils to implement bilingual policies. Dublin has proved to be supportive of the language revival in Northern Ireland, but has been unwilling to contribute financially to the revival in any significant way. Official recognition of the Irish language would meet massive resistance from Unionists, who would view it as a cultural convergence with the Republic in advance of a British withdrawal. Unionists are also hostile to the concept of 'parity of esteem' for Nationalist culture, suspecting that it would provide a cultural justification for joint authority over Northern Ireland by the British and Irish Governments. The Government has claimed that its existing Irish language policy 'reflects a parity of esteem between the cultural traditions of the two main sections of the community' (Letter to Councillor Máirtín Ó Muilleoir from Simon Rodgers on behalf of the Secretary of State 15 May 1995, p. 2). Most Nationalists, apart from some language activists, rarely campaign for legislation to make the Irish language a co-official language with English in Northern Ireland. Furthermore, even if Northern Ireland became officially bilingual, Nationalists may shift their demands to other issues, as has been the case in the Basque region in Spain (Williams 1984: 205). Thus state-sponsored bilingualism may not contribute to a resolution of the conflict in Northern Ireland.

The Government-appointed advisory body, the Standing Advisory Commission on Human Rights (SACHR), stated that there were 'strong countervailing arguments' against the proposal to grant full equality of status to the Irish and English languages: Northern Ireland is not a bilingual country in the same sense as Wales, Canada or Belgium; given the low levels of comprehension in Irish among large sections of the population, such a development would be expensive and difficult to implement; and thirdly, such a proposal would be highly divisive, particularly if the whole population was compelled to learn or take examinations in Irish (SACHR 1990: 8.44). The Secretary of State for Northern Ireland's response to the SACHR report stated that the Government recognised the importance of the Irish language, particularly to the minority community, and would fund the development of the language 'in a cultural context', but that he was 'not persuaded that legislation is necessarily the best way to develop the Irish language' (SACHR 1992: 301).

The discourse of 'community'

This discourse emanates from the separate social institutions developed by the Nationalist population in Northern Ireland, leading to communalism and the articulation of a demand for community justice (Todd 1990: 34). The community's rights and not the Irish nation's are asserted. The Irish language movement presents itself as a group of tax-payers demanding fair-play for a linguistic community. The connection between the language and Nationalism is under-communicated; as an endangered language, interest in Irish is welcome from all quarters, including Unionist ones. Irish language activists concentrate on specific issues, presenting the language as their sole concern. Proponents of this discourse utilise international pronouncements on the protection of linguistic and cultural minorities by organisations such as the UN and the EU; a favourite document is the 1992 European Charter for Regional or Minority Languages (Committee on the Administration of Justice 1993), which obliges all signatories to promote the use of indigenous languages. Activists also use the 'pro-rata' argument, claiming that Irish is discriminated against in comparison with Scots Gaelic and Welsh.

Language activists who believe the Government may become more favourable to the language issue represent themselves as a weak linguistic minority, in urgent need of Government support. Other activists who doubt the good intentions of the state adopt the self-representation of a strong vibrant community, demanding state recognition. The latter approach is more common. Irish language speakers claim that they constitute a community in which the language is used in day-to-day interaction, rather than a scattered group of second language learners. The Northern Ireland Census of 1991 included questions on knowledge of the Irish language which did not attempt to measure competence. The language movement maximised the results, which indicated that 142,003 people had some knowledge of Irish (Department of Health and Social Services 1993: 1).

Activists use this discourse to lobby for separate Irish language facilities and institutions, including media, schools, and entertainment. Some also use it to make similar demands to those of the proponents of the discourse of nation, campaigning for state recognition of the Irish language community through the implementation of bilingual policies in communities with large numbers of Irish speakers, such as West Belfast. This discourse is believed to be beneficial in that it weakens the ideological link between Irish and Nationalism, thus arousing less hostility among Unionists. The demand for separate domain provision for Irish language speakers arouses less Unionist hostility than state-sponsored bilingualism. The discourse also has the advantage of drawing on existing Government practice to highlight the apparent inconsistency of language policies in different parts of the United Kingdom. Minorities often draw on the ideological terms of reference of the elites to pressurise for change, a tactic which the latter find difficult to deflect as they are made to feel hypocritical (Scott 1990: 105). The discourse of community has become increasingly sophisticated in recent years, and is preferred by Constitutional Nationalists, though Republicans will utilise it if they believe it will be more effective. This discourse is the only one used by the ULTACH Trust.

In British society no formal recognition is normally given in politics or the legal system to categories or groups of people based on their culture, language or race; rather, the focus is on individual rights and equality of opportunity (Baker 1993: 251). Many countries ignore international declarations on the rights of linguistic and cultural minorities. The European Charter for Regional or Minority Languages consists of a set of principles which are vague enough to allow each signatory state to choose its language policy (Tabouret-Keller 1991: 50). Furthermore, it is primarily a matter of principles and does not involve any international obligations (Tabouret-Keller 1991: 45). The British and Irish Governments have refused to sign the treaty.[7]

Although the language movement maintains that the language is for everyone, the vast majority of Irish speakers are Nationalist, and very few Unionists with an interest in the language have more than an elementary knowledge of it. They are also reluctant to publicise their interest in Irish, or comment on the demands of the language movement in public, leaving the impression that Irish language speakers are entirely Nationalist in orientation. Furthermore, many language projects, such as Irish-medium education, are based entirely within the Nationalist community.

The funding of private-domain language activities in the absence of official recognition leads to fears that the language will be 'ghettoised' into segregated institutions, which would do little to alleviate Nationalist feelings of inequality in Northern Ireland. Such a policy may result in Irish speakers feeling that they are second class citizens. On the other hand, calls for official recognition of Irish on a par with Welsh and Scottish Gaelic may seem to Unionists to cloak Nationalist aspirations.

The pro-rata argument does not take into account the differing socio-linguistic circumstances of Scotland, Wales, and Northern Ireland. In Scotland the Gaelic language has no legal status and the language movement concentrates its efforts on Gaelic-medium education, arts, and television programming. Welsh has received a high degree of official recognition and protection. The language has been permitted for use in Welsh courts since 1941, though this was only in circumstances in which the use of English would prejudice a defendant, a situation that hardly obtains in Northern Ireland where most Irish speakers are secondary bilinguals. Although census returns indicate that there are half the number of Gaelic speakers in Scotland than Irish speakers in Northern Ireland, Gaelic is not considered an integral part of Scottish nationalist ideology; consequently, there is less danger of census returns in Scotland indicating group loyalty, rather than linguistic competence. The British Government has been favourable to the Scottish Gaelic lobby, which is perceived as 'politically innocuous' since it distances itself from nationalist politics (McKee 1995: 96).

In Wales the situation is the reverse of that in Scotland; the language issue is a central, uniting theme of Welsh nationalism, which has failed to create an image of 'Welshness' that admits the majority who do not speak Welsh (Jenkins 1991: 34–5). Welsh and Scottish Gaelic both have traditional community bases for their languages. In Wales, Welsh is an important language of everyday life, thus providing a large pool of fluent Welsh speakers for language activities, including state-sponsored bilingualism. In Northern Ireland, traditional Gaeltacht areas had all but vanished by 1921; modern neo-Gaeltachts are in an early and precarious state of development. One Government report indicates that although a knowledge of Irish is quite high among northern Catholics, levels of competence are quite low, indicating little use of the language outside the educational context (Sweeney 1988: 24). Thus language activists have difficulty in claiming that Irish speakers comprise a strong community.

Furthermore, Northern Ireland's position within the United Kingdom is more uncertain, as it contains a growing Nationalist minority supported by an adjacent state. Northern Ireland is occupied by two mutually antagonistic ethnic blocks; in Wales and Scotland the situation is less conflictual. Welsh and Scottish language movements use peaceful tactics to achieve their aims; in Northern Ireland Irish is associated by many with the Republican movement. The Irish language is thus a very sensitive political issue in comparison with its 'mainland' British counterparts.

The development of the discourse of community by the Irish language movement in the 1990s indicates a more pragmatic approach, in contrast to the earlier
incorporation of the discourse of nation into a rhetoric of resistance. Although the
Irish language movement has often invoked the discourse of nation, since the
paramilitary cease-fires the discourse of community is commonly drawn upon as
well. Government policy has been largely favourable to the discourse of community. Nevertheless, the justification of state-sponsored bilingualism in terms of the
promotion of a non-aligned linguistic minority would appear difficult because of
Unionist suspicions and the belief of many members of the language movement
that the Irish language is an important element of Nationalist culture. The British
Government has not favoured the discourse of nation, as it challenges the cross-
community interpretation of the language and could fuel political unrest. The
Local Government (Miscellaneous Provisions) (NI) Order of 1995 permitted the
erection of street signs in Irish in areas in which the views of the occupiers were
taken into account. The Environment Minister for Northern Ireland justified the
decision 'as part of Government policy' of encouraging greater respect for, and
appreciation of, cultural diversity in Northern Ireland' (Northern Ireland
Information Service 1994: 2). The Government therefore drew on the discourse of
'community' and 'common heritage' in explaining its decision to permit the erection of street signs in Irish.

Conclusion

We have seen how the Irish language can be used to symbolise Irish nationalism,
Ulster nationalism, or a cultural Irish identity divorced from political separatism.
The nature of the competition to define the symbolic significance of Irish can be
interpreted by reference to Harrison's delineation of four types of symbolic competition among social groups (1995). In a 'valuation contest' a group attempts to
diminish the prestige of the opposing group's symbols, while attempting to raise
the status of its own. In a 'proprietary contest' a group attempts to monopolise its
symbols, and treats the efforts of another group to copy or acquire them as an act
of hostility. A precondition of a proprietary contest is a consensus among the rivals
on the prestige of the symbolic property for which they compete. Thus a proprietary contest is the reverse of a valuation contest; in the former the prestige of the
symbol is unchallenged but its ownership is contested, while in the latter the
reverse occurs. 'Innovation contests' involve the invention of new motifs or their
importation from other communities in an atmosphere of competitive inventive-
ness. In an 'expansionary contest' a group tries to displace its competitor's symbols with its own in an attempt to absorb the other group into its own
socio-political identity.

Many Irish-speaking Nationalists engage Unionists in an expansionary contest by trying to replace the symbols of Unionism with their own, including the
Irish language. Others confront Unionists in a valuation contest by attempting to

diminish the status of Unionist culture and elevate the prestige of the Irish language as a symbol of Nationalism. Unionists respond by denigrating the prestige of the Irish language in a valuation contest, or, if they agree on the prestige of the language, they unite with the British Government and some Irish-speakers to contest its symbolic association with Nationalism in a proprietary contest. Some Unionists who regard language as a valuable symbol of nationhood promote their own language, Ulster Scots, in an innovation contest with Irish-speaking Nationalists.

Language planning can be understood to be a form of conflict management (Haarmann 1990: 123). The British Government's approach to the Irish language issue has largely been cautious and gradualist, avoiding publicity where possible, in an attempt to meet the needs of the language lobby without generating resentment elsewhere. Personal bilingualism in the private sector has been encouraged, largely removed from the eyes and ears of suspicious Unionists; calls for the institutionalisation of Irish have been resisted. Many Unionists and Nationalists are expressing their identities in cultural terms, with Government encouragement and support. Northern Ireland has become an arena of cultural competition, in which Gaelic and counter-Gaelic movements accuse one another of the spurious politicisation of divisive and retrograde cultural forms, while attempting to validate their own political viewpoints in cultural terms.

Nationalists are suspicious of the state policy embracing Irish, and cultural pluralism, viewing it as an attempt to absorb them into the body politic of Northern Ireland. For their part, Unionists view pluralism as an attempt to prepare them for a United Ireland. Pluralism and assimilation are not dichotomous concepts, but are in fact closely related (Gleason 1984). The Irish language movement has adopted pragmatic discourses in addition to dogmatic ones as a result of improved state funding for language projects.

According to an interview which I conducted with a representative of CCRU in 1993, Government policy is not to promote Irish language projects, but to respond to what it regards as soundly based requests where practicable. If the Government is perceived to take the initiative in Irish language projects, it alarms Unionists who fear a British withdrawal. It therefore justifies aiding projects in the utilitarian terms of catering for a legitimate demand. The Irish language seems set to remain in the political arena: while state funding of Irish language activities seems to many Unionists to reflect a Nationalist agenda, the non-funding of language activities invite Nationalist accusations of Government 'politicisation' of the language.

Notes

1.   I will use the following terms in this chapter. *Nationalists* seek the unification of Ireland. *Constitutional Nationalists* wish to unite Ireland by peaceful means. *Republicans* justify, or justified, the unification of Ireland by armed insurrection. *Unionists* wish Northern Ireland to remain a part of the United Kingdom. *Loyalists* are Unionists who believe, or

believed, that force should be used to maintain the union with Great Britain. Most Nationalists are ethnically Catholic and most Unionists are ethnically Protestant.

2.   While media and Government organs often portray the population of Northern Ireland as being divided into Unionist and Nationalist 'communities', I find the use of this term to be extremely problematic. These 'communities' are internally divided in terms of ideology, residence and social interaction. Affective social interaction is often facilitated by a common aversion to political violence, rather than a shared Nationalist or Unionist outlook. Thus some Constitutional Nationalists would prefer the company of Unionists to that of Republicans. Those who draw upon the 'two communities' discourse also tend to equate all Protestants with the Unionist community, and all Catholics with the Nationalist one, though a minority of Protestants are Nationalist and a minority of Catholics are Unionist.

3.   Daniel Corkery wrote, 'Languages do not die natural deaths; they are murdered, and their murderers are those who would destroy the soul of a nation' (Khleif 1979: 348).

4.   Many Unionists equate 'Ulster' with the six counties of Northern Ireland, though Nationalists point out that the ancient province of Ulster included three counties that are presently in the Republic of Ireland. A minority of 'Unionists' who are deeply suspicious of Westminster's intentions for Northern Ireland wish to create an independent state in the region.

5.   It is not within the scope of this chapter to examine major Irish language campaigns in detail, though they can be summarised as follows: in 1988 the Irish language lobby fought Department of Education proposals to diminish the status of the language in Northern Ireland's schools; in 1990 a campaign was launched to restore state aid for *Glór na nGael*, an Irish language organisation whose ACE funding was withdrawn due to Government suspicions that the organisation was connected with paramilitary activity; and since 1991 the Irish language movement demanded state recognition for *Meánscoil Feirste,* an Irish language secondary school in West Belfast. All of the above campaigns were successful.

6.   Máirtín Ó Muilleoir, a Sinn Féin councillor, accused the ULTACH Trust of being responsible for the Government decision to withdraw funding from *Glór na nGael* (Ó Muilleoir 1990: 97). He has also referred to the Trust's director as '*fear an* NIO' ('the NIO man') (*Lá 14 Meitheamh* 1990, p.3).

7.   Commentators believe that the British Government has refused to sign the Charter as it would require major policy changes in the official status of the Scottish Gaelic and Irish languages in the United Kingdom. The Irish Government has not signed the Charter, as the state refuses to consider the Irish language as a minority language. The 1937 Irish constitution embodied the discourse of nation, declaring Irish to be the 'national' and 'first official language'; English was recognised as the 'second official language' (Ó Huallacháin 1991: 44).

References

Adamson, I. 1985. *The Identity of Ulster.* Belfast: Pretani Press.

Baker, C. 1993. *Foundations of Bilingual Education and Bilingualism.* Clevedon: Multilingual Matters.

Cadogan Group 1992. *Northern Limits: Boundaries of the Attainable in Northern Ireland Politics.* Belfast: The Cadogan Group.

____. 1995. *Lost Accord: The 1995 Frameworks and the Search for a Settlement in Northern Ireland.* Belfast: The Cadogan Group.

Cathcart, R. 1984. *The BBC in Northern Ireland 1924–1989.* Belfast: Blackstaff Press.

Chapman, M. 1992. *The Celts: The Construction of a Myth.* London: Macmillan.

Cohen, A. P. 1994. *Self Consciousness: An Alternative Anthropology of Identity.* London: Routledge.

Committee on the Administration of Justice 1993. *The Irish Language in Northern Ireland: The UK Government's approach to the Irish Language in light of the European Charter for Regional and Minority Languages.* Belfast: CAJ.

Department of Health and Social Services 1993. *The Northern Ireland Census 1991: Irish Language Report.* London: HMSO.

Eastman, C.M. 1984. Language, Ethnic Identity and Change. In J. Edwards (ed.), *Linguistic Minorities, Policies and Pluralism.* London: Academic Press.

Edwards, J. 1985. *Language, Society and Identity.* Oxford: Basil Blackwell.

Edwards, V. 1984. Language Policy in Multilingual Britain. In J. Edwards (ed.), *Linguistic Minorities, Policies and Pluralism.* London: Academic Press.

Fitzgerald, T. K. 1991. Media and Changing Metaphors of Ethnicity and Identity. *Media, Culture and Society* 13 (2), 193–214.

Gleason, P. 1984. Pluralism and Assimilation: A Conceptual History.' In J. Edwards (ed.), *Linguistic Minorities, Policies and Pluralism.* London: Academic Press.

Grillo, R. 1989. *Dominant Languages: Language and Hierarchy in Britain and France.* Cambridge: Cambridge University Press.

Haarmann, H. 1990. Language Planning in the Light of a General Theory of Language: a Methodological Framework. *International Journal of the Sociology of Language* 86, 103–126.

Hadden, T. and K. Boyle 1989. *The Anglo-Irish Agreement: Commentary, Text and Official Review.* London and Dublin: Sweet and Maxwell in association with Edwin Higel Ltd.

Halliday, M. 1978. *Language as Social Semiotic.* London: Routledge.

Harrison, S. 1995. Four Types of Symbolic Conflict. *Journal of the Royal Anthropological Institute* 1 (2), 252–72.

Hindley, R. 1990. *The Death of the Irish Language: A Qualified Obituary.* London: Routledge.

Jenkins, R. 1991. Violence, Language and Politics: Nationalism in Northern Ireland and Wales. *North Atlantic Studies* 3 (1), 31–40.

Kennedy, D. 1988. *The Widening Gulf: Northern Attitudes to the Independent Irish State 1919–49.* Belfast: Blackstaff Press.

Khleif, B. 1979. Language as Identity: Towards an Ethnography of Welsh Nationalism. *Ethnicity* 6, 346–57.

McDonald, M. 1989. *'We are not French!' Language, Culture and Identity in Brittany.* London: Routledge.

McGimpsey, C. 1994. Untitled contribution in P. Mistéil (ed.), *The Irish Language and the Unionist Tradition.* Belfast: Ulster People's College/ULTACH Trust.

McKee, V. 1995. Contemporary Gaelic Language Politics in Western Scotland and Northern Ireland since 1950: Comparative Assessments. *Contemporary Politics* 1, 92–113.

Maguire, G. 1991. *Our Own Language: An Irish Initiative.* Clevedon: Multilingual Matters.

Mayhew, P. 1992. Culture and Identity: Text of a speech delivered by the Secretary of State, Sir Patrick Mayhew, MP, at the Centre for the Study of Conflict, University of Ulster at Coleraine on 16 December 1992. Belfast: Northern Ireland Information Service.

New Ulster 1993. *New Ulster: The Journal of the Ulster Society* 21.

Northern Ireland Information Service 1994. *Proposal for Draft Local Government (Miscellaneous Provisions) (NI) Order.* Belfast: Northern Ireland Information Service.

Ó hAdhmaill, F. 1985. *A Survey of the Irish Language in West Belfast.* Belfast: Glór na nGael.

Ó Huallacháin, C. 1991. *The Irish Language in Society.* Coleraine: University of Ulster.

Ó Muilleoir, M. 1990. *Comhad Comhairleora.* Coiscéim: Baile Átha Cliath.

O'Reilly, C. 1992. *Teanga Dhúchais:* The Irish Language and Ethnic Identity in West Belfast. Dissertation submitted in part fulfilment for the degree of Master of Arts in Social Anthropology, Queen's University, Belfast.

Scott, J. C. 1990. *Domination and the Arts of Resistance: Hidden Transcripts.* London: Yale University Press.

Sinn Féin 1985. *Learning Irish: A Discussion and Information Booklet.* Belfast: Sinn Féin.

_____. 1989. *Response to The Reports of the Curricular Working Groups on (1) Education for Mutual Understanding (2) Cultural Heritage.* Belfast: Sinn Féin.

Smith, A. D. 1971. *Theories of Nationalism.* London: Duckworth.

Standing Advisory Committee on Human Rights (SACHR) 1990. *Religious and Political Discrimination and Equality of Opportunity in Northern Ireland.* London: HMSO.

_____. 1992. *Report for 1991–2.* London: HMSO.

Sweeney, K. 1988. *The Irish Language in Northern Ireland 1987. Preliminary Report of a Survey of Knowledge, Interest and Ability.* Belfast: Policy Planning and Research Unit.

Tabouret-Keller, A. 1991. Factors of Constraints and Freedom in Setting a Language Policy for the EC. In F. Coulmas (ed.), *A Language Policy for the European Community; Prospects and Quandaries.* Brussels: Mouton de Gruyter.

Todd, J. 1990. Northern Irish Nationalist Political Culture. *Irish Political Studies* 5, 31–44.

Tovey, H., D. Hannan and H. Abramson 1989. *Why Irish? Irish Identity and the Irish Language.* Dublin: Bórd na Gaeilge.

Ulster Unionist Party 1984. Devolution and the Northern Ireland Assembly: The Way Forward. Discussion Paper presented by the Ulster Unionist Party's Report Committee. Belfast: UUP.

Whyte, J. 1990. *Interpreting Northern Ireland.* Oxford: Clarendon Press.

Williams, C. H. 1984. More than Tongue can Tell: Linguistic Factors in Ethnic Separatism. In J. Edwards (ed.), *Linguistic Minorities, Policies and Pluralism.* London: Academic Press.

8   'Nature's way': coping with early pregnancy loss

Rosanne Cecil

> Pregnancy, induced and spontaneous abortion (miscarriage), stillbirth and infant death all take their meanings from the lives of those who experience them and the social worlds in which they occur (Simonds and Katz Rothman 1992: 252).

This chapter outlines the experiences of a specific group of patients and their perceptions of the care given to them by various health professionals. These patients were not suffering from a disease, but were women who had undergone an event which involved hospitalisation, namely miscarriage. The findings presented here are drawn from a study of women who miscarried during the first trimester of their pregnancy (i.e. during the first thirteen weeks) and who previously had had no more than two clinically recognised miscarriages. The chapter thus examines the experiences of women who tend not to be of great medical interest and whose distress tends to be poorly recognised in contrast to women who have had recurrent miscarriages or a later pregnancy loss, such as a second trimester loss or a stillbirth.

There is no attempt here to examine the views of policy-makers or health professionals regarding the care of women who miscarry. Pregnancy loss is looked at solely from the perspective of the women, and it is their feelings about some aspects of the provision of hospital and community-based services which are reported.

The loss of a pregnancy through miscarriage or stillbirth raises a number of questions of anthropological interest, yet has been the focus of very little anthropological investigation. This may seem surprising, for pregnancy loss is clearly related to reproduction and birth (subjects which have, for a number of years, been areas of anthropological concern) and to death, and thus to the long-standing anthropological interest in funerary rites and rituals.

It may be that it seems self-evident that a pregnancy loss cannot have the social impact of either a birth or a death. It does not result in the creation of a new person who will be incorporated into the society, nor is it the loss of one who had already achieved membership and recognition within the social order. Yet how a miscarriage is viewed, experienced and managed may rest upon a range of social and cultural factors. Recent comparative studies into pregnancy loss in a number of different cultures and different historical periods have revealed an array of attitudes, beliefs and practices (see Cecil 1996).

Northern Ireland differs from other parts of the United Kingdom in a number of respects which could have a bearing on how miscarriages are experienced, perceived and dealt with. Families tend to be larger in Northern Ireland than elsewhere in the United Kingdom. Consequently, the significance of a pregnancy and of the loss of a pregnancy may not reflect the significance of such events to women in Britain and elsewhere. The specific social and cultural context of Northern Ireland needs to be considered. The legislation on abortion in Northern Ireland differs from that of Great Britain. The 1967 Abortion Act, which allowed abortion on so-called social grounds, was not extended to Northern Ireland. Thus it seems reasonable to suppose that the possibility of terminating a pregnancy with relative ease does not form part of the world view of fecund women in Northern Ireland as it may elsewhere (although women from Northern Ireland may make various arrangements in order to secure an abortion). Finally, the provision of hospital beds is currently higher in Northern Ireland than in Britain, which may result in a higher level of hospitalisation and medicalisation of the miscarriage event, and women's experiences of hospital care may thus differ from those of women hospitalised elsewhere in the United Kingdom.

Method

The women who constituted the sample on which this study was based were contacted through two hospitals: a large teaching hospital in Belfast (Hospital A) and a general hospital in a provincial town (Hospital B). Fifty women were selected for the study on the following grounds: that they had been in the first trimester of their pregnancy at the time of the miscarriage; that they had had no more than two clinically recognised pregnancies; that the current miscarriage was not due to an ectopic pregnancy. The women (35 from Hospital A and 15 from Hospital B) were initially contacted after they had returned from theatre following surgery (all the women in the sample underwent the surgical procedure of evacuation of the retained products of conception—ERPC—which is more commonly referred to as dilatation and curettage or 'D & C'). Three further interviews took place with the women over a period of six months. The second interview took place two to three weeks after the initial contact, the third approximately three months after the first contact, and the final interview after six months. A considerable number of women dropped out of the study between the first and second interview. Of the 23 women who dropped out at this stage, six had refused further contact at the first interview;

three were undecided and refused a further interview when contacted by telephone; ten agreed to further interviews but were impossible to contact; and four, who had initially agreed to a further interview, changed their minds when contacted. Twenty-two women were interviewed at 3 months (the third interview) and 20 of these were interviewed for a fourth time at six months.

The interview procedures consisted of the administration of a questionnaire at the first interview (which included questions on the woman's social and personal characteristics, her pregnancy and miscarriage, and hospital procedures), and of guided discussion at the later interviews at which a number of themes were covered (such as, emotional and physical well-being, the response of the partner to the miscarriage, the response of the family and friends, the reaction of any existing children, particular problems and anxieties, and what they had found most helpful and most difficult). Spielberger's State-Trait Anxiety Inventory (STAI) (Spielberger 1983) was administered at each contact (the results of these tests have been reported elsewhere, see Cecil and Leslie 1993).

Initial findings

The ages of the women in the sample ranged from 16 to 43: six were in their teens; 24 were between 20 and 29; 18 were between 30 and 39; and two were 40 or over. While 20 of the women had no children, the number of live births among the remaining 30 women ranged from one to six.

In terms of the Registrar General's classification of social class, 32 women were categorised as being in classes I, II and III non-manual, and 11 were in III manual, IV, V and VI, and seven women were unclassified. No relationship was found between the social class position of the women and the length of time spent in discussion with them by medical and nursing staff. However, while it would be unusual for a woman experiencing a first trimester miscarriage to be given an explanation as to the specific cause of the loss of her own pregnancy, over a third of the women said that they had not even been given an explanation as to the causes of miscarriage in general.

Catholic women were over-represented in the sample relative to the population of Northern Ireland, which was not unexpected given that the majority of the sample were attending Hospital A, situated in the predominantly Catholic area of West Belfast. A range of variables was cross-tabulated with religion. No significant relationship was found between the number of children a woman already had and her religious affiliation. Indeed, only one effect of religious affiliation was found; this was the length of time which women had been trying to conceive: 19 per cent of Catholic women but no Protestant women had been trying for more than two years.

Results from the questionnaire data indicate that only 50 per cent of the pregnancies were planned. This is a low figure in comparison with another recent Irish study on miscarriage where 19 out of 27 women had planned their pregnancy (Jackman, McGee and Turner 1991). However, the women in both studies were overwhelmingly pleased to be pregnant and upset at miscarrying.

Differing perspectives: fatalism and science

Pregnancy was considered by many of the women in my sample to be a condition largely beyond their own control. Fatalism clearly constitutes a perspective which is at odds with the scientific worldview largely held by health professionals.[1] For some women, this fatalistic attitude was expressed in a religious idiom. A 40 year old woman who had miscarried twice and who already had one child said:

> When I lost that one I started to feel guilty . . . there was too much planning gone into it by me, and I felt that, really, children are a gift, they are not something that you sort of plan one day to have . . . I see them more as being a gift from God and I started to feel a wee bit guilty that I had planned this (pregnancy). I sort of felt that it was God's way of saying to me: 'If you have a child it will be on my terms, not on your terms'.

A young childless woman said, 'it's just God's way'. With other women, the religious idiom was missing but the sentiment was much the same: 'if it happens, it happens'.

For some women it was their experience of miscarriage that led them to feel that they had little personal control over their own bodies. A twenty-two year old woman with one child said:

> I don't think you can really plan these things. I think it just happens . . . I used to think you could plan it until I had the miscarriage. I mean it's alright saying 'well, we'll plan to have another one', start trying and then get pregnant, but after that it's in somebody else's hands; it's not in your hands anymore what happens after that.

A further aspect of early pregnancy loss which is crucial to take into account in the attempt to understand the differing perspectives of the event held by the women themselves, and by medical and nursing staff, is that for most women being pregnant means that they are carrying a *baby* however incipient. This is clearly expressed in the women's use of language in describing miscarriage. None of the women used the medical term 'abortion', with its connotations of a deliberately induced termination of pregnancy. Some women avoided referring to the miscarriage by any specific term and used euphemisms such as 'this business'. The term 'mis' or 'miss' was used by a number of women, with its double meaning of an abbreviation of the word miscarriage, and of a lack of success as in the phrase 'hit or miss'. Many women referred to the miscarriage as the loss of a baby (even when, as in a small number of cases, the miscarriage was due to a blighted ovum or suspected hydatidiform mole, and was thus never a viable pregnancy). One woman reflected on her own use of language as follows: 'It is funny the way I am actually explaining things now. The way I say it would be "I was three months pregnant and I lost the baby"; I don't use the word "miscarriage"'.

Women were aware that their view of their pregnancy was not necessarily shared by other people, even by members of their own family. One childless woman of 28 remarked:

> I have the notion that nobody knows what it is like until it actually happens to them. Because different ones have said to me it is not the same when you didn't hold a baby, and you can't explain to them just, you know they don't understand. They said it would have been worse if you had actually carried it nine months and it died, or if you had been holding it, but it is the very same thing to me.

To hospital staff a first trimester miscarriage is an everyday occurrence that requires only routine medical and nursing care. However, for the woman who miscarries the event may be of overwhelming significance. It may be the most distressing event she has hitherto experienced and may well be her first experience of bereavement. A great need was expressed by women for explanations and discussion about miscarriage.[2] A number of women in the sample expressed dissatisfaction with the way in which the information that they had miscarried was given to them. A twenty-two year old woman with one child spoke of the unsympathetic manner in which a female doctor broke the news to her of her pregnancy loss: 'She just said "this pregnancy is terminated" and . . . said "I'll see if I can get you booked in tomorrow". It was cold to me. Maybe she had to say it that way . . . but . . . I was breaking my heart.'

Another woman was angry at the manner of one of the doctors who had dealt with her, 'One of them I found very abrupt . . . just her attitude . . . just as if you were a number'. Even basic practical explanations were considered to be inadequate by some of the women. A thirty-five year old Protestant woman with three children complained that: 'I wasn't really explained a lot . . . I had to call the doctor (i.e. her own General Practitioner or GP) and ask him what did I have to do, have I to wait a while and take precautions before I have another baby'. For a thirty-year old childless woman, the lack of an adequate explanation resulted in confusion and fear: 'I would love them ones to explain what is happening to me . . . I am bleeding all the time . . . I'm just worrying and worrying about that bleeding so I am. I'm frightened of that bleeding'.

Nature's way

While dissatisfaction with basic explanations and the manner in which they were given was expressed, many women mentioned a more fundamental need to know the cause of their miscarriage. A thirty-seven year old woman with one child spoke of her search for a reason for her miscarriage in the events preceding it, and said: 'Although I've been told that it was just one of those things, it couldn't be helped, there was no reason for it, and we would never know the reason for it . . . it was the first thing in my mind when I woke up in the morning and it was the last thing when I went to bed at night'.

Causal explanations for a specific pregnancy loss were rarely given. However, it was fairly common for women to report that they had been told, by hospital medical or nursing staff, or by their own GP, that miscarriage was nature's way of getting rid of something that was not perfect. 'Nature's way' was clearly a phrase frequently used by health professionals and sometimes adopted by the women themselves as an explanation for pregnancy loss. For a few women it seemed to have provided some comfort. As one woman said, 'I accept everything that I have been told by the doctors, that there was something wrong with the baby and it was just nature's way of getting rid of it and starting again'. But for many women it was of little comfort, for implicit in the 'nature's way' explanation is the suggestion that a woman who has miscarried can be grateful that she has been spared the distress of giving birth to a less-than-perfect baby and the difficulty of raising a disabled child. Not only does this express an attitude towards disability which may not be shared by the woman, but it ignores the fact that when a woman conceives, she hopes, and generally expects, to be carrying a healthy baby. For a woman to be told that she has been carrying a baby who was too ill to live and which thus died *in utero*, may be of very little comfort.

There is a paradox here that it is from the realm of the health professionals that the 'explanation' of 'nature's way' is offered. Pregnancy, childbirth and pregnancy loss occur increasingly within the medical sphere of influence, and the role of 'nature' tends not to be cited with any great frequency in references to pregnancy and childbirth, except in critiques of the medicalised system. Advances in tests for pregnancy have enabled women to learn of their pregnancy at a very early stage. Early visits to the doctor for confirmation tend to lead to early involvement with some of the technologies associated with reproduction, such as the ultrasound scan. Yet when pregnancy fails, as around 20 per cent do, the early involvement with medical care is of no avail, for 'nature' takes its inevitable course. Nevertheless, expectations of a successful pregnancy may have been raised unrealistically high.[3] The use of the ultrasound scan to enable the operator to detect a range of abnormalities and assess the development of the foetus, also enables the woman to see an image of the baby weeks or months before birth. It is unclear whether this results in early 'bonding' and whether, should the pregnancy subsequently fail, such early bonding as may have occurred helps or hinders the woman in coping with the loss. What is surprising is that, in a context where medical, scientific and technological perspectives and procedures are paramount, 'nature' is called upon as an explanatory device.

An examination of belief systems regarding reproduction in other societies has revealed diverse explanations and reasons for pregnancy loss (Cecil 1996). For example, in Jamaica pregnancy loss may be attributed to the work of *duppies*, the spirits of those who recently died, who for reasons of their own, or due to the requests of others, wish to do harm (Sobo 1996). Amongst the Abelam of Papua New Guinea, offending the spirits (*wala*) may lead to pregnancy loss (Winkvist 1996). These explanations for pregnancy loss are readily understandable when considered within the framework of the whole spectrum of beliefs of the society. In Northern Ireland it appears that the lay, predominantly fatalistic, perspective on reproduction is one that is implicitly, and sometimes explicitly, rejected by health professionals; yet a version of fatalism—'nature's way'—is sometimes offered by the professionals as an explanation of pregnancy loss.

Hospital procedures

Many women found their stay in hospital to be distressing, although a number of them spoke highly of the care given by the nursing staff, and a smaller number of the care given by the doctors. Hospital procedures may function to foster an acknowledgement or a denial that, in a miscarriage, an event of some significance has occurred. From the women's observations it appeared that three areas of hospital care were of particular concern, namely accommodation, the use of ultrasound scan and the D & C operation.

Women who miscarry may be accommodated in a gynaecological, ante-natal or post-natal ward. There is no ideal hospital location for the woman who has miscarried (Moulder 1990: 76). The decision regarding accommodation for women undergoing an early miscarriage is largely governed by the availability of beds. In Hospital B, all the women in the sample were admitted to the gynaecological ward. In the busier Hospital A, some women were admitted to the ante-natal or post-natal ward. A number of women felt very strongly about their accommodation. A thirty-one year old childless woman explained that the reason she found being in the ante-natal ward so upsetting related directly to her own recent experience:

> I had been told 'there's no heartbeat, the baby doesn't have a heartbeat' . . . every pregnant lady in the ward had that ultrasound test done . . . all I heard for a good solid hour was the nurse going round each mum-to-be and you heard this wee tiny heartbeat . . . to me it was rubbing salt into the wound.

In contrast, two women who were admitted to the ante-natal ward for a second miscarriage compared this favourably with being placed in a gynaecological ward, as they both had been on the earlier occasion. For one of these women, a forty-year old with one child, this was because she felt that it had helped her to confront her loss:

> I think that putting somebody with a miscarriage into a gynae ward is trying to pull
> the wool over their eyes. You are trying to defer the trauma of it until later. Whereas
> putting somebody into a maternity (ante-natal) ward, you are helping them to con-
> front it there and then.

The other woman considered that being admitted to the ante-natal ward was in a
sense an acknowledgement that she had been pregnant and had the potential to be
so again: 'I think I felt better this time . . . I felt that when you were in maternity
you were able to relate to it better . . . even though you can't carry a baby at that
time, it's possible you can'.

Those women who were admitted to the post-natal ward tended to find it
rather distressing. One found it awkward being asked by the other women in the
ward, who did not know that she had miscarried, whether she had had a boy or a
girl. Another, who was put in a room next to the nursery, became upset by the
sound of the babies crying. Women who were given a single room generally were
appreciative and welcomed the privacy. But one woman, a mother of two children,
found it more helpful to be with the newly-delivered mothers than to be by herself:

> They were talking about their childbirth, I mean that could have been me, I could
> have went through that and then I was relating to what I had been through years ago
> . . . I felt better that I was sitting listening to other people rather than tormenting
> myself in my room . . . I felt if I sat in that room any longer I would have went nuts
> . . . so I went in to see one of the other girl's babies.

For some women, being placed in the ante-natal ward or, particularly, the post-
natal ward, was very distressing, and this was a view shared by at least some of
the nursing staff. For those women who were not upset, admittance to either the
ante-natal or post-natal ward appeared to implicitly acknowledge the potentiality
of motherhood and, consequently, the significance of the loss.

The way in which technology, such as the ultrasound scan, is used may contribute to the distress associated with having a miscarriage. For example, a twenty-
eight year old mother of three who had miscarried on an earlier occasion without
having seen the baby on the scan, spoke of her distress at her second miscarriage:

> Seeing the child in the scan, that's what made me worse . . . If I hadn't have seen
> the child . . . I don't think it would really have annoyed me so much. It's just know-
> ing that the child was alive that night and then about an hour later, you know what
> I mean. I'm disappointed more this time.

Clearly the same piece of technology may have a different impact upon different women.[4] A woman whose second miscarriage was detected by a scan found
the experience less traumatic than her first miscarriage: 'The consultant . . . saw
on the scan that things weren't going well and he just said "You might as well go
into hospital". So it happened very quickly and was a much simpler exercise
really'.

Most women accepted the D & C as an inevitable, although not necessarily expected, part of the hospital care. A small number of women had to return to hospital for a second D & C and this they found distressing: until the physical symptoms of the miscarriage had abated, it was clearly difficult for them to put the experience behind them. A successful D & C appeared to act as a marker between on the one hand, the state of being pregnant and the liminal state of miscarrying, and on the other hand, the state of not being pregnant. By means of the D & C, women were clearly returned to a state of non-pregnancy; they were 'back to normal' and ready to 'try again'.

Marking the event

Miscarriage is not only the loss of a potential baby, it is also, for the childless woman, the loss of potential motherhood. Miscarriage robs a woman of one of the major, if not *the* major life cycle event of her life. Miscarriage involves not only bereavement but also loss of status. Lovell (1983) argues that throughout pregnancy there is a 'social process of identity construction' which abruptly stops if the pregnancy fails. For the woman who is already a mother, the loss is of experiencing again the state of new motherhood, and for them, it may also be the loss of a longed-for child of a particular sex.

Many women who have had an early miscarriage feel that a funeral service would be inappropriate, while nevertheless desiring some publicly expressed acknowledgement of their loss.[5] Early pregnancy may be known to very few people other than the woman herself, her partner and close family. Consequently, when an early miscarriage occurs, it too will probably be known only to a few. Apart from the medical procedures which, in the absence of anything else, may serve a ritual function by clearly marking the end of the pregnancy, it is not an event which is generally acknowledged or observed by any kind of ritual process.[6]

The study did find a small number of exceptions, all of which concerned Catholic women; one woman had been told of a Mass held on the Feast day of the Holy Innocents for stillborn babies and those lost due to miscarriage and abortion. Other women, when asked, reported that they had not heard of anything similar, though one spoke of a service during Catholic Schools Week at which prayers were said for those who died young, and commented, 'I thought to myself "What about all the ones that were miscarried?" They weren't even mentioned and it crossed my mind it would be nice if you had some way of remembering them'. An example of a small action of ritual significance which had taken place within the private domestic sphere was recalled by a 35 year old woman with five children. Speaking of her first miscarriage, which had occurred a number of years before, she recalled her mother's behaviour at that time: 'I didn't really know I had lost it because I didn't know I was expecting and I just sort of flushed it down the toilet, and she (her mother) was away with 'holy water', blessing it and all'. Another woman spoke of being given prayers and holy medals from women who had made pilgrimages to shrines such as that at Knock. For a small number of women it appeared that Catholicism offered a means by which they could express their loss. Not all Catholic women spoke of these things, however, and nothing comparable was reported by any Protestant women. Only a small number of the total sample of women reported receiving any support from their clergyman.

There is no shared cultural consensus as to the significance of miscarriage. The reason for this must lie, in part at least, in the lack of consensus regarding the status of the foetus. How the foetus is categorised has a direct bearing on the significance attributed to the loss of a foetus, whether or not the loss is considered to constitute a bereavement and, consequently what is considered to be an appropriate response. Does the foetus fall into the category of 'baby' or not? If it does, at which stage of gestation does it do so: at conception, or at 24 weeks (that is, at the legal age of viability), or at some stage in between? Despite the debate surrounding the issue of abortion and the considerations expressed in the Warnock Report (Great Britain Committee of Inquiry 1985), there exists no coherent system of belief regarding this matter.

In their cross-cultural study of post-natal depression, Stern and Kruckman (1983) observed that major life cycle changes such as puberty, pregnancy, childbirth and death are in many cultures 'socially dramatised' events. Their importance is acknowledged by a ritual process which constitutes a *rite de passage*. Stern and Kruckman attribute the prevalence of post-natal depression in the West (specifically in the USA), and the lack of it in many other places, to the fact that in North America little attention is paid to the post-partum period. Their own observations and the anthropological literature suggest that this is not the case elsewhere. They identified common elements in the social structuring of the post-partum period in a number of other cultures, which include social recognition of the new social status of the mother, social seclusion and mandated rest, and an acknowledgement of a distinct post-partum period. They suggest that these may be 'basic components which provide necessary social support and which cushion or prevent the experience of post-partum depression' (Stern and Kruckman 1983:1039).

It would be illuminating to examine pregnancy loss from a similar cross-cultural perspective. Studies undertaken so far do indicate great diversity in the management of pregnancy loss, in how the event is perceived and in the appropriate behaviour associated with it. In stark contrast to successful childbirth, a pregnancy loss does not involve a change of status from childless woman to mother. It is not in that sense, an event worthy of social acknowledgement. It may also be that as an event experienced exclusively by women, miscarriage has been largely neglected. Women, as members of a 'muted group' (Ardener 1975), have not had a forum in which to express publicly their feelings about the loss of a pregnancy and the significance which it holds for them. There have been, thus, no shared rites or rituals undertaken at the time of a pregnancy loss which endow the event with social significance. In recent years, however, this lack of ritual activity has been addressed. In some hospitals in the United Kingdom it has become the practice, in the case of late miscarriages and stillbirths, to take a photograph of the infant and/or a lock of hair or footprint for the parents to keep. A book of remembrance is available in some hospitals and a cremation or burial service is conducted, at the parents' request, even for losses of early gestation in some instances (Kohner 1992). The development of parental-inspired ritual activities of remembrance has been more extensive in the United States of America, especially the writing of poetry and the planting of trees (see Layne 1990; 1992).

Pregnancy loss and policies of care

Policy requirements regarding pregnancy loss are not easy to formulate. Individual responses to miscarriage on the part of women, their partners, and the medical and nursing profession differ widely. Consequently, it is very difficult for policy decisions to be made which will be appropriate for everyone involved. Two British publications which address this issue (Henley and Kohner 1991; Moulder 1990) emphasise the need for a flexible and sensitive response to be made in each individual case, while suggesting general guidelines in such matters as the place of care (i.e., the ward in which the mother is placed); the naming of the child; the gathering of mementoes, photographs etc.; disposal of the remains and the question of a funeral service; and follow-up care.

Simonds and Katz Rothman (1992) point out that pregnancy and birth are social and physical experiences which women do not share with men. Thus, in the past, when pregnancy and pregnancy loss were contained within the private domestic domain, women would have comforted other women in the event of a loss. The grief of women who have lost a pregnancy has recently entered a more public domain. In part, they argue, this is due to the 'discovery' of the foetus: 'As modern science and medicine discover the world of the foetus, foetuses become "real". . . . Sonography . . . constructs women's private knowledge for public consumption' (Simonds and Katz Rothman 1992: 256). Simonds and Katz Rothman draw an analogy between the way writers such as Aries (1962) have written about childhood, and how pregnancy and the unborn child are now viewed. Aries suggests that in the tenth and the eleventh century 'childhood was a period of transition which passed quickly and which was just as quickly forgotten' (1962: 34). In response Simonds and Katz Rothman (1992: 254) ask how:

> At a time when most women spent most of their adult lives as the mothers of young children, can one really speak of childhood as a period of transition that passed quickly and was just as quickly forgotten? For whom did it pass quickly and by whom was it quickly forgotten?

Thus it was only 'when men discovered childhood, childhood came into existence' (Simonds and Katz Rothman 1992: 255):

> The discovery of the foetus and the newborn no more empower women as mothers
> than the discovery of the child did—no more, for that matter, than the discovery of
> any 'new world' has empowered the people who lived there first. Power is lost with
> this kind of discovery, for with it comes the discoverer's control (Simonds and Katz
> Rothman 1992: 256).

Simonds and Katz Rothman are consequently wary of the way in which the
grief of the mother, now that it has been recognised, depends on the construction
of the foetus as an entity separate from its mother. In response to the prevailing situation among some social groups in the United States, they suggest that while the
provision of mementoes of the lost child may be helpful if they are wanted, it is
more important to focus on the feelings of each individual mother (Simonds and
Katz Rothman 1992: 259). They argue that care-providers should allow women
the freedom to express the meaning which pregnancy and pregnancy loss has for
them in their own lives: 'For a woman who experiences a pregnancy loss as a
tragedy, it is a tragedy; and for a woman who experiences a loss as a relief, it is a
relief' (Simonds and Katz Rothman 1992: 259).

The findings from this study indicate that while women were appreciative of
the care and support which they received from medical and nursing staff, it was
not always felt to be appropriate or adequate. The changing technologies associated with pregnancy have led to an early identification of pregnancy and high
expectations of a successful outcome. Consequently, it seems likely that greater
feelings of loss are felt at an early miscarriage than in the past. Although the onset
of pregnancy may, for many women, be the result of 'God's will' or luck (good or
bad), the premature ending of a pregnancy increasingly takes place within a medical context. The increasing medicalisation of pregnancy and of miscarriage has
resulted in a shift of responsibility for the care and support of women from the
informal sphere of family, friends and neighbours to the formal sphere of medical
and nursing professionals.[7] It is thus to health professionals that women now look
for help. Health professionals need to be responsive to this, and to acknowledge
their responsibility to provide ongoing support to women who have miscarried, as
required.

Whatever policy decisions may be taken regarding the specific care of women
who miscarry, it follows from what has been presented here that a change of policy is needed at a very early stage in the pregnancy, or even prior to a pregnancy.
The medical profession has fostered a dependency which is unwarranted, and
unhelpful to women. The way in which the role of medicine in the field of
pregnancy and childbirth is presented to women needs to be modified in order to
incorporate some acknowledgement of its limitations regarding pregnancy loss, as
well as needing to reflect an awareness of the unique circumstances of each
woman.

Notes

The research on which this chapter is based was funded by the Economic and Social Research Council (award number R000233062) to whom I am very grateful. I am also very grateful to the Sir Halley Stewart Trust, the Sir Samuel Scott of Yews Trust, The TSB Foundation for Northern Ireland and the Elmgrant Trust. My sincere thanks go to all the women who participated in the study. Ethical approval for the study was obtained from the Research Ethical Committee of The Queen's University of Belfast.

1. Martin (1989) argues that working class women are more likely than middle class women to be critical of, and resistant to, the existing organisation of society. In terms of reproductive medicine this suggests that working class women are less likely to internalise the medical viewpoint.
2. It is known that the way in which information is conveyed to a patient may affect her immediate sense of well-being and possibly her long-term coping behaviour (Kaplan et al 1989).
3. 'There is no indication that there has been any significant decline in the frequency of miscarriage and stillbirth as a result of medical intervention' (Layne 1992: 33).
4. Petchesky (1987: 73), in her critique of the use of visual imagery in the field of reproductive medicine and politics, suggests that: 'Women's relationship to reproductive technologies and images differs depending on social differences such as class, race and sexual preference, and biological ones such as age, physical disability and personal fertility history'.
5. For miscarriage *not* to be acknowledged as significant can exacerbate distress. Lovell (1983: 756) found that health workers dealing with late miscarriage, stillbirth and perinatal death considered that 'the earlier the pregnancy failed, the "lesser" the loss, making miscarriage less sad than stillbirth; and stillbirth less sad than losing a baby who had lived. It followed that miscarriage and stillbirth were not viewed as proper bereavements'. However, Lovell's own findings challenge what she calls this 'hierarchy of sadness', for she found that mothers whose babies were born alive were 'better able to make sense of the tragedy . . . better able to mourn . . . Acceptance was linked to the way that the baby's existence, though short, had been acknowledged and made tangible' (1983: 759).
6. While miscarriages which occur at a later stage of a pregnancy *may* involve a funeral service, these are very rare for early miscarriages (see Kohner 1992), and none took place for any of the cases in this study.
7. Support from the family has been found to be rather piecemeal and of limited duration (see Cecil 1994).

References

Ardener, E. 1975. The 'Problem' Revisited. In S. Ardener (ed.), *Perceiving Women*. London: J.M. Dent and Sons Ltd.

Aries, P. 1962. *Centuries of Childhood*. (transl. Robert Baldick). London: Jonathan Cape.

Cecil, R. 1994. 'I Wouldn't Have Minded a Wee One Running About': Miscarriage and the Family. *Social Science and Medicine* 38, 1415–22.

Cecil, R. (ed.) 1996. *The Anthropology of Pregnancy Loss: Comparative Studies in Miscarriage, Stillbirth and Neonatal Death*. Oxford: Berg.

Cecil, R. and J. Leslie 1993. Early Miscarriage: Preliminary Results from a Study in Northern Ireland. *Journal of Reproductive and Infant Psychology* 11, 89–95.

Great Britain Committee of Inquiry into Human Fertilisation and Embryology 1985. *A Question of Life: The Warnock Report.* Oxford: Blackwell.

Henley, A. and N. Kohner 1991. *Miscarriages, Stillbirth and Neonatal Death: Guidelines for Professionals.* London: Stillbirth and Neonatal Death Society.

Jackman, C., H. M. McGee and M. Turner 1991. The Experience and Impact of Early Miscarriage. *Irish Journal of Psychology* 12, 108–120.

Kaplan, S.H., S. Greenfield and J. E. Ware Jr. 1989. Impact of the Doctor-Patient Relationship on the Outcomes of Chronic Disease. In M. Stewart and D. Roter (eds.), *Communication with Medical Patients.* Beverley Hills, CA: Sage.

Kohner, N. 1992. *A Dignified Ending.* London: Stillbirth and Neonatal Death Society.

Layne, L.L. 1990. Motherhood Lost: Cultural Dimensions of Miscarriage and Stillbirth in America. *Women and Health* 16, 69–98.

_____. 1992. Of Fetuses and Angels: Fragmentation and Integration in Narratives of Pregnancy Loss. In D. Hess and L.L. Layne (eds.), *Knowledge and Society: The Anthropology of Science and Technology.* Greenwich, CT: JAI Press Inc.

Lovell, A. 1983. Some Questions of Identity: Late Miscarriage, Stillbirth and Perinatal Loss. *Social Science and Medicine* 17, 755–61.

Martin, E. 1989. *The Woman in the Body.* Milton Keynes: Open University Press.

Moulder, C. 1990. *Miscarriage: Women's Experiences and Needs.* London: Pandora Press.

Petchesky, R.P. 1987. Foetal Images: The Power of Visual Culture in the Politics of Reproduction. In M. Stanworth (ed.), *Reproductive Technologies.* Cambridge: Polity Press.

Simonds, W. and B. Katz Rothman 1992. *Centuries of Solace: Expressions of Maternal Grief in Popular Literature.* Philadelphia: Temple University Press.

Sobo, E.J. 1996. Cultural Explanations for Pregnancy Loss in Rural Jamaica. In R. Cecil (ed.), *The Anthropology of Pregnancy Loss.* Oxford: Berg.

Spielberger, C. D. 1983. *Manual for the State-Trait Anxiety Inventory.* Palo Alto: Consulting Psychologists Press.

Stern, G. and L. Kruckman 1983. Multi-Disciplinary Perspectives on Post-Partum Depression: An Anthropological Critique. *Social Science and Medicine* 17, 1027–41.

Winkvist, A. 1996. Water Spirits, Medicinemen and Witches: Avenues to Successful Reproduction among the Abelam, Papua New Guinea. In R. Cecil (ed.), *The Anthropology of Pregnancy Loss.* Oxford: Berg.

9   Equal opportunities, the clothing industry and the law

Kate Ingram

In this chapter I demonstrate that there are serious problems involved in any attempt to rectify inequality of employment opportunity through the legal process. These problems are intensified by the nature of women's work in Ireland and the United Kingdom, as well as being compounded by the implementation of the two laws which are designed to redress inequality there. The legislative process of the United Kingdom further exacerbates the difficulties. I examine conditions within the Northern Irish clothing industry and show how these conditions exemplify certain of the difficulties discussed in general terms.

Women's work

In the United Kingdom women tend to be segregated horizontally and vertically within the labour market (Worsley 1987). In Ireland, too, according to Wickham (1986), men and women participate in the labour market in different ways. In Ireland, women's work encompasses 'semi-skilled jobs entailing fairly high levels of manual dexterity' (Harris 1984: 156), and areas of female employment have either remained largely unchanged, or have become increasingly feminised (O'Hara 1987). Perrons (1979) notes that female labour is particularly important in textile multi-nationals in the Republic of Ireland, where women, having been freed from patriarchal control at home, find themselves dominated by male supervisors. Although the economic activity rate of married women in Ireland has increased considerably in recent years, women's jobs generally remain part-time (O'Dowd 1986). Where full-time work is available, as in the textile industry, it is largely based on the traditional pattern of a male working life, which assumes that there is a woman at home 'to feed him, wash his clothes, keep house and soothe him after the working day' (Beale 1986: 151).

Employers perceive the labour force participation of women as intermittent, and see jobs requiring little training as the best option. Many of the popular jobs for women are one-level occupations, with little opportunity for promotion or sideways movement. Nevertheless, in the United Kingdom, young women appear more favourably disposed to training than young men (West and Newton 1983). However, little investment has been made in equipping women with the formal training required for higher level work, since they are perceived as providing a poor return when compared with men (Cavendish 1982).

McCarthy (1987) found that in the Republic of Ireland some managers believed that women who were more committed to work than men became less so after the age of twenty-five. They attributed this to the characteristics of the women themselves, rather than to the nature of the work or the absence of training. Commitment was sometimes judged by a willingness to relocate. Unsurprisingly, many married women are not free to show such a level of commitment. Managers also believed that it was because women stayed a shorter time with their company that their promotional opportunities were limited (McCarthy 1987).

The pursuit of equal opportunities has broadened from an initial concern over pay differentials to looking at job-sharing, flexi-time, childcare facilities and reduced working hours. Given the present structure of labour force involvement, the achievement of equal opportunities is almost impossible (Beale 1986). Perhaps because of a belief that the ideology of the family contradicts and compromises the notion of married women working outside the home, the move towards equal opportunities has gone much further for single women, and has left married women lagging far behind.

Reasons for equal opportunities legislation

According to Carter (1988), the chief reason for having laws on equality of opportunity is to change the behaviour of employers and employees. This can be done by influencing the tone of official and public comments, which in turn influence the attitudes of the general public and, more specifically, employers. Equal treatment for men and women then begins to be seen as a right, not a privilege. Ending discriminatory behaviour is likely to bring about the acceptance of equal treatment of the labour force. Additionally, the law protects people who may not themselves be prejudiced, but who may have to work in a prejudiced society.

Lustgarten (1989) disagrees, however, arguing that the emphasis on defining minimal compliance, which is part of the legal process in the United Kingdom, may discourage people from developing and implementing more imaginative measures for improving equality of opportunity. He suggests that legal regulation ultimately works in a negative fashion, and that financial inducements are more likely to overcome resistance and stimulate voluntary innovation in this field (Lustgarten 1989: 23).

Nevertheless, Zabalza and Tzannatos (1985) maintain that the average relative pay of women in the United Kingdom in the 1970s increased by 15 per cent, and that the main factor behind this remarkable increase was the anti-discriminatory legislation. They admit, however, to being unable to identify any further increases as a result of the legislation.

The laws

There are two laws in the United Kingdom which relate to equality of opportunity: the 1970 Equal Pay Act (NI) and the 1975(6) Sex Discrimination Act. The 1970 Equal Pay Act was designed to prevent inequalities in terms and conditions of employment between men and women. It stated that men and women should be paid the same amount if employed on the same, or broadly similar, areas of work. The concept of 'broadly similar work' was later widened to include jobs which had been rated 'the same' under a job evaluation scheme, though this concession was only achieved through the intervention of the European courts. The Central Arbitration Committee was empowered to remove discrimination in collective agreements, employers pay structures and statutory wage orders, with provisions which applied separately to men and women.

The 1975(6) Sex Discrimination Act was introduced to ensure equality of opportunity in access to jobs. In the field of employment, the Sex Discrimination Act prohibits discrimination with respect to hiring, opportunities for promotion, transfer and training, and dismissal on the grounds of gender or marriage. The provisions relate to direct and indirect discrimination. This act applies equally to men and women, which means that discrimination against men is also unlawful. There are no affirmative action proposals as used in the United States, except in the provision of special access to training facilities; women, or men, may be positively helped to train for a particular job if one or other was under-represented in that area of work within the previous twelve months.

Under both these laws, the individual has the right to take his or her case to an industrial tribunal. In the event of an action being brought, the burden of proof is on the complainant to demonstrate the existence of a particular requirement (for example a minimum height or chest measurement), and that this requirement operated to his or her detriment. If the case is accepted, the burden of proof is transferred to the employer, who must demonstrate that the alleged discriminatory requirement is justified.

Deficiencies in the laws

To monitor these Acts a quango was established, the Equal Opportunities Commission (EOC). The EOC has the power to conduct formal investigations into organisations which have been the subject of complaint from the public, and to issue non-discrimination notices. In addition, 'as the "guardian" of the legislation, the EOC has the power to commission research to discover whether these Acts are being implemented' (Collinson et al 1990). Certainly the emphasis on commissioning research has grown stronger as the EOC has grown older, but this in itself may reflect the failure of the legislative process. Arguably, the establishment of the EOC is where the deficiencies in the legal process began.

It can be argued that quangos compartmentalise and marginalise the issue of equal opportunities. Instead of impinging on every aspect of governmental business, agencies such as the Commission for Racial Equality (CRE), the Fair Employment Agency (FEA), and the EOC are marginal to the basic agenda of government, and the issues with which they deal have been successfully isolated from mainstream policy (Jenkins and Solomos 1989). A further problem inherent in the EOC is the need for it to establish its own priorities and emphases. Some of these problems stem from the breadth of its remit, combined with the smallness of its allotted budget.

Employer bias

Another limitation of the equal opportunities laws is the way in which they are weighted in favour of the employer. The invoking of the legislative process involves skills which large-scale employers may be expected to command more readily than complainants. This helps to explain the large number of Equal Opportunities cases which have been defeated. The figures given by Chiplin and Sloane (1982) indicate that almost 60 per cent of cases were settled by conciliation, or withdrawn prior to tribunal hearing; 11.6 per cent of complaints were upheld, whereas 29 per cent were rejected. It is unlikely that this is due to a 'culture of complaint', which finds problems where they do not exist, since cases are more likely to win if help is given by the EOC, who indeed frequently do present the cases. Nevertheless, the responsibility for taking cases to the Tribunals under both Acts lies with the person who feels he or she has been discriminated against, and many complainants receive no expert help in presenting their case (Carter 1988).

The effectiveness of industrial tribunals

The Policy Studies Institute (PSI) has published its findings on a group of employers in Britain, each of whom was found to have broken the law on sex discrimination or on equal pay (Chambers and Horton 1990). The PSI established that the loss of a case by an employer was unlikely to bring about improvement in equality of opportunity. Only one in five employers introduced an equal opportunities policy or reviewed an already existing policy as a result of a tribunal decision. Tribunals failed to use their powers to recommend change to employers. Changes in equal opportunities policy and practice were more likely among large employers and among those in the public sector. The PSI also found that the majority of sex discrimination and equal pay applications were not successful. Even where they were successful, the low compensation payable meant that employers were unlikely to act on the findings. Improvement in employment practices we greater where there was follow-up pressure from trade unions or employees, though trade unions have only infrequently utilised tribunal decisions to raise awareness of inequality of opportunity (Chambers and Horton 1990). If management attitudes remained hostile, successful cases did not result in improvements. There is no official monitoring of employers who have contravened the legislation in any part of the United Kingdom.

Common law ideology versus equal opportunities

Alongside the difficulties which occur because the enforcement of equal opportunities has been handed over to quangos, there is a contradiction between the ideology of the common law and the ideology of equal opportunities. By definition, discrimination is the antithesis of individualised decision. The person is discriminated against because of his or her involuntary membership of a group. There is a collective dimension to every discrimination case which is difficult to fit within the traditional processes of the legislature. The British legal system, unlike the American one, conventionally proceeds along the lines of individuation, but additionally there is an ideology at work, the exaltation of individualism by the common law (Lustgarten 1989).

The equal opportunities legislation is restricted in several ways by the concept of individuation which informs it. The most important restriction concerns the scope of the remedies which can be imposed on the offending employer. In America, if an employer is adjudged to have discriminated, he faces a large monetary bill for all those who are within the class against which he has discriminated. In consequence, it is often cheaper and easier for him to obey the law. In the British legislative process, compensation is only payable to 'the individual who has had the courage, persistence and patience to bring the action' (Lustgarten 1989).

Interpretation of the laws

Initially there was a tendency for the Equal Opportunity Laws to be interpreted very narrowly by the legislature, but this has now broadened considerably because the British legal system has been supplemented by the mechanism of appeal to the European Courts (Carter 1988). Article 119 of the Treaty of Rome requires member states to apply the principle of equal pay for the same work, or for work to which equal value is attributed by the courts. In other words, work could no longer be defined as worth more simply because it was performed by male operatives, though broadly the same as that performed by women. As a result of various cases of sex discrimination being referred to the European Courts of Justice, the EOC commented that a number of claims for a woman to earn the same pay as her male predecessor were satisfactorily settled before reaching a tribunal. The European Court also found that part-time working by itself did not provide grounds for lower hourly rates of pay, and once again a number of women throughout the United Kingdom were assisted by this ruling and their cases settled out of court. In 1982, the European Economic Community (EEC) commission ruled that the Equal Pay Act did not meet the requirements of Article 119, and under the European Communities Act an order was issued for the British Government to change its domestic law. This produced the 1984 amendment to the 1982 act, stating that equal pay was to be given for work of equal value.

The legislature is a very cumbersome instrument, the due processes of which are notoriously lengthy, whilst all loopholes are explored and delaying tactics employed. This is standard defensive procedure, and must be accepted if defence is to be admitted at all. One example of this is evident from the 'Casebook of Decisions on Sex Discrimination and Equal Pay' (EOC 1990). Since 1984, when the amendment to the Equal Pay Act was passed, a number of important cases have been lodged before industrial tribunals in Northern Ireland.

> However, due to the complexity of the legislation only two cases have been concluded in the first five year period (EOC 1990: ii).

The reason that proceedings have been so slow is that, in order to claim work of equal value, an independent expert appointed by the Labour Relations Agency must visit the workplace to assess the two allegedly equivalent jobs (unless an employer has already undergone a comprehensive job evaluation scheme, in itself an inordinately lengthy process as we shall see later). The assessment is usually considered under five headings: physical skills, mental skills, decision-making, effort, and working conditions, although training may also be taken into account on some occasions. I shall return to the issue of training later.

Economic forces and social factors

So far I have concentrated on the restrictions of the legal processes in the enforcement of equality of opportunity, rather than on the position of women in the labour market, or on the reasons for this position. Arguably it is this, at least as much as the cumbersome nature of the legal process, which means that the inferior position of women has not been much improved after twenty years of equality legislation. 'Laws cannot alter the way the economy functions' (Carter 1988). Economic recession has undermined women's bargaining position and increased job segregation, always a key cause of inequality (and, incidentally, one which is very evident in the Northern Ireland clothing industry). Indeed, economic conditions are becoming increasingly unfavourable to women achieving equality at work (Carter 1988).

As Chiplin and Sloane (1982) point out, it is rarely optimal for employers to ensure that women are given the same opportunities as men among all occupational groups, given the higher rates of absenteeism and turnover among women. They go on to suggest that the theory of human capital regards the acquisition of skill as an investment decision made in anticipation of future returns. It then becomes less profitable for firms to invest in the training of women, since the period over which the return can be reaped is shorter than for men. A woman who has to bear the cost of training herself may also feel this (Chiplin and Sloan 1982). I consider this issue below in relation to the clothing industry.

Davis (1988) has argued that for most women family obligations take priority over work, or exist in an uneasy relationship with work. Culturally, women carry the responsibility for childcare and domestic chores. This ensures that men are free to compete in the workforce, and even if women were given exactly the same treatment as men (in itself frequently an elusive objective), they would still be disadvantaged. Either the burdens of men and women must be better balanced before they arrive at the marketplace, or women should be privileged once they enter it. Women often need more than equality. They need maternity leave, refresher programmes and chances to brush up their skills. They need child-care facilities. They also need special training courses to enable them to compete with men. All of the above could be conceded through the legally acceptable policy of positive action. In practice, it is scarcely ever used. There is a further demand to restructure jobs, and to provide a shorter working day and flexible hours, as well as part-time working under better conditions and at all levels. It is impossible to ensure equality of opportunity for women when it comes to jobs, because these jobs are structured as male jobs. The system assumes that women will be elsewhere than in the labour market. Conway (1992) argues that women who have children are obliged to withdraw, if only temporarily, from full-time paid employment, in order first to bear and then to look after the children in their early years.

According to Moore (1988), household organisation and gender ideologies play a crucial role in determining women's entry into the labour market. The need for maximum economic output, together with firmly held beliefs about women's capabilities, has led to the confinement of women workers to particular sectors of the economy and to particular levels within these sectors. It is not only the failure of the legislative process which hinders the implementation of equal opportunities, but economic and cultural factors, working on women's position in society.

The clothing industry in Northern Ireland

I now turn to the clothing industry in Northern Ireland as an extended illustration of the difficulties which have not yet been overcome by equal opportunities legislation. The material presented derives from a study undertaken on behalf of the

Equal Opportunities Commission (McLaughlin and Ingram 1991). This study involved a postal survey of employers, which collected information on the terms and conditions of employment in 46 production units. The survey was supplemented by in-depth studies of three production units.

In 1990 the industry accounted for 37 per cent of all manufacturing employment for women, and six per cent of all female employment (DED 1990). In contrast, it provided four per cent of male manufacturing employment and only one per cent of all male employment. It is the second most important source of employment for women outside the public sector (McLaughlin and Ingram 1991). Given this fact, prospects for equality of opportunity do not look bright if we look at it from Davis's (1989) position. Women are not privileged when they are employed in the clothing industry.

Only 6 firms in the survey made special arrangements for pregnant women, 29 did not. Not one of the units covered by the survey had ever operated a crèche or nursery, though two had discussed the possibility. None had ever contributed to sponsored or concessionary places at local community nursery schools or crèches. None of the firms paid anything more than statutory maternity pay (SMP) to their workers, and there was very limited provision for unpaid maternity leave. Only three of the larger units permitted such leave. The few benefits which were available within the industry were targeted at the higher (disproportionately male) occupational grades (McLaughlin and Ingram 1991).

The industry is highly segregated. Men and women work in different areas, with women generally working in tasks of lower status. The industry is characterised by a shop-floor which is predominantly female and a mainly male management, this in itself illustrating the failure of the equal opportunities legislation. In 1971, 91 per cent of the shop-floor operatives were women, with 88 per cent of managerial staff being men. By 1987 the position had changed little, with 92 per cent of the shop-floor operatives being women, while 70 per cent of managerial staff were men. In 1987, although women represented 86 per cent of all employees, only 30 per cent of managerial staff were women (McLaughlin and Ingram 1991).

Horizontal segregation

Whereas the vertical segregation, with women sitting mainly at the bottom of the industry hierarchy, demonstrates a failure to deliver equal opportunities, the prevalence of horizontal segregation gives an indication of why the failure has occurred. 94 per cent of the workforce were employed in sex-segregated occupations or occupations where at least two-thirds of employees were of the same sex. 83 per cent of the workforce were employed in highly sex-segregated occupations, where 90 per cent or more of the employees were of the same sex. This segregation has implications for the implementation of equal opportunities legislation, since it is difficult, unless a full-scale job evaluation is undertaken, to compare men's work with women's work or to argue for higher pay for women on the grounds of equal pay for equal work. I look in more detail at the criteria for job evaluation later. The high level of sex segregation within the industry was evident from the physical location of male and female workers within the production units. These were studied individually. Entire areas of the shop-floor were either all male or all female.

This physical separation is of some significance, since it may prevent employees knowing the terms and conditions of other employees who, though of similar occupational levels, work in separate and distinct areas of the production unit.

> Lack of knowledge about and contact with employees of the other sex may struc-
> ture the way male and female workers perceive their jobs, and in particular may
> reduce the likelihood of and the ability to make comparisons across jobs, or
> between groups of workers (McLaughlin and Ingram 1991: 16).

Finlay (1987) has argued that the traditional separation between cutting room and sewing room has performed this very function in the past.

Women workers who perform a variety of functions (pressers, packers, sewing machinists and quality control) are likely to occupy one large, open-plan space. The physical layout of production units thus reflects sex segregation more than it does occupational divisions. At present, the physical separation of men and women mirrors their occupational segregation and may contribute to the problems of breaking down traditional occupational barriers between men and women.

Training

One of the most interesting aspects of the clothing industry is the interaction between the perception of training and the notion of skill which seems to be dependent on training. As we shall see, this has implications for equal opportunities, in particular when job evaluation is in question. Men typically enter the industry as apprentice mechanics or as apprentice or trainee cutters. Women enter as 'service girls', which is followed by movement into one of the female-dominated production areas of sewing, pressing or quality control. When women move from 'service girl' to production line, they typically receive training of from five weeks to seven months. The length of training depends on the job into which they move. If a woman becomes a presser, it is unlikely that training will take more than six weeks, whereas training for sewing jobs varies greatly depending on the complexity of the specific task.

There are two main differences between the training received by cutting production workers and mechanics, and that received by sewing and pressing workers. Cutting workers and mechanics are more likely to receive 'off the job' and day release training. Sewing and pressing workers receive in-house training, generally through exposure methods or formal in-house training programmes. The second difference concerns recognition of training received. After the initial training period of between five weeks and seven months, most sewing workers continue to undergo training. However, unlike young cutters and mechanics, they will no longer be considered trainees. The further instruction they receive is not necessarily considered as 'training', and they do not progress up a clearly defined occupational ladder.

> As apprentices and trainees each cutter and mechanic participates in a formally designed training programme which results in the individual acquiring a comprehensive body of skills and knowledge . . . Each fully trained mechanic or cutter is thus an individual repository of all the skills which may be needed by the production unit. In contrast, sewing workers are trained initially for specific jobs, and then subsequently trained for other jobs on an ad hoc basis as the production unit requires. The result is that an individual sewing worker may, over an extended period, acquire a comprehensive body of skills, or some part of the total possible body of sewing skills, but she does not do so as part of a planned programme, nor will the full range of skills she possesses be recognised (McLaughlin and Ingram 1991: 34).

In the large production unit which formed part of the study there were two patterns of training. The first applied to managerial staff, workstudy staff, mechanics and cutters. It gave formal trainee status to the employee for a recognised and fairly lengthy period, and during this period the individual moved from simple to complex tasks with appropriate increases in pay. At the end of this period of training the employee was recognised as skilled and experienced. The second pattern of training applied to sewing and pressing production workers. It involved an initial move from servicing (wheeling trolleys of 'work' to the appropriate production areas, as and when they were required) to the production process. This was accompanied by an increase in status and pay and a short period of formal training. After that, neither status nor pay increased with the additional training received. So, for example, a sewing worker who had been working for five years and who had been trained to perform several complex tasks might well be earning the same as a pressing worker who had only been trained for six weeks and could only pack garments.

Moreover, during the time in which the experienced worker was undergoing training, she often suffered a reduction in wages, since, at least while she was growing accustomed to the different and frequently more complex task, she worked at a slower rate than usual and so earned less. She was never compensated for this reduction in earnings.

Although it would not be entirely true to say there was one pattern of training for women and one for men, since some women were employed as cutters and managers, it was only women who experienced the second pattern of unstructured and largely unrecognised training. Thus, as Chiplin and Sloan (1982) claim, clothing firms invest less of their capital in training women.

Promotion

The procedure for promotion, to quote the personnel officer of the large production unit, was 'the tap on the shoulder' approach. Promotion to supervisor from
production worker frequently took no account of the amount of training the
women had received, and therefore of how skilled they were as sewing machinists. In the large production unit the two most recent promotions were of women
who had been working on quality control, and were in fact quite unable to use a
sewing machine. One woman was told that her application for the job of supervisor had failed, because at twenty-one she was too young for the post. The women
who were promoted had been selected for their acceptability rather than their suit-
ability (Jenkins 1986).

There was little enthusiasm for promotion from production worker to supervisor. Management, workers, and trade union officials noted a reluctance among
sewing machinists to apply for supervisory posts. All saw this as being, at least
in part, the result of monetary considerations. When a woman was first promoted
from the floor, she would earn less than she would have earned if she had previously been a 'good' production worker working at around 140 per cent performance (that is, 40 per cent faster than the rate expected for the job.) In contrast
with the sewing machinist's ability to control her own earnings level (the harder
she worked, the more she earned), the supervisor's take-home pay was dependent on the performance of others. The harder she could persuade her section to
work, the more she earned. Initially at least there was little or no financial gain
in taking on the more stressful job of organising production. This was in sharp
contrast to promotion incentives in all the other occupations in the factory. Not
all women experienced this financial disincentive (those in management and
workstudy did not), though it was only women and not men who experienced
it.

I have already mentioned the strongly segregated nature of the clothing
industry. In the large production unit, I was told that men would not be allowed to
work as sewing machinists. The test which determined whether a trainee would be
taken on as a machinist discriminated against men, since only those who had previously operated a domestic sewing machine would be likely to obtain an acceptable grade on the test, and until recently men were unlikely to have had such prior
experience.

The result of this occupational segregation is that if a woman enters a claim
under equal pay for work of equal value, her employer will either have to agree to
take part in a complete evaluation scheme, or an independent expert will have to
be appointed to adjudicate the claim.

> ... the Equal Value Regulations provide a means whereby a woman can make com-
> parison with any man engaged in the same employment ... whom she thinks is
> doing work of equal value, although it is not like work (Bourn 1992: 22).

The more favoured method is that of appointing an independent expert. On the occasions when this has happened, one of the factors which is consistently taken into consideration is the degree of skill required for the jobs which are being compared. For example, in the case of Tennants Textile Colours Ltd versus Todd, the independent expert who was brought in to adjudicate evaluated the jobs according to the demands made upon the job holders, and used the five characteristics mentioned earlier: physical skills, mental skills, decision-making, effort and working conditions (EOC 1990). In the case of Winton versus Northern Ireland Electricity:

> the Respondent argued that the jobs were not of equal value under various headings, such as effort, skill and decision-making (EOC 1990: 169).

The only other case where a claim for work of equal value was involved—McCauley and Others versus Eastern Health and Social Services Board—cited an evaluation scheme undertaken in England where once more the headings under which the jobs were assessed were 'effort, skill and decision-making' (EOC 1990: 172).

The emphasis placed on skill when job evaluation is carried out is very worrying for women workers. When we look at the clothing industry, we see ways in which a woman's skill consistently goes unrecognised.

As already mentioned, to obtain employment in the factory women must achieve a certain score on the sewing machine before they are accepted as a 'service girl', a score unlikely to be achieved by men. A certain level of expertise with the sewing machine is thus assumed in those who apply for the job of a sewing machinist. This contrasts with the apprentice engineers, who take no test before they commence their apprenticeship. They may have studied technical drawing at school but they are not expected to have done so, nor are they tested on their knowledge at the point of entry into the factory. It is assumed that their lengthy training will provide them with the necessary expertise in the job. Women, on the other hand, are already expected to have a certain level of expertise before they begin their training.

It is notoriously difficult to arrive at a definition of skill as it relates to employment. There are various ways of measuring and defining jobs as skilled and unskilled but one consistently used, and around which the concept of a 'skilled job' has arisen, is that of successfully emerging from an apprenticeship, or an extended and structured training period.

> . . . unions and management have tried to reduce the evaluative term 'skilled' to a descriptive one, by confining it to the jobs which require a certain clearly defined and labelled (apprenticeship) length of training, or which entail the use of certain machines (Ingram 1989: 56).

In the light of this, we should look again at the pattern of the women sewing-machinists' training. I have already mentioned that women initially undergo a brief period of training when they move from servicing to using the sewing machine, and that this is the only occasion when their training is accompanied by an increase in pay and status. The training is quite unstructured, in that it is under-taken on an ad hoc basis, as and when a vacancy occurs on a different job. The result is that a sewing machinist with great expertise may well not be recognised as skilled. She may have spent more than two years on periods of training, but since these periods are rewarded neither by higher pay nor increased status, they are unrecognised. The sewing-machinist's training is hidden. Consequently, since skill is frequently defined by length of training, so is her skill.

This hidden skill of women in the clothing industry has obvious negative implications for equal opportunities when it comes to job evaluation. Since one of the elements of job evaluation is the amount of skill required to perform a certain job, and since the skill of the women is both learned before they enter the factory and hidden once they are in the factory, and, moreover, not even necessarily rewarded by promotion, then the women sewing machinists are unlikely to be compared favourably with men, whose skill can be clearly seen after they emerge from structured training programmes.

A variety of difficulties beset those who wish to ensure equal opportunities for women in the workplace. There is the position of women in the home, and with relation to children. This position means that equality in the marketplace is not enough. Women should have special facilitatory conditions, but economic con-siderations mean they are unlikely to receive even bare equality. Moreover, full adult status is not accorded to women until they have married and borne children, whereas for men it is achieved simply by entry into the labour force. There are also the limitations of the legislative process and the laws themselves, which make tak-ing cases to law a lengthy and unwieldy process, weighted against the employee if she acts on her own. Finally, there are specific conditions within certain indus-tries, particularly the Northern Irish clothing industry, which mean that the ideal of equal pay for work of equal value is virtually impossible to implement.

Nevertheless, it is important to note by way of conclusion that the unrecog-nised nature of women's skill due to the hidden nature of their training may now be changing. Since the research discussed above was undertaken, National Vocational Qualifications have been introduced. These are designed precisely to reward participants in the labour force for the skills they are using, in the job they are doing. In these qualifications practical skills are underpinned by theoretical knowledge, with an emphasis on flexibility. There is a progression from level one to level five (managerial level). As yet, these qualifications are still in their infancy and their impact has not been assessed. If they work as they are designed to, they could mean that women's skill in the labour market is finally recognised.

References

Bourn, C. 1992. *Sex Discrimination Law: A review.* The Institute of Employment Rights.
Beale, J. 1986. *Women in Ireland: Voices of Change.* Dublin: Gill and Macmillan.

Carter, A. 1988. *The Politics of Women's Rights*. London: Longmans.

Cavendish, R. 1982. *Women on the Line*. London: Routledge and Kegan Paul.

Chambers, G. and C. Horton 1990. *Promoting Sex Equality: The Role of Industrial Tribunals*. London: Policy Studies Institute.

Chiplin, B. and P. J. Sloan 1982. *Tackling Discrimination at the Workplace: An Analysis of Sex Segregation in Britain*. Cambridge: Cambridge University Press.

Collinson, D., D. Knights and M. Collinson 1990. *Managing to Discriminate*. London: Routledge.

Davis, C. 1989. Workplace Action Programmes for Equality for Women. An Orthodoxy Examined. In C. Hussey (ed.), *Equal Opportunities for Men and Women in Higher Education in Ireland*. Dublin: University College Dublin.

Conway, D. 1992. Do Women Benefit from Equal Opportunities Legislation? In C. Quest (ed.), *Equal Opportunities: A Feminist Fallacy*. London: IEA Health and Welfare Unit.

Department of Economic Development (DED NI) 1990. Census for Employment Register. Belfast: DED (NI).

EOC 1990. *A Casebook of Decisions on Sex Discrimination and Equal Pay*. Equal Opportunities Commission.

Finlay, A. 1987. The Cutting Edge: Derry Shirtmakers. In C. Curtin, P. Jackson and B. O'Connor (eds.), *Gender in Irish Society*. Galway: Galway University Press.

Harris, L. 1984. Class, Community and Sexual Division in North Mayo. In C. Curtin, P. Jackson and B. O'Connor (eds.), *Culture and Ideology in Ireland*. Galway: Galway University Press.

Ingram, K. 1989. Hidden Training, Hidden Skills. Queen's University Belfast: unpublished MSSc Dissertation.

Jenkins, R. 1986. *Racism and Recruitment: Managers, Organisations and Equal Opportunity in the Labour Market*. Cambridge: Cambridge University Press.

_____. and J. Solomos (eds.), 1989. *Racism and Equal Opportunities Policies in the 1980s*. Cambridge: Cambridge University Press.

Lustgarten, L. 1989. Racial Inequality and the Limits of the Law. In R. Jenkins and J. Solomos (eds.), *Racism and Equal Opportunities Policies in the 1980s*. Cambridge: Cambridge University Press.

McCarthy, E.N.D. 1987. *Transitions to Equal Opportunities at Work: Problems and Possibilities*. Dublin: Employment Equality Agency.

McLaughlin, E. and K. Ingram. 1991. *All Stitched Up: Sex and Skill in the Northern Irish Clothing Industry*. Belfast: Equal Opportunities Commission.

Moore, H. 1988. *Feminism and Anthropology*. Cambridge: Polity Press.

O'Dowd, L. 1986. Beyond Industrial Society. In P. Clancy et al (eds.), *Ireland: A Sociological Profile*. Dublin: Institute of Public Administration.

O'Hara, P. 1987. What Became of Them? Women in the West of Ireland Labour Force. In C. Curtin, P. Jackson and B. O'Connor (eds.), *Gender in Irish Society*. Galway: Galway University Press.

Perrons, D. 1979. Ireland in the New International Division of Labour. *Sussex University Paper* 15.

West, M. and P. Newton 1983. *The Transition from School to Work*. London: Croom Helm.

Wickham, J. 1986. Industrialisation, Work and Unemployment. In P. Clancy et al (eds.), *Ireland: A Sociological Profile*. Dublin: Institute of Public Administration.

Worsley, P. (ed.) 1987. *The New Introduction to Sociology*. Middlesex: Penguin.

Zabalza, A. and Z. Tzannatos. 1985. *Women and Equal Pay: The Effects of Legislation on Female Employment and Wages in Britain*. Cambridge: Cambridge University Press.

10 'Counselling' the unemployed in Belfast

Hastings Donnan and Graham McFarlane

During the 1980s unemployment emerged as one of the most contested areas of social science research, both academically and politically. Obviously, much of this research was initiated because of its potential public policy relevance, and took as its focus the causes, consequences and long term impact of both short term and chronic unemployment on, *inter alia*, labour markets, social life in local communities and national budgets. Equally obviously, social science discussions of the issues revolving around unemployment became caught up in more general debates about the potential future of the entire state welfare system. The contours of these general debates are well known, with opinions spread between two extreme positions. At one extreme, the welfare system needs better targeted, and streamlined, since the number and level of benefits fail to distinguish between the 'deserving' and 'undeserving' and have produced a dependency culture which is sapping feelings of personal responsibility, destroying the family, distorting the true logic of labour markets and enabling massive fraud. At the other extreme, the welfare system remains an essential safety net, but one in need of reform for other reasons: benefit levels are too low; the bureaucracy works to ensure that many benefit entitlements are either unclaimed or delivered slowly; the system stigmatises its clients and does not empower them to deal with their own or their communities' futures.

Irrespective of one's position in these debates as they apply to the strategies of unemployed people, it is certainly arguable that evidence adduced to support notions that those who are clients of the welfare system are either disproportionately devious manipulators of the system or relatively powerless victims of it should include some knowledge about information flow and the contexts in which it occurs. It is surprising, therefore, that while social science research has included work on some of the *kinds* of information and advice required by unemployed people (about benefit entitlements, training, the job search etc.), it has given rather less attention to the *ways* in which this advice and information is communicated. Of course, pieces of research look at these issues in passing (see, for instance, many of the papers in Finemen 1987, and the observations made by Howe 1985;

1990), but there have been few specific studies of the dynamics of the flow of advice and information between the various agencies (statutory and non-statutory) and the heterogeneous population which makes up 'the unemployed'.

This chapter derives from a project rather loosely called 'Counselling and the Unemployed in Belfast', carried out in 1987–88. The aim of the project was to map out the sources of information and advice made available to those unemployed people served by one Department of Social Security local office in Belfast, and to identify the kinds of social and cultural factors which either hinder or encourage successful communication of that advice and information. We argue that a study of counselling and information provision for the unemployed must examine both sides to the relationship, the counsellors and their 'clients', as well as the cultural presuppositions and social contexts which frame their meeting. As part of their effort to understand complex societies, anthropologists have long been interested in the relationships between clients and bureaucrats of various kinds, and have shown how a distinctively anthropological approach can be especially useful in understanding the ways in which official policy and official actions are mediated into everyday terms and responses (see, for example, Cullen 1994; Edwards 1994; Handelman and Collman 1981; Handelman and Leyton 1978; Herzfeld 1993; Howe 1985; 1990; Long and Long 1992; Robertson 1984; Turner 1981). This work has become dominated by Foucauldian analyses of situated practices and other cultural 'work' which not only function to reproduce the asymmetrical power relations between officials/bureaucrats and their clients, but also function to ensure that certain ideologically loaded discourses or ideas hold sway in the policy fields under investigation, all this being achieved irrespective of whether researchers find compliance or resistance in the practices of clients. Relations of dominance are reconstituted not least because the paradigms and understandings of the more powerful penetrate or encapsulate those of the less powerful. As Escobar (1995: 41) eloquently puts it:

> In sum, the system of relations establishes a discursive practice that sets the rules of the game: who can speak, from what point of view, with what authority, and according to what criteria of expertise: it sets the rules that must be followed for this or that problem, theory or object to emerge and be named, analysed and eventually transformed into a policy or plan.

Without becoming too involved with the theoretical lacunae about what is to count as evidence of compliance, resistance and domination in different cultural contexts, issues recently teased out by Morrow (1996), this chapter finds itself in the same theoretical territory as this kind of literature. Here we are trying to go some way towards understanding communication and translation between what might be called 'official' and 'lay' models of counselling for unemployed people in Belfast, by analysing people's talk about the relationship. Our data are constructed out of a mixture of in-depth interviews and systematically collected everyday accounts of a range of actors' experiences and perceptions of the process of counselling the unemployed. Perhaps obviously, a full account of the process of counselling would depend not only on analysing people's talk about their experiences, but also an analysis of actual encounters between professionals and their 'clients', as well as an analysis of how these routine practices relate to actors' representations. Recording the details of actual encounters was not open to us for various reasons, but we believe that the talk which was recorded during our research does at least give us pointers towards the kinds of differences which might exist in how people theorise counselling provision.

Below we analyse, first, how the statutory and non-statutory agencies which offer counselling and their clients viewed each other in stereotypical terms; and second, the differing perceptions of the counselling process (and of unemployment) held by all concerned. These are examined in an effort to determine the extent to which the various 'models' which underlie the talk about the practice of counselling and seeking counselling accommodate or fail to accommodate to each other. Although, for example, the counselling interviews carried out by particular agencies were conducted on a one-to-one basis, the meanings which they had for counsellors and for clients, were conditioned by broader understandings. In part, this was a matter of the expectations which they brought with them; in part, it was because the interviews were later discussed with others and their implications reinterpreted. Thus, one feature of this approach to counselling is the way in which it extends the apparent context of the communication to include pre-existing cultural assumptions and subsequent discussions and interpretations. The 'meaning' of the communication is seen not to inhere solely in the communication event but in the broader cultural context within which the people make sense of that event.[1]

On 'counselling'

There has been a vast amount of literature produced on counselling, reflecting the growth of this social phenomenon in the industrialised west since Halmos first noted the emergence of a 'personal service society' in 1965 (Halmos 1965). Counselling has emerged as a highly theorised area of expertise with various schools of thought, much academic debate and a huge body of specialised literature. It is unnecessary to rehearse here the various arguments in this literature, though it is important to provide some operational definition of 'counselling' as it was conceptualised by the various people with whom we talked.

Such conceptualisations were retrievable from verbal statements, both from those explicit statements made in response to direct questioning and from indicative statements which were made as asides in many interviews. For most of those involved in counselling practice with whom we spoke, 'counselling' meant the in-depth, extended, supportive and mutually-directed giving of advice and information in a manner which allowed the recipients to set realistic goals for themselves, and to develop sensible ways of achieving these goals. However, while these varied elements collectively 'make up' counselling, so too can any one of them stand for, or represent, counselling. Thus the giving of advice, in a short encounter, was sometimes construed as counselling by those with whom we talked. The distinction between counselling which has all the elements and counselling which has only one or two of these elements was usually expressed as a distinction between 'real counselling' and 'counselling'. People's definitions were, therefore, simultaneously both exclusive and inclusive.

The commonsense, more multi-functional understanding of counselling resonates with the definition proffered by many specialists in the field of counselling. Broad understandings of counselling are also retrievable from literature provided for counsellors in Belfast, especially in the statutory sector. For instance, for the Restart Programme organised by the Jobmarket, a circular included the following ideas:

> Counselling the long term unemployed does *not* mean conducting deep, psychological sessions with them, nor does it mean giving out endless 'tea and sympathy'. What counselling *does* mean is achieving a *positive* outcome by helping the long term unemployed to:
> (i) think clearly about their situation
> (ii) talk about their problems and help solve them
> (iii) realise what is available for them
> (iv) regain self-esteem
> (v) consider change by being realistic
> (vi) set priorities
> (vii) accept responsibility for helping themselves.

The counsellors

It was initially tempting to categorise agencies according to the statutory/non-statutory distinction on the naive assumption that counsellors in the non-statutory sector would be more likely to be radical in their approach to counselling than their colleagues in the statutory sector; that they might be more committed to their work; and that supervisory staff at least might be more concerned with keeping up to date with background literature and newspaper reports bearing on their job. We also assumed that the two sets of counsellors might have clearly distinctive images of the unemployed. However, while there are certain differences between the two sets of counsellors in some attitudes and practices, what impressed us were the similarities.[2] In both sectors we found individuals who took their jobs home with them, and in both sectors we found people who had similar views about how unemployment happens and about its consequences for people. This will become apparent below, when we outline the views or 'culture' of the counsellors.

Furthermore, while the counsellors with whom we spoke clearly saw the relevance of the statutory/non-statutory distinction for such things as funding, many argued that the distinction is a difficult one to maintain given the amount of 'statutory' money which supports 'non-statutory' agencies. In addition, when counselling *practice* was considered, all saw the various counselling agencies as forming one large system, activated by a formal and personal network of relationships which cuts across the statutory/non-statutory division. For this reason also it makes sense not to raise this legal distinction to a crucial analytical distinction, and instead to distinguish the agencies according to the kind of service which they offer. Thus agencies are differentiated here in terms of whether or not they offer incidental provision of information, general welfare advice, advice on a particular issue or issues, or advice to a specific group, such as young people, the local community, one-parent families, women, the less able, ex-offenders, professionals, or unemployed people.

Of course, counsellors vary in the degree to which they reflect upon the problems experienced by unemployed people, such variation reflecting many factors, from the extent to which their work focuses specifically on the unemployed to personal career ambitions. Many counsellors were able to articulate and elaborate upon a diverse range of problems which they thought or knew to be associated with unemployment, while others were unable to mention more than one or two clichés about their situation. However, all were able to say something about these issues, and those who were less articulate about their ideas in response to direct questions indicated in casual chat that they had some ideas.

Though most of those interviewed stressed that unemployment confronts a person with a bundle of interconnected problems which is best treated as a package, rather than being broken down into its different elements, many considered some problems to be more pressing than others. Not surprisingly, the difficulty of finding work was mentioned by everyone as the major problem facing unemployed people and this was obviously represented as the core of their difficulties; by definition, only employment with a reasonable wage could resolve the problems of unemployment. Also not surprising was the fact that problems were thought to be more pressing in the area of finance, particularly in relation to budgeting, benefits and debt. These were the issues which were most commonly and consistently mentioned, and where interviewees made efforts to prioritise the need for advice at all, it was with regard to these issues. Less frequently mentioned were issues related to the more private face of unemployment: personal relationships within the home, relationships to friends and neighbours, and the importance of social contact. If measured by the frequency with which they were mentioned, therefore, these issues were clearly weighted less heavily than financial affairs by many of the agencies. Even agencies which quite explicitly recognised this side of unemployment often pointed out that financial matters were prioritised in practice, as a result of resource constraints which did not allow time to explore all areas of possible concern. This meant that they often had to compromise their philosophy of treating unemployment problems as a package.

Counsellor perceptions of the unemployed

Plainly not all unemployed people have the same problems and hence needs. Some bodies recognise these distinctive needs both in their practice and in their literature. An Open University (1987–8) study pack for unemployed people, for example, recognises:

> the extra disadvantage felt by unemployed people who belong to the following groups—black people, women, older people, the disabled, and those recently out of prison.

Other agencies, as we have indicated, are targeted at different groups (e.g. women, single parents, the less able, the middle class professional, ex-offenders). However, as a backdrop to a discussion of counselling activities and goals, it will be useful here to look briefly at the heterogeneity among the unemployed which *all* counsellors perceived, irrespective of the specific agency to which they were attached.

The category most often cited as being important by all counsellors was long term unemployed men. It was felt that the most immediate need for these men is to encourage them to transcend the lifestyle to which they might have become resigned: to get 'out of the rut' as one local advice worker put it. In statutory discourse at the time of our fieldwork the 'long term unemployed' were people who had been unemployed for six months or more, but for the counsellors with whom we talked, it would take much longer than six months to develop the kind of lifestyle to which they referred. All the problems associated with unemployment—such as the absence of employment opportunities, the problems with benefits, debt and budgeting, progressive demoralisation, boredom, risks to health, and loss of identity and social isolation—are felt to affect long term unemployed men: not only are real job opportunities needed for this category, but 'other things to do' to relieve boredom must be developed. Psychological counselling is needed, both to help these people cope with their situation and, according to some counsellors, to change their negative attitudes. Some in the non-statutory sector believed that many men in this category needed to be encouraged to see benefits as entitlements rather than as 'state handouts' and charity. It was realised that many of these men may never be in paid employment again. Local advice workers especially thought that this category was least in need of counselling on career development and most in need of advice on benefits, budgeting, and ways to fill time.

When discussing the long term unemployed as a category, or even 'older workers', *men* tended to be the focus in our interviews with counsellors. No doubt this was because of the importance placed on the man's occupational role in Northern Irish society as a whole, especially in the overall assessment of the community status of families and households. When specific groups of unemployed women were identified as having problems, usually widows, divorcees and other unmarried mothers were identified as having the most pressing needs for advice. One counsellor in the Jobmarket pointed out that they need help to break down their 'isolation', not only to increase their psychological well-being, but also to encourage their use of informal networks which are vital 'to hear about the wee jobs which might suit them'.

As we might expect, young people were a group for whom unemployment was felt to have deleterious affects. All counsellors specified this group as having special needs, especially the need to overcome the lack of hope and to experience real work. For some counsellors the problem derives as much from young people's own unrealistic aspirations as from society letting them down, but others blamed society in general for the situation, since it is society which creates young people's aspirations and society which constrains their ability to achieve them.

A dominant theme in all the imagery used by the counsellors is that the unemployed are in a sense one of the weakest groups in society. Of course, counsellors varied in the degree to which they placed responsibility on individuals for their own situation, but it was clear to all the counsellors with whom we spoke that society has a responsibility to help everyone in the group identified. The image of 'weakness' pervaded all our interviews, to such an extent that the well-established view that there are 'deserving' and 'undeserving' unemployed was only occasionally expressed. This is surprising in one sense, since there does seem to be evidence that this distinction is operative in the broader society and among some Department of Health and Social Services desk clerks (see, for instance, Cullen 1994: 144; Howe 1985; 1990). Perhaps this playing down of the distinction was a product of the interview situation: no doubt all the professionals presumed that our apparent liberal tendencies might be challenged if they appeared anything else but concerned with helping the weak (and not the undeserving).

That the distinction did exist in their minds could be discerned from casual asides, as when one counsellor involved in the Restart Programme pointed out the difficulty of dealing with 'people who come in better dressed than you and with a suntan'. 'Timewasters' were also likely to be seen as 'undeserving', as a Jobmarket desk clerk recounted:

> You get ones come over with the numbers [of job advertisements] and tell you they want work as a driver or labourer or whatever. That's fine, I can help immediately. Others come over with four vacancies but no numbers and you ask what sort of jobs were they, and they say 'Och, I don't know, I can't remember', and they expect you to know. And immediately you think, this guy doesn't really care, and that's the sort of guy you won't go out of your way for. Because he's creating more work for you, though I don't really care about that, but he just doesn't give, he's not interested . . . Even if they'd some idea of what job they wanted, it'd be alright, but just 'Och, I don't know'. Our impression is some people come down and they don't really want a job, yet they go through the whole rigmarole of going up to those boards, writing the numbers down, coming over, getting us to tell them all about the jobs, see if they're interested, see if they have the experience, arrange the interviews. But I would estimate that half of them don't turn up for the interviews.

However, it would be unfair to argue on the basis of this scant evidence that the distinction between deserving and undeserving unemployed underlies every-day counselling practice in a crucial way. It is the theme of 'weakness' which seems to dominate the counsellors' opinions of the unemployed. Even when the middle class were discussed by one counsellor in a charitable organisation (they were mentioned very rarely it must be said), the theme of weakness is still present:

> There is what they call the 'new poor', many people who have had small businesses and shops who had a fairly decent standard of living, suddenly in the last two or three years, there they are in trouble. I know there's a debate going on in society over it . . . so the nature of people coming for help is changing. Given this, people are coming who have had a good standard of living and no longer have a car. Because they've no car, they can't take the children to school, various things like that, which would've been unthinkable ten years ago. Holding on to a telephone, and that type of thing. So we have to keep changing our attitudes all the time . . . but at the same time not to forget the real poor who are always with us, and who are getting poorer all the time because of cut-backs in the social services.

In the following section we look at the general themes which can be discerned in counsellors' attitudes to their work.

Counsellor perceptions of counselling the unemployed

As already mentioned, for all of the counsellors the only real solution to the needs of the unemployed is paid employment. Given this view, we expected to find counsellors who saw counselling the unemployed as a kind of placebo, as a process to make people feel better in the short term and to satisfy the general public that the government is doing something. However, while paid employment is the ultimate solution for the counsellors, and while some felt that counselling is working only at 'one end' of the problem, as one person put it, no one denied that counselling in the broadest sense is a necessary activity (of course, one would hardly expect a majority of professionals to deny the importance of their activities). Most argued that the in-depth, lengthy style of counselling of people 'in the round', even with their families, (the 'real' counselling) would be of benefit for everyone, but no one felt that such an ideal situation could ever be attained. So it is counselling in the broadest sense which concerns us here. While counselling was deemed an important practice, it was easy to discern different emphases or basic assumptions about how it was to proceed. There is first of all a difference between those who emphasise achieving employability and those who put their emphasis on extending and improving life skills (we should stress here that we are dealing with emphases in counsellors' perceptions, not with exclusive viewpoints).

One set of counsellors see their task principally in terms of assisting unemployed people obtain work. As one voluntary worker expressed it, 'what we need to do is find them real work'. This body of professionals tends to see unemployment in terms of improved competitiveness in the labour market; if people are failing to find the jobs that will improve their lot, it is because they are poorly equipped to compete with other applicants. Counselling is thus mainly about improving employability and those who hold this view emphasise the need for unemployed people to be trained in interview skills, the use of the telephone, writing letters, preparing a curriculum vitae, and so on.

There are also counsellors who are much more pessimistic about the labour market and who believe that the declining number of jobs is a trend likely to continue. In these circumstances, training people to be better candidates for jobs that do not exist is not only a waste of time but is, for some, politically suspect. For this body of professionals, counselling the unemployed thus means exploring alternatives to paid employment, as well as offering moral support, boosting confidence, and promoting self-help. In a few cases it may even mean making efforts to raise people's political awareness about the causes of unemployment, though generally there seems to be an uneasiness about this. One advice worker expressed this body of opinion as follows:

All we can do is try and improve the life of the unemployed—it'd be a lie to say there's a job at the end of it.

The existence of these two views is consistent with what has been reported elsewhere in the literature. Research among professionals working with young people, particularly in the area of careers guidance, has reported a similar variation of opinion and approach. Some youth counsellors apparently adopt what has been called a 'job-placement-oriented' approach which focuses on the importance of work, while others are more 'client-oriented', trying to encourage self-help and offering more general kinds of support (Gladstone and Etheridge 1981: 58). Elsewhere, basically the same two positions have been called 'conservative' (job-search focused) and 'radical' (exploring avenues other than wage labour) to highlight the different interpretations of unemployment from which they stem (Fleming and Lavercombe 1982: 30).

As we have said, these two views are not mutually contradictory and some advice workers make efforts to reach a balance between advising people about finding work and exploring alternatives to paid employment. Nor do these views correlate simply with voluntary and statutory agencies; both shades of opinion can be found in both types of agency, though in the case of the latter actual practice is, of course, constrained by job description and by official policy.

Apart from contrasting perceptions about the direction which counselling the unemployed should take, there are also differences in views about *how* the unemployed are to be helped. Some presume that help can be given directly to the unemployed, others that help can be given to the unemployed so that they can help themselves. Each of these views can again be discerned among counsellors in both the statutory and non-statutory agencies.

How is help to be given directly? Perhaps most important, the unemployed were thought to need 'go-betweens', brokers who could record their needs and present them to powerful bodies in an increasingly complex society (and who could translate the viewpoints of these powerful bodies for the unemployed). One worker had the following to say:

> We need to let people see that we can do something for them. We can offer them direction and contacts when they are looking for work (Restart counsellor).

The problem of dependency was raised in this context. For counsellors in both the statutory and non-statutory sectors, the helping role has the capacity to produce a hierarchy, a kind of clientelism. This worries them:

> People expect an awful lot of you personally. They sometimes get to want to see you and no one else (Jobmarket desk clerk).

This problem is felt most acutely by those who work in advice centres in the non-statutory sector. They find themselves in a dilemma. On the one hand, they want to be seen to be useful, to have many 'comebacks' ('any advice centre without its comebacks isn't worth its name' as one worker put it), but they also do not want to be seen to be 'above' people, to be the provider of largesse. There is an egalitarian ethos among local advice workers which makes them embarrassed by the use of words like 'clients' when they discuss the people with whom they work.

The identification of the problem of dependency makes sense of the other aspect of how people are to help the unemployed. For some counsellors, it is not only the specialists who must help the unemployed, it is up to everyone. Some workers felt that successful counselling of the unemployed would involve making much more effort to bring them into contact with people in employment. The distance between the employed and unemployed was thought to be one of the contributing factors to the package of problems and difficulties which face the latter. Any advice service which separates off the unemployed as a distinct category of people would therefore be likely to aggravate the situation rather than relieve it. The life styles of employed and unemployed people already tend to separate them, as previously mentioned.

Some local advice centres emphasised the need for unemployed people to move away from a position as passive recipients of advice towards one of becoming active agents who can pursue matters and resolve them themselves, since only in this way can confidence be restored. People were thus encouraged to develop their own sense of motivation in the Jobclub scheme initiated by the Jobmarket. Although the principal aim of the Jobclub was to assist people to find work rather than helping them to deal with other problems related to unemployment, its organisation was founded on a philosophy which recognised the value and importance of a degree of self-help in job search. Schemes based on this model have been developed in some local advice centres as a necessary adjunct to the self confidence which they wish to instil in dealing with the benefit maze.

These then are some elements in the 'culture' of the counsellors which inform their practice as outlined in the following section.

Counselling activities

The kind of counselling activities characteristic of different agencies reflects both the philosophical or cultural assumptions of the counsellors themselves and the constraints (and opportunities) present in the different agencies in which they work (cf. Cullen 1994: 152–5). But before examining the different 'styles' of counselling practised by different agencies, it is first useful to recall the broader context within which counselling of any kind takes place. When people receive counselling, they are obviously likely to be already at least partly informed about the issue that concerns them and to have their own ideas about it. The information and advice imparted during counselling is filtered through a screen of pre-conceived ideas and existing knowledge about the matter in hand, ideas and knowledge which are acquired from many different sources, including information gathered from friends, relatives and neighbours, as well as that from leaflets, pamphlets and the media.

One important source of information for most unemployed people about their situation is the vast array of published material which deals with unemployment and related matters. Much of this kind of information is produced by the statutory bodies, and almost all of the agencies in this study displayed a fairly comprehensive selection. It is obviously impossible to say how many people actually read this material, though comments from unemployed people and advice workers suggest that such information is important. Nevertheless, its value in helping people actually resolve their problems is limited; each group thus emphasises the need for using this literature in conjunction with some other form of advice provision.

Television and radio may also inform unemployed people about their situation and influence the way they think about themselves. While again it is difficult to assess precisely how useful are these media, a content analysis of letters written to a general advice programme on local radio indicates that information delivered in this way is especially important for the socially isolated and geographically less mobile (Donnan and McFarlane 1988: 54–55).

By itself, however, factual information delivered by electronic and print media may not always be sufficient, 'since without counselling [people] may not be able to make adequate use of the material presented to them' (Osborne 1983: 85). In Belfast two kinds of more specific counselling practice supplement the printed and other media: group counselling and individual counselling.

Some of the chief advantages and disadvantages of counselling unemployed people in groups are immediately obvious: the loss of confidentiality and, unless the group is small enough, the loss of personal attention. Set against this, however, is the possibility of developing peer group support and mutual trust, and of countering any feelings of loneliness and isolation. In fact, groups successful in developing these qualities may find that they develop enough momentum to extend their life-span beyond the original counselling period. While a number of different ways of counselling groups of unemployed people exist in Belfast, we mention only two here by way of example.

One way is the seminar format. Northern Ireland was one of four areas in the United Kingdom targeted by the Open University in an effort to alleviate some aspects of unemployment. Participants in seminars were encouraged to think more deeply about their situation and were provided with the knowledge and skills to resolve many of the more ordinary and routine difficulties likely to arise in the wake of redundancy. Using local organisers to arrange and convene the seminars, groups of self-selecting unemployed people were led through the contents of a specially designed study pack the stated goals of which were to:

> tackle the immediate practical problems associated being unemployed; assess their
> interests, achievements, skills and potential; explore options open to them in the
> future; choose which option to pursue; draw up and implement an action plan.

The aim of the Open University seminars was to enable unemployed people to 'take a fresh look at their lives'. It was therefore very pragmatically oriented, but clearly depended for its success on the quality of the local leaders it was able to recruit and on the degree of literacy of those who participated. The seminar is a style of group counselling adopted by very few agencies, despite the mutual support which participants could potentially offer one another.

A second kind of group counselling is to train people while at the same time allowing them to put that training into practice as they learn, something which few agencies have the resources to offer. In fact, the only agency in this study which ran a programme designed to equip people with certain skills while simultaneously requiring them to put these skills into practice was the Jobclub organised by the Jobmarket. The Jobclub offered small groups of people who had been unemployed for six months or more a short course on job-search techniques, which it backed up by providing access to basic job-search facilities such as typewriters, photocopiers, paper and telephones. The aim of the Jobclub was to help those who had some clear ideas about their goals to learn the skills to achieve them, rather than waiting passively for job advertisements to appear.

Participation in the Jobclub was thus intended to help people structure their search for work and to encourage them to be persistent; participants were expected to follow up at least ten job leads a day. Though by its nature the Jobclub was clearly job-focused, once the abilities to be self-motivated and self-reliant had developed, they could be applied to situations other than the search for work. Job-search success rates at the Belfast Jobclub were estimated to be between 60 and 65 per cent. In 1987, there were two Jobclubs operating in the province, although plans existed to open more, and a number of local advice and community centres had developed their own 'jobclubs', using the model of the statutory agency.

Personal counselling is distinct from group counselling in being focused specifically on a particular individual's needs and problems. Defined broadly, it includes personal interviews and inquiries of relatively brief duration, as well as fully-fledged in-depth explorations of a person's difficulties over an extended period. A wide range of agencies in Belfast offer personal counselling, though we include here only three as examples.

At some stage, all of those defined here as unemployed were personally interviewed by social security staff at their local Department of Health and Social Services office. Initial interviews when first signing on lasted approximately 15 or 20 minutes, which allowed enough time only to take an individual's personal details and explain briefly the benefits they could expect. At subsequent visits further information could be obtained about special benefits and allowances or about the consequences of a change in circumstances. All interviews were by appointment and were conducted in a private booth. Given the nature of the organisation, the bulk of advice and information offered obviously concerned benefits, though occasionally people were referred to other statutory and non-statutory bodies for different kinds of specialised advice. From Howe's (1985) work on the encounter between claimants and counter-staff it does appear, however, that the distinction between the 'deserving' and 'undeserving' poor exists in the minds of at least some staff dealing with counselling.

Interviews in the Jobmarket were similarly conducted on a personal and one-to-one basis. Since 1982 (and during the period of our research) attendance at the Jobmarket had been voluntary, though before this it was compulsory to attend when registering as unemployed. The standard interview with desk staff lasted less than half-an-hour and mainly provided information about the jobs advertised in the Jobmarket and recorded the job skills, qualifications and personal details of those looking for work. According to desk staff, dealing with these two tasks left little opportunity to give details of other possible forms of employment such as training schemes, or to explore any other interests which the interviewee might have by asking the open-ended questions which they were taught to ask during their week's counselling training. Even the full range of job options might not be covered.

Jobmarket staff recognised that they were further constrained in advising those looking for work by the fact that part of their responsibility was towards employers as well as to potential employees:

> You're doing the employer's job for them. We're actually screening people for them
> . . . I feel it's a bit of a con for the people themselves, because they're coming in
> here and they don't realise we're doing the selection, doing the screening. So
> they'll just come in off the street in whatever they're wearing.

Since they must apply guidelines laid down by employers, desk clerks often felt unable to provide entirely disinterested advice to unemployed people looking for work. Thus some staff pointed out that balancing legal obligations to employers against obligations towards those applying for work was not always the best recipe for successful counselling of the latter.[3] Like the Department of Social Security counsellors in Britain described by Cullen (1994: 154), it is not surprising that some felt themselves propelled towards a strategy of 'control through care'.

Not all interviews in the Jobmarket were conducted along the same lines and in some kinds of interviewing there was much more room to explore a particular individual's needs. This was the case with those consulting the Disablement Resettlement Officer or registering with Professional and Executive Personnel. According to one employee who had worked in these areas, interviews were usually longer than in the ordinary Jobmarket interview, because 'more is expected of you', whereas 'in the Jobmarket the person is easier satisfied'. This view was shared by Jobmarket and Professional and Executive Personnel staff alike, both of whom recognised the constraints which the large numbers of people attending for interview in the former put on staff there; equally, they recognised that because Professional and Executive Personnel staff dealt with fewer people, they could engage in longer interviews with them, developing a relationship across a series of meetings. In this sense, Disablement Resettlement and Professional and Executive Personnel interviews more closely approximated what professionals considered to be 'real counselling'.

The Restart Programme introduced by the Jobmarket in 1986 to counsel those defined as long term unemployed (initially those unemployed for one year or more; in 1987–8 those unemployed for more than 6 months) was also considered by those involved to be closer to 'real counselling', even though it did not have all the ingredients necessary. Restart provided individual help to the long term unemployed in the form of a counselling session during which participants were offered a range of options directed towards finding employment. Response to this style of counselling among those unemployed people interviewed who had participated in Restart was generally positive, a view more or less consistent with the conclusions of a survey which found that for 95 per cent of respondents 'the counselling interview had helped them in some way' (Barry 1987: 7). However, while the counselling style itself was generally appreciated, the element of compulsion which attended the invitation to participate was not, as one participant remarked:

> They sent for me and I went down and I joined the Jobclub . . . they invite you to join the Jobclub, but at the same time they also threaten you. If you fail to come down, your benefit may be withdrawn. So, apart from that I did think it was a good idea.

Moreover, on the counsellors' side there is the possibility that a counselling programme such as this can quickly produce a 'burn-out' syndrome amongst those required to counsel for long periods.

Three basic styles tend to characterise the personal counselling offered in the non-statutory sector. Most common is the drop-in facility whereby people bring particular well-defined problems or requests for advice which can usually be dealt with by providing information. Local advice centres reportedly spent much of their time handling personal inquiries of this kind and assisting people with claiming benefit and completing forms. The second two types both involve more in-depth and extended counselling sessions which review a person's overall circumstances, one type conducted on agency premises, the other in the community itself through outreach programmes. It is in the context of these second two styles of counselling especially that the voluntary sector is in some respects better placed than statutory agencies to provide a more satisfactory service. Since the voluntary sector is less tied to offering advice on a specific topic than most of the statutory agencies, it is better able to counsel 'in the round' and to tackle an individual's problems within the context of their general circumstances.

We presume this counselling 'in the round' to be vital for those who work in local advice centres, since a large part of their role was considered to be successful brokerage between the state and individuals. Local advice workers in the non-statutory sector felt that they were not taken seriously by the professionals in the statutory sector unless they got their facts right and could demonstrate that they were at least as familiar as those in the statutory agencies with the relevant rules and regulations. The many informal ties between advice workers and contacts in the various statutory agencies (see Belfast Law Centre 1987: *passim*) depended as much upon competence, as upon personal social skills, on the part of local advice workers.

Yet workers in local advice centres argued that they faced an uphill struggle in gaining such competence, given the way in which staffing was organised. The local advice centres depended extensively on workers recruited through the Action for Community Employment scheme, which usually meant a one-year contract or, at best, a two-year contract for those classified as key workers. According to supervisors whom we interviewed, advice workers have just about managed to establish expertise in the rules of the game and to build up a good reputation vis-a-vis the statutory agencies (and locally), when their period of employment is ended.

Advice workers also recognised what one could call the local cultural constraints on their practice. For some sections of their public (the more elderly especially, though not exclusively), it was thought, the image of local advice centres was that they were full of radicals. As one worker put it, '[People say] there goes that lefty, self-help crowd again'. There was also a general assumption that people were reluctant to give up their independence by making initial contacts with local advice centres. Counsellors argued that it was often only some kind of crisis that brought people in. Not only that, but the issue of confidentiality was thought to work against people coming to advice centres. Such fears about confidentiality were believed to increase where advice workers were local people (and, it must be said, such fears were supposed to increase if local workers were women).

Even apart from these constraints, it was also true that relatively few voluntary sector agencies had the resources to offer the more in-depth kind of counselling on a regular basis. Even the better funded voluntary agencies, such as the Citizens Advice Bureaux, found their resources stretched in the face of an increasing number of enquiries.

Psychological counselling in the voluntary sector tended to be as poorly represented as among the statutory agencies. Few facilities existed specifically to counsel people on the psychological effects of unemployment, despite the recognition that such effects could be grave. In fact, such counselling often seemed to take place only outside those agencies directly concerned with unemployment, in agencies where psychological counselling on other issues was a major part of their work. Thus, for example, Contact and, we were told, the Marriage Guidance Council (now 'Relate') and Parents' Aid occasionally counselled on the psychological dimensions of unemployment as part of their more specific tasks of counselling youth and counselling people about relationships.

The unemployed and counselling

We now turn to 'client' perceptions and experiences of counselling, examining people's orientation to the acquisition of information in relation to life while unemployed, detailing the information and advice sought by those we interviewed, as well as the identities of the organisations and individuals approached. It seems that the range of information sought, at least as declared by the interviewees themselves, was relatively narrow and that only a very limited number of those organisations offering information were actually utilised. Not surprisingly perhaps, the interviewees were tied to those organisations with greatest visibility and to those with which they had had some previous dealing. This often meant that the local social security office was a first stop whatever the information sought, despite the fact that perceptions of the information which it provided were largely negative (something which hardly surprised us given previous research on views of the Department of Health and Social Services), and despite the view held by many that more 'go-betweens' are necessary, especially in the complex area of welfare benefits. We explain this pattern through an analysis of people's reckoning of the cultural constraints on using other agencies.

No doubt it was partly a result of the very nature of our interview topics, but nearly everyone we contacted thought that it would be generally useful to have more information on the kinds of problems which they faced. This was closely tied in with the generally negative view of information provision by the local social security office which we outline below. 'More' information on benefits, on everyday financial problems and, for very few, on psychological problems would be a 'good thing'. However, what our material consistently shows is that it is not simply more information which people requested, but 'personalised' information, information interpreted according to their particular needs and circumstances. In other words, it is not so much that interviewees identified a gap in the kinds of information already available, which could be met by providing information of a particular type, as that they expressed reservations and criticism of the style of delivery of existing information. This call for personalised information seemed to be more acute for some groups (the first-time unemployed, the single parent, the elderly) than for others, as one might expect. For some it would be a 'good idea' also to have more 'go-betweens', since go-betweens 'have more clout', 'if the office don't like your face, they can sort things out', and 'they could really speed things along'.

The overall tenor of views expressed on local social security office practice is relatively clear and tends to be critical rather than laudatory: not only were negative factors more frequently mentioned in the interviews than positive factors, but interviewees consistently identified more negative characteristics than positive ones. Attitudes towards the Department of Health and Social Services thus fairly clearly group around positive and negative poles. Perhaps not surprisingly the most positive view of the Department of Health and Social Services was expressed by those who had had no problems receiving their benefit and who had had few or no visits to them other than to sign on. One or two interviewees said that they thought of the Department of Health and Social Services as a public body to which anyone could turn should the need arise. They pointed out that the Department of Health and Social Services was reasonably accessible by being open during office hours and provided a sense of security to those unsure of where else to turn; as one woman remarked 'at least you can go over there if there's a problem'.

Interviewees who took this positive view of the Department of Health and Social Services felt that there were no barriers to their seeking information from their local social security office and that such information was easily and readily available for the asking, particularly in relation to benefits. However, only a minority of those who had actually sought information or assistance from the Department of Health and Social Services remained unequivocally positive about the reception which they had received there. Moreover, even those who were positive were aware that others were extremely critical, and they maintained their positive tone only by being defensive: 'they're only doing their job like anyone else'.

Those interviewed clearly found it much easier to be critical of the service offered by social security offices and were much more forthcoming and loquacious about what was wrong with the service than about its positive aspects. Consequently, negative ideas towards the Department of Health and Social Services are much more highly elaborated and evince certain quite dominant and consistent themes. As with the positive evaluations, it is once again possible to identify a spread of ideas from more to less negative.

At the least negative end of the scale are remarks about the length of time that must be spent waiting to have a query answered. This kind of criticism is well known and was one which was frequently voiced by the interviewees. When the length of the wait is combined with the amount of bureaucracy involved, obtaining information or advice from a social security office is viewed even more negatively: 'you don't get the problem solved on the spot—it's the red tape again'. Many interviewees believed that there was an unnecessary number of forms to complete and that the amount and kind of information required were superfluous. Repetition of the same questions and collecting information apparently for the sake of it were cited as particularly galling:

> After about twenty minutes he says, well, you don't qualify for a grant for insulating your house because if you've over £ 500 in the bank you don't. Now, when I told him I had that could he not have said, well that's alright and stopped there. Now did he have to go through all the [bank and building society] books and all? And record all that. And he went through it and he says no, you don't qualify for it . . . but he went through everything, and I just felt sick, you know, going through all your personal affairs and all. And then saying, no, you're not getting it. He should've said, ah well, if you've over £ 500 in the bank you won't get it and stopped there. And I could've withdrew the claim there and then and said I'm not claiming, just forget about it. But he went through all these questions and everything, you know.

This kind of experience encourages the idea, as one man put it, that 'the bru is not where you get the information, it's where you give it'. A more negative connotation was given to this view by some of the interviewees who felt that extensive questioning was the means by which the Department of Health and Social Services could 'check up on' claimants. In fact, it was a practice that several interviewees interpreted even more negatively, as an attempt by the Department of Health and Social Services 'to trick you'. This suggests that at least some claimants thought of the social security office's role in providing information and advice as a two-edged sword; every consultation involved a bargaining in which each side exchanged certain information to which they had sole access for certain other information which they desired. There was therefore always the possibility of asymmetry in the relationship.

Almost all the interviewees who claimed to have sought advice in their social security office expressed the view that active 'dissemination of information is very poor' and that 'the ones who are unemployed have to do all the running'. Some even suggested that this seemed to be a policy which pervaded all aspects of the Department of Health and Social Services work: while there were leaflets in racks, claimants were not directed to them; while there were notices on walls, 'you'd need spyglasses to see them'; and while there were signs that were legible, they gave nothing away—'there isn't even a sign up "New Claimants", there is simply a sign which says "Claims"; but that doesn't mean anything, since everyone's there to claim!'

All of this appeared especially negative to those interviewees who felt that their benefit had been wrongly calculated. Though none of the interviewees had been told how their benefit would be calculated when they initially registered as unemployed, even those who had returned specifically for this purpose expressed their dissatisfaction with what they had been told:

> No one cares . . . it's all a hustle and bustle, everyone wants to get on with it.
> They're only interested in get you in, get you paid, and get you out.

Viewed in this light, the Department of Health and Social Services was considered to attribute provision of information and advice a low priority.

Given such views, one might expect that people would not use the Department of Health and Social Services office as their first stop for information, but instead go 'armed' with the correct questions. Given the desire expressed by many for 'go-betweens', one would expect some other agencies to be contacted either before or simply *as well as* the local social security office. But surprisingly, the practice of advice-seeking did not appear to follow this pattern.

Although there was considerable demand for information and advice as indicated above, analysis of self-declared take-up rates suggests that relatively few availed of existing information services. In other words, demand appeared to exceed take-up. For many interviewees, the Department of Health and Social Services was actually the first stop when looking for assistance. Of the 70 people interviewed, 41 said that they contacted their local social security office for information or advice subsequent to their initially signing on. Obviously many of these inquiries concerned benefits of one form or another, but not all of them were benefit-related. Apart from the local Department of Health and Social Services office, other statutory agencies were contacted, although this was only a small range and involved only 26 of the 70 individuals interviewed. Moreover, it was frequently the same individuals who visited several different statutory bodies.

The pattern of advice-seeking from non-statutory organisations or individuals frankly surprised us, given the overall views towards the local social security office. Only 20 out of the 70 individuals interviewed sought advice in the non-statutory sector.

The gap between the negative attitudes towards the provision of information by the local social security office and the apparently low take-up of mediators' advice needs to be explained, especially because the same individuals who expressed negative attitudes also sought information from the local office, usually without direct contact with non-statutory agencies (who would, of course, in their eyes be useful). There is little evidence that this gap is the result of a skewed sample. Nor does the gap seem to exist because of an unwillingness among people to admit to using voluntary agencies; fear of a lack of confidentiality and a cultural value on not being seen as 'dependent' did not inhibit people from discussing their problems with us, and no one suggested that seeking information is in any way stigmatising *in itself*. Instead, under-use of advice centres seems to be a result of other factors. A few people, for instance, said that they did not know of the existence of brokers who could work on their behalf. However, it was the cultural costs incurred in seeking counselling that inhibited the majority of people from seeking advice locally. These costs were multifarious: not wanting to appear 'stupid'; fear of lack of confidentiality (especially when women from the area were working in the local centre); sectarian bias; not wanting to be 'beholden' to people; suspicions that they were 'all part of government anyway'; or suspicions that they were staffed by young radicals totally against the state.

This pattern of advice-seeking should not be taken to mean that the advice centres and the specialised groups of all kinds were not fulfilling a key role in the dissemination of information. That would be an outrageous claim. What seemed to be happening was that they were in a sense pumping information into the total reservoir of information provided by other sources like the statutory agencies and the media.

Job search and the unemployed

Obviously the main issue for many people whom we interviewed was the search for paid employment. Here too attitudes to the statutory agencies involved were broadly negative, irrespective of how the staff in the agencies were perceived. Practice in job search was consistent with the pattern of attitudes, displaying the emphasis on informal channels (and newspapers), so readily apparent in the literature on employment strategies in Northern Ireland. We describe here unemployed people's views of the statutory agencies, chiefly the Jobmarkets, and outline some of the assumptions underlying the practice of job search.

Attitudes to the Jobmarkets conveyed a generally negative flavour, though for slightly different reasons than those underlying the attitudes to the local social security office. Not surprisingly, everybody's expectation of the Jobmarket was that it was there to provide advice on employment, and it was evaluated accordingly. Apart from several interviewees who said that they had never visited the Jobmarket and did not know where to find it, interviewees considered the Jobmarket 'a quite good idea' and were generally positive about the idea of a central location which could assist with finding work. However, criticism outweighed praise, and interviewees expressed their dissatisfaction with two issues in particular: the kind of employment about which the Jobmarket was able to offer information, and the manner in which that information was offered or withheld.

Views about the kinds of employment on which the Jobmarket was able to offer information centred on two themes, both of them negative. Firstly, very few interviewees actually believed that the Jobmarket was in a position to offer them information which could actually lead to what they considered a 'real job' or the 'right job'. Even those who were positive about the idea of Jobmarkets in theory, could not see 'any sense in creating a lot more Jobcentres [sic] . . . when there are no jobs to be got'. The idea that Jobmarkets provided information only on training schemes was commonly held by young and old, male and female alike, as was the idea that such schemes, and thus such information, ultimately led nowhere.

Interviewees were equally sceptical about the information they were given about forms of employment other than training schemes. Either this was low paid work, for which the net income would have been less than that on social security, or it was unskilled work which someone with a trade was reluctant to accept. Moreover, information about some kinds of work was thought to flow through other channels, such as personal contacts. In fact, the majority of interviewees believed that the information on employment available in the Jobmarket was available elsewhere anyway, in newspapers for example. That is why, some argued, many jobs were already filled before they even reached the Jobmarkets.

The second general theme relating to the kinds of jobs about which the Jobmarket was able to offer information was the idea, particularly apparent among older interviewees, that the Jobmarket directed its attention mainly towards certain segments of the population. Almost all older interviewees felt that their age 'went against them' and that the Jobmarket was 'trying to help the younger element'. A number of interviewees agreed that extra effort should be made to help the younger unemployed find work but expressed annoyance when then they themselves had to deal with a system which seemed exclusively designed for the young. Certainly many older interviewees felt little point in seeking information really meant for others, and could not understand why the Jobmarket apparently failed to pinpoint the kinds of information which they needed. Interviewees were therefore sceptical about the employment information offered by the Jobmarket and often felt that they could more easily and more readily obtain better information about work elsewhere.

The second issue about which a number of interviewees expressed dissatisfaction was the manner in which they were given information in the Jobmarket. This was viewed more or less negatively depending on whether or not the interviewee felt that matters were beyond the control of Jobmarket employees themselves; in other words, some tempered their criticism by pointing out that 'even with the best will in the world', the Jobmarket could not offer their clients work where there was none. When those who took this view encountered lack of optimism and enthusiasm on visiting the Jobmarket, this was a lamentable but nevertheless understandable response:

> They seemed to be quite despondent too. You know, it seems to be affecting them
> as well as the people coming in.

Others were less understanding, and took this lack of enthusiasm as an indication that staff 'did not care'. Similarly, the idea expressed by some interviewees that 'the Jobmarket keeps promising but do not produce results' was regarded more or less negatively depending on whether the interviewee saw this as a consequence of the fact that 'there are so many looking', or as due simply to staff callousness. Certainly a few interviewees felt that the Jobmarket sometimes unnecessarily set themselves up as gate-keepers who blocked rather than facilitated people's access to jobs:

> One thing I don't like in the Jobmarket is—I went down for a couple of application forms and they give me some forms and reply envelopes, and the reply envelopes they give me was to the Jobmarket. It wasn't to the firm. it was to the Jobmarket. And the Jobmarket goes through those applications, which I think is quite personal documents, and they go through them. And they even ask you can they use them again for any other prospective employers that they may feel could benefit you. But nobody writes the same application form for all different jobs. It's crucial that you gotta fill in sometimes to what people want.

Other interviewees claimed to have had even more negative experiences of how the Jobmarket appeared to hinder rather than promote people's access to jobs:

> I tripped over the information. Nobody offered me anything. And were very reluctant to tell me anything. I was told by a friend of a friend who had done this [training] scheme years ago that this [particular scheme] was possible . . . So I went down to Gloucester House and asked the girl about it. She didn't know anything about it and asked someone else. She came back and asked what sort of training I was looking for . . . but no, there was no such training scheme. I waited, so she said she would go and ask someone else. So she came back eventually after phoning upstairs and said go and see Mrs. so-and-so, because there might be a training scheme. So I went and she passed me on to somebody else. And she said there was such a scheme . . . and I got it. But it was only because my feet were firmly planted on the ground and I was not budging. You know, they'd have fobbed me off and shown me the door very handily.

Even positive efforts on the part of the Jobmarket to provide innovatory forms of assistance to clients were tainted in the eyes of some of the interviewees, as we noted earlier in relation to its Restart Programme: while most of the interviewees involved with the Restart Programme were positively disposed to the counsellors involved and thought the scheme a good idea (see Barry 1987: 8), they were unhappy about the manner in which it had been implemented.

The strategies involved in job search were broadly consistent with the views expressed in our interviews with job-seekers. The Jobmarket was seen as only one option among many for obtaining information about jobs. The pattern reported in studies done elsewhere was replicated in Belfast too: initial frequent visits were followed gradually by declining attendance, until people only called in whenever they were 'passing'. Very few claimed that they never went into the Jobmarket, since most agreed that there was always 'the chance' of a job. This pattern was so entrenched that those who used the Jobmarkets exclusively were presumed to have little chance of gaining work: the Jobmarkets were a less favoured option.[4]

The logic underlying the practice of using informal links to gain information about jobs, or to have some degree of 'pull' vis-a-vis employers, seemed reasonably clear to many of the people we interviewed. This approach has various advantages: it enabled one to hear about work and job requirements prior to makin⌐ approaches about the job; it provided information about who best to target wi applications; it meant that one had social contacts in the workplace; it was generally easier than aimlessly 'running around' looking for work. There was a general assumption too that many employers preferred their workforce to have existing relationships with one another: 'everyone gets along better'. People were clearly aware that not everyone had the right connections to get jobs in this way, and many would lament that this was why they found it difficult to obtain work. The labour market was perceived as one in which people competed with unequal resources, not only their personal attributes (including their ethnic label), but also because of their contacts. It should be pointed out that this perspective went together with the view, held by some of our interviewees, that the 'Government' or 'Society' should provide more work for people, *and* with the apparently contradictory and more individualistic view that it was up to the individual to seek his or her own way in the world.

Conclusion

In this chapter we have tried to identify the different 'models' of unemployed people's needs and problems which were held both by the representatives of the counselling agencies and by the unemployed themselves, and to assess how well or how badly these 'models' matched up with, or reflected, one another. It seems to us that the models were congruent or compatible with one another on most of the key issues: there was a shared understanding of problems and needs; there was a shared view that the ultimate or ideal solution to some of these information needs would be highly personalised counselling (counselling 'in the round'); there was a generally shared idea that information and counselling should be targeted at particular groups; there was a shared idea that counselling is a useful idea (even if it is not the ultimate solution to the problems deriving from unemployment, since for most people the problem can only be solved by employment). In other words, there appear to be no extensive areas where the 'culture' of the unemployed and the 'culture' of the counsellors on the issue of information and advice radically diverge.

Nevertheless, a degree of 'distance' is discernible between the agencies which offered counselling and those who said they needed it. In the area of advice and information on general welfare there were cultural barriers among the unemployed against their use of the advice services which *they* themselves believed would help them in their encounters with the Department of Health and Social Services (there were, of course, also problems with the Department of Health and

Social Services itself). It is clear that counsellors in local advice centres were aware of some of these cultural barriers. Local advice centres were only one of the sources of information and advice among many which included kinship, friendship and neighbourhood networks. These agencies seemed to be valued less by the unemployed in the sense that they were not seen to have all the cultural values of confidentiality, egalitarianism, and accessibility characteristic of the personal networks. Given these actual 'disadvantages', it is not surprising that few individuals in our sample of unemployed people regularly made use directly of the counselling agencies available to them.

Pathways to advice did not seem to begin at the agencies themselves, but they sometimes led there. More often, unemployed people drew on information and advice originating in the agencies but filtered through a third party: friend, relative or neighbour. This may have certain consequences. The comparative under-use of advice agencies in our sample could mean that the point at which unemployed people might approach the 'experts' is beyond the point which would be recommended by the 'experts' themselves. This could mean that agencies end up counselling more for problem management than for problem avoidance.

Yet our impression is that the counselling agencies are still heavily used, and our evidence seems to suggest that when they *are* used, their work is favourably regarded. In other words, the problem in the field of welfare advice seems to be one of delivery: going to advice-giving agencies would be a 'good thing' if only certain barriers could be broken down, or at least the 'cultural costs' relatively devalued.

In the area of job search, the problem seems somewhat different, and this derives from the fact that counselling in this field is still dominated by the statutory agencies. It is clear from our research that no matter how favourably people might view the workers in the Jobmarket (and many do view them favourably), there are negative attitudes towards the general work of the Jobmarkets among the unemployed, attitudes which lead them to perceive them as useless or redundant, given the fact that the ideal way of getting jobs seems to be to use one's own contacts and initiative. The more specialised agencies existing under the umbrella of the Jobmarket seem to be *less* negatively viewed, and despite the problem associated with the Restart Programme, there does not seem to be such a *total* rejection of its efforts to get people into jobs and training. What we have among the unemployed seems to be a problem of at least partial disengagement from the statutory agencies' work.

But partial disengagement implies partial engagement, a feature for which we have to give an account. To some extent, the appearance of mutuality between counsellors and their clients could be largely a product of the fact that our analysis is based upon talk about counselling, rather than an analysis of its practice. It would not be unlikely that what we were presented with in most of our discussions was a kind of partial 'public transcript', designed to deal with inquisitive researchers, rather than to give a complete account of what people think. This may indeed be so, but even if we have succeeded in recovering only a partial account, it is still interesting that elements in this 'public transcript' seem to be widely shared among clients and counsellors alike: ideas about who is deserving and who is undeserving, about what constitutes ideal counselling provision, and about what constitutes good and bad advice are widely shared across the divide between counsellors and those who are exposed to them. How can we account for this? The temptation might be to present this as evidence of the penetration of bureaucratic ideas into the views of those who are clients or, in other words, the production of a discursive practice about counselling in which the powerful dominate the less powerful. This may be so to some extent, but this kind of argument seems very deterministic to us, since it not only presents implicitly a picture of a world where there are discrete bureaucratic cultural models about counselling, separable from other models (in a sense waiting to dominate the views of clients), but it also downplays the possible interaction between the sets of ideas which make up the models of counselling held by counsellors and their clients. While there *are* bureaucratic models set out in agency documentation and existing in the more unofficial rules of the workplace, it is clear to us that these 'bureaucratic' ideas are not seen by counsellors in either the statutory or non-statutory sectors as providing enough information for them to carry out their work. The counsellors' reports on their practices are based not only on ideas deriving from the agencies in which they work, they also derive from, and are mediated by, counsellors' wider representations of Northern Irish society, and their suppositions about the unemployed's place within it. All kinds of issues related to unemployment had entered into high profile public debate in the 1980s when the research was undertaken. These issues had become public currency; they had become part of the way unemployment was talked about in the United Kingdom, and even part of the way unemployed people viewed themselves by the time we did our research. Given this, it is at least arguable that both counsellors and their clients have been engaged in a continual process of co-production of their models.

Notes

The research on which this chapter is based was carried out between March 1987 and June 1988, and was funded by the Department of Economic Development. It also draws on information collected between December 1987 and February 1988 for a DHSS-funded evaluation of the Belfast Centre for the Unemployed. The authors would like to thank Karen McCartney for her assistance in the latter project.

1. The interest in locating communication in its cultural context could readily be extended to other agencies where there is an official interest in how advice, information, and instruction are actually taken up by clients. This would build upon existing work by anthropologists in the broad field of evaluation studies (see, for example, Britan 1978a; 1978b; 1979; 1981; Britan and Cohen 1980; Donnan, McCartney and McFarlane 1988; Knapp 1979).

2.   See Edwards (1994: 199) who describes how some Housing Aid advice workers in
     Britain distinguish their practical, experiential knowledge of their clients' worlds from
     the 'theoretical' knowledge held by 'bureaucrats'.
3.   The sectarian geography of Belfast also raised some concerns for counsellors, although
     they had developed skills to deal with them. It cannot always be assumed, for instance,
     that a Catholic interviewee interested in a particular job will know that that job is in a
     Protestant neighbourhood, nor can it be assumed even that the location matters to the
     interviewee. However, the suspicion that such matters might concern the interviewee has
     made some counsellors develop sensitive ways of finding out. As one desk clerk put it:
     "You know what it's like in Belfast. You have to ask 'will that area suit you?' Often
     they'll smile when they answer and you know why."
4.   We have no clear evidence that the pattern of visits to the Jobmarket varies by gender,
     though some of the literature suggests that those women who are diligently seeking work
     find less use for these kinds of agencies than men (for various reasons to do with their
     perceptions of their 'right' to paid work). No one expressed such views to us, at least
     explicitly.

References

Barry, R. 1987. *Counselling and Restart survey: interim report.* Belfast: Policy Planning and
     Research Unit.
Belfast Law Centre 1987. *Advice services in Northern Ireland.* Belfast: Belfast Law Centre.
Britan, G. M. 1978a. The place of anthropology in program assessment. *Anthropological
     Quarterly* 51: 120-28.
_____. 1978b. Experimental and contextual models in program evaluation. *Evaluation and
     Program Building* 1: 229–34.
_____. 1979. Evaluating a federal experiment in bureaucratic reform. *Human Organization* 38
     (4): 319–24.
_____. 1981. Contextual evaluation: an ethnographic approach to programme assessment. In
     R.F. Conner (ed.), *Methodological advances in evaluation research.* London: Sage.
_____. and R. Cohen (eds.) 1980. *Hierarchy and society: anthropological perspectives on
     bureaucracy.* Philadelphia: Institute for the Study of Human Issues.
Cullen, S. 1994. Culture, gender and organisational change in British welfare benefits ser-
     vices. In S. Wright (ed.), *Anthropology of organisations.* London: Routledge.
Donnan, H. and G. McFarlane 1988. *Counselling and the unemployed in Belfast.* Belfast:
     Policy Planning and Research Unit.
_____., K. McCartney and G. McFarlane 1988. *The Outreach Project organised by the Belfast
     Centre for the Unemployed: an evaluation.* Belfast: Department of Health and Social
     Services.
Edwards, J. 1994. Idioms of bureaucracy and informality in a local Housing Aid office. In S.
     Wright (ed.), *Anthropology of organisations.* London: Routledge.
Escobar, A. 1995. *Encountering development: the making and unmaking of the Third World.*
     Princeton: Princeton University Press.
Fineman, S. (ed.) 1987. *Unemployment: personal and social consequences.* London:
     Tavistock.
Fleming, D. and S. Lavercombe 1982. Talking about unemployment with school-leavers.
     British Journal of Guidance and Counselling 10 (1): 22–33.

Gladstone, D. and J. Etheridge 1981. Counselling the young unemployed: the experience of "Just the Job". *British Journal of Guidance and Counselling* 9 (1): 56–64.

Halmos, P. 1965. *The faith of the counsellors*. London: Constable.

Handelman, D. and J. Collman (eds.) 1981. Administrative frameworks and clients. *Social Analysis* 9.

——. and E. Leyton 1978. *Bureaucracy and world view: studies in the logic of official interpretation*. St Johns, Newfoundland: Institute of Economic and Social Research.

Herzfeld, M. 1993. *The production of indifference: exploring the symbolic roots of Western bureaucracy*. Chicago: University of Chicago Press.

Howe, L.E.A. 1985. The 'deserving' and the 'undeserving': practice in an urban, local social security office. *Journal of Social Policy* 14: 49–72.

——. 1990. *Being unemployed in Northern Ireland: an ethnographic study* Cambridge: Cambridge University Press.

Knapp, M.S. 1979. Ethnographic contributions to evaluation research. In T.D. Cook and C.S. Reichardt (eds.), *Qualitative and quantitative methods in evaluation research*. London: Sage.

Long, N. and A. Long (eds.) 1992. *Battlefields of knowledge: the interlocking of theory and practice in social research*. London: Routledge.

Morrow, P. 1996. Yup'ik Eskimo agents and American legal agencies: perspectives on compliance and resistance. *Journal of the Royal Anthropological Institute* 2: 405–23.

Osborne, K. 1983. Counselling requirements in a voluntary advice agency. *British Journal of Guidance and Counselling* 11 (1): 82–85.

Open University 1987–8. *Action Planning: a course for unemployed people*. Milton Keynes: Open University.

Robertson, A.F. 1984. *People and the state: an anthropology of planned development*. Cambridge: Cambridge University Press.

Turner, R. 1981. Models of good government. In L. Holy and M. Stuchlik (eds.), *The structure of folk models*. London: Academic Press.

11   Unemployment, labour supply and the meaning of money

Eithne McLaughlin

> . . . the specialised sciences involve a kind of abstraction . . . it is seldom, after such a conceptual scheme has become well worked out, that its abstractness does not sooner or later become a crucial source of difficulty in relation to some empirical problems . . . This has been notably the case with economics . . . the problem of the motivation of economic activities . . . has inevitably become involved by implication (Parsons 1964 [1940]: 50-1).

This chapter is about the limits of economic theory in relation to labour supply issues. As Parsons noted in the 1940s, motivation in economic activities can rarely be adequately understood within the limits of conventional economic theory (see also, Lane 1991 and Ormerod 1994 for recent critiques in similar vein). In this chapter, I suggest that a better understanding of the way many unemployed people, especially those with children, approach labour supply and the generation of household incomes can be achieved by drawing on anthropological analyses of money and income generation, in particular, the work of Bloch and Parry (1989). The latter is helpful in highlighting the differences, and the relationship, between long-term and short-term motivational elements in the attitudes to, and behaviour towards, paid employment among unemployed people.

The behaviour and motivations of long-term unemployed people have been among the most contested and controversial territories for social science research, academically and politically, during the 1980s and early 1990s. The reasons are partly practical and partly ideological. The cost of unemployment is huge, both for those people directly affected, and for society as a whole. For example, the cost in total public expenditure terms of 1991 levels of registered unemployment in the United Kingdom was £ 21 billion (McLaughlin 1992: 4). To this must be added poor returns on public investments in education and training, a national output lower than would otherwise be the case, and income and opportunity inequities between population groups. The latter is particularly significant in Northern Ireland where levels of unemployment between the Nationalist and Unionist communities continue to differ greatly, with the male Catholic rate around 2.2 times that of the male Protestant rate in 1991 (see McLaughlin and Quirk 1996).

Government response to high unemployment in Britain in the 1980s and early 1990s, however, was largely to abdicate state responsibility for the workings of the labour market and emphasise instead the role of individual motivation. The adoption of a brand of monetarism from the USA, based on nineteenth-century theories of how money moves in modern economies, has provided legitimacy for this response. In monetarist approaches, inequalities in employment and unemployment are caused by exogenous non-market factors—the key culprits usually being individual 'choice', personal (in)efficiency, excessive labour power and the political intervention of the state. Accordingly, government policy towards unemployment in the 1980s has had four strands (McLaughlin 1992): making social security benefits for unemployed people more difficult to get (for example, through more stringent availability-for-work tests), as well as lower relative to earnings; the promotion of incentives to take low-paid work (for example, the promotion of Family Credit); remotivation programmes for the unemployed (for example, Restart); and deregulation of the employment contract. Under the guise of parity, these same policies have been effected in Northern Ireland as well as in Great Britain.

Characteristically, these policies pay scant attention to the nature of the labour markets within which unemployed people seek work. That is, these policies, and the theoretical approach underlying them, presume that there is what might be called equality of choice between individuals. Such a notion is difficult to square with statistics on the nature of localised geographical labour markets, which display extreme differences in the overall level of demand as well as in the nature of that demand.

In addition, the theoretical underpinnings of the 1980s policy approach to unemployment makes three further dubious assumptions: that a person will only take work, and hence forsake leisure, if there is a financial return for that effort (work as a disutility); that all forms of income are equal because all are reducible to their common denominator—money; and that people make their decisions about whether to take paid work, and which kinds of work to take, with reasonably complete information on the alternatives before them. We can instead describe these three assumptions as two: that the amount of money available in and out of work is the only or the major determinant of labour supply; and that the conditions for 'rational' choice can be met in the real world. Given these assumptions, it makes logical sense to conclude that the level of money available when one is in a state of 'leisure'—that is, unemployment—must affect the decision-making process in the direction of reducing the incentive to take paid work. Despite the appealing simplicity of such models, a large amount of econometric work has been unable to find effects of this kind to the extent predicted among key population groups, such as prime-age unemployed married men.

In contrast to econometric work based on these assumptions, in the late 1980s a small number of qualitative research projects were conducted exploring the decision-making of unemployed and low income men and women. These included McLaughlin, Millar and Cooke (1989) in Coleraine, Northern Ireland, and West Yorkshire; Smith with McLaughlin (1990) in Nottingham and York; and Jordan, James, Kay and Redley (1992) in Exeter. The remainder of this chapter summarises the empirical results of these studies and reflects on grounded theory derived from it, focusing in particular on the finding that not all forms of income are treated as equal, as they 'should' be in terms of Western conceptions of money.

Qualitative research on incentives and disincentives to work among the unemployed

The key empirical findings of qualitative research on attitudes to, and behaviour towards, paid work among unemployed people have been:

1. a remarkably high commitment to employment from even the very long-term unemployed (though this can also be found in quantitative work), in principle even if wages will yield the same as benefits when unemployed;

2. a surprisingly high level of search activity among even the very long-term unemployed and even in depressed labour markets such as Coleraine (though this too can also be found in quantitative work);

3. at the same time, barriers to taking employment caused by the social security system (these barriers involve both the low incomes people have while out of work and related structural difficulties in making the transition between unemployment and employment);

4. a significant degree of resistance to relying on in-work benefits (which runs counter to Government policy and the promotion of Family Credit as the 'solution' to low-paid work and to theories of incentives);

5. a gap between what people say they need financially from work and what they do (that is, when applying for particular jobs). This has also been found in quantitative surveys, such as Dawes (1993), and again runs contrary to theories of incentives;

6. some responsiveness to the conditions of the local labour market; chiefly, some reduction of the wages sought from employment in more depressed labour markets, but within the context of a high priority given to protecting basic household needs.

Analysing the decision-making process

The first two findings listed above are commonplace in both quantitative and qualitative research on unemployment. The most usual way in which economists, psychologists and sociologists have explained these kinds of findings is that employment is preferred to unemployment for a host of 'non-economic' reasons, such as pride, self-respect and social conformity (for example, Atkinson 1981). According to this perspective, although people may appear irrational in strict economic terms (by preferring paid work even if it does not yield more income than benefits), they do appear rational once the validity and importance of non-economic factors and needs are accepted. Some economists are beginning to go further than this and accept work as a utility rather than a disutility—the most prominent example is probably Hutton (1995). The problem with the standard interpretation—that is, acceptance of the importance of 'social' factors—is that it embodies acceptance of a dichotomy between 'the social' and 'the economic', leaving no obvious way to integrate 'social' motivations and attitudes with 'economic' calculations about jobs and wage offers vis-a-vis material needs. Later in this chapter, I will argue that application of Bloch's and Parry's (1989) concept of short-term and long-term transactional cycles would allow—indeed demand—integration of the economic and the social in the way that we think about individuals' and households' income generation and expenditure strategies and decisions.

In terms of motivation, the three qualitative studies cited above found that, despite a high level of commitment to paid work, unemployed men and women did not necessarily jump at every opportunity which appeared to be available. Certain kinds of jobs were often not considered viable—many part-time jobs, many temporary jobs and a few very low-paid full-time jobs. This has often been regarded by politicians and policy-makers as 'proof' that many unemployed people do not 'really' want to work, or are not prepared to work for less than they would receive in benefits, an interpretation in keeping with the simple labour supply assumptions underpinning econometric work. However, as we have argued elsewhere (McLaughlin et al 1989; Millar et al 1989), the selectivity found in unemployed people's attitudes to certain kinds of vacancies, operating alongside high levels of commitment to paid work in principle, can be substantially explained through an analytical framework of risk and decision-making under conditions of uncertainty, familiar in economic anthropological work such as that of Ortiz (1973).

Unemployed people, like most people in other situations, have less than perfect knowledge, and in that sense literally cannot make the same decisions that econometric models predict they should; and therefore decision-making takes place under conditions of (greater or lesser) uncertainty. The majority of people in McLaughlin et al's (1989) study, for example, said that they would 'do anything', and indeed analysis of the jobs which they had recently applied for showed that the majority had applied for jobs in areas in which they had no previous experience. Only a minority (16 per cent of men) was very specific about the kind of work (either economic sector or occupational level) they were prepared to accept. In this they were the same as unemployed people nationally. High proportions of unemployed people returning to work exhibit 'occupational flexibility' (for example, two-thirds of the short-term unemployed changed industry in their return to work in 1978; Layard and Nickell 1987: 152).

However, when unemployed men said they would 'do anything', they were not including 'women's jobs' or part-time or very short-term casual jobs. This kind of 'occupational inflexibility' on the part of unemployed men was important, in light of the nature of economic restructuring over the last decade, which has led to growth in precisely those kinds of work which unemployed men did not apply for (McLaughlin 1991). The causes of that inflexibility were not only men's perception of some jobs as 'women's work' or their (reasonable) belief that employers would not consider a man for 'a woman's job'. Rather, the dominant reason given for not applying for these jobs was that such jobs were too low paid and/or often less than full-time (the two, of course, being closely associated).

It is important to consider how men (and women in a rather different way) defined what was 'too low paid'—that is, to identify the factors they considered when they thought about what they 'needed' to get financially from paid work. The theory underpinning the policy preoccupation with incentives suggests that 'benefit levels' determine what will be considered 'too low-paid'. Increases or decreases in benefit levels are therefore held to raise or lower the wage sought, and lead to longer or shorter durations of unemployment. However, for most of the families in the empirical studies under discussion, the primary determinant of wage levels sought was an estimate of the income needed to cover basic family needs. In other words, the majority thought not about what they ought to be paid or, most significantly, about what they were receiving in benefits, but instead they thought in terms of a level of income based on household 'need'. This did not generally result in unrealistic or inflexible wage levels but it did mean people thought principally about managing the practicalities of moving off benefit and into work, and this was where the nature of social security payments (rather than their level) became important.

Sources of income

People did not think about all sources of income in the same way. There was a fundamental difference in the value attributed to earnings and to means-tested in-work benefits for low earners, a difference which runs completely contrary to assumptions which have been incorporated into both research and policy. The whole point of in-work benefits such as Family Credit is that the household income sought or needed can be higher than the wage for which a person works. At the time of McLaughlin et al's (1989) study, it would not have mattered (hypothetically) in net income terms whether the men concerned had applied for jobs offering only £60 gross per week or offering £100 gross per week, since their net incomes, after tax, national insurance and in-work benefits, would have been the same. Yet the jobs these men had applied for were generally not at the very low gross wage levels of £60 or £70 a week, though they were low paid by most definitions, averaging about £85 net or £100 gross a week. Why was this the case? In the rest of this chapter I will suggest that the reason is that sums of money which are numerically the same are not necessarily worth the same amount; and that the value of a sum of money depends on its capacity to help achieve longer-term household expenditure objectives.

The capacity of a sum of money to help attain a person's objective (whatever that might be) is dependant on several factors. The size or amount of money is only the most obvious one. A second factor is the amount of control the person believes they have over the amount of money which is, or will be, available, and this was an issue in relation to means-tested in-work benefit income. Most families had a general idea of the existence and function of means-tested support for low wage earners but few had enough detailed knowledge to exploit this support with confidence. A few people were resistant in principle to continuing benefit dependence after the return-to-work, but for the majority the issue was more pragmatic. The families attached weight to the ways in which relying on different sources of in-work income could have different consequences. In the case of means-tested in-work benefits, they could not be sure whether they would receive them, how long they would have to wait before receiving them, exactly how much they would be, or whether they would subsequently be able to 'hang onto' them (that is, whether they might be withdrawn). The perception of the risks involved in accepting a low paid job supplemented by an unknown and uncertain quantity of benefits put barriers in the way of adopting the wages-plus-benefits strategy promoted by Government in the 1980s as central to the solution of long-term unemployment.

Related to such control issues is the third factor which was important in terms of how effectively a sum of money could help attain household expenditure objectives. This was the degree of stability attached to it. The importance to families of avoiding excessive financial risk is abundantly clear from these qualitative studies. Financial stability, even if on a low income, was something unemployed families of necessity valued highly and could not readily sacrifice. Most unemployed families rely on income support, together with child benefit for those with children. The low level of income provided by these sources means that only a very small margin is left for expenditure other than on food and fuel. The majority of unemployed families have no savings, some are in debt and most just 'get by'. 'Getting by' is achieved partly by using credit (usually mail order catalogues) but mainly by very rigid and scrupulously careful budgeting from week to week. The precarious balance of families' budgeting is commonly reported in studies of long-term unemployed people. The finding is emphasised here because it has important implications (not previously explored) for our understanding of how people think about the financial consequences of returning-to-work. Paradoxically, if they had had a larger margin of income left after expenditure on necessities and more savings to cushion the impact of the transition to work, they would have been better placed to take risks in the labour market. Unemployed parents in particular were concerned about risks, because they placed even more value than single people on protecting basic household expenditures such as heating, food, and so on, so as to protect their family life and the welfare of their children.

Not every pound was perceived to be equally able to fulfil whatever strategy people were pursuing, which raises the issue of the non-equivalence of apparently equal sums of money. Some social scientists have challenged the purely rationalistic economic definition of modern money, particularly the idea of fungibility, by emphasising 'mental accounting'—the ways individuals distinguish between kinds of money (for example, Douglas 1967). For instance, people treat a windfall income differently from a bonus or inheritance, even when the sums involved are the same (for a review of the psychological literature on money see Lea, Tarpy and Webley 1987). Zelizer (1989: 352), too, notes that

> Even identical sums of money do not 'add' up in the same way. A $ 1,000 paycheque is not the same money as $ 1,000 stolen from a bank or $ 1,000 borrowed from a friend.

Thus the value of money is regulated by more than rational market calculation. It is regulated instead by source, timing, and predictability, all of which are significant because of the different expenditure possibilities to which they give rise.

It was because people were concerned with the extent to which different sources of income could support perceived household expenditure needs that they typically considered potential jobs in terms of a best and second-best strategy. Under the best strategy, the man of a couple would ideally obtain a wage high enough to avoid the need for means-tested in-work benefits. This strategy—a job at a wage sufficient to keep all of the family—is recognisably based on the 'family wage' concept which has featured (for different reasons and different purposes) in trade union wage bargaining and in discussion of access to resources within households. Considered from the subjective viewpoint of the families themselves, this strategy was rational because of the perceived risks associated with the second-best strategy, which was to rely on a combination of in-work benefits and earnings in the way that current policy attempts to encourage.

The safer strategy, then, is the one in which as much as possible of the family's needs are secured out of earnings and out of the earnings of one partner only. The difference between the earnings potential of men and women (and to a much lesser extent the work aspirations of the partners) meant that the prospective earner was invariably assumed to be the man, despite the fact that the local labour markets described in McLaughlin et al (1989) and Smith (1990) offered better chances for women to obtain paid work.

It has been a powerful assumption in both theory and policy that it is simply the level of benefits which determines the level of wages which unemployed men are prepared to accept. These studies suggest that an important determinant of employment behaviour is the way in which the structure and nature of benefits (both in and out of work), together with a highly gendered labour market, sets the parameters of the choices which unemployed people perceive to be available to them.

In summary, the assumption of rational choice under conditions of certainty which underpins traditional labour supply theory does not appear to be valid on the basis of detailed empirical evidence. Uncertainty derives from imperfect knowledge and particularly, if paradoxically, from being aware that one probably has imperfect knowledge. However, it also derives from the degree of control which a person has over the various components of the income equation. To return to the concrete example of Family Credit, people may have less than perfect knowledge about the workings of Family Credit and hence feel uncertain about the outcome of their application. They may also recognise that the success of their application, the amount of money they get, and the continuation of payments are in the hands of others. Thus there is a recognition that the claimant has little control over this source of income, generating grounds for uncertainty which are not due to 'imperfect knowledge' as such.

Therefore not all sources of income are the same and there is a clear contrast between wages and benefits. A person assumes (sometimes wrongly) that if they agree to work for £ x a week, then so long as they turn up and do their work each week, they will in fact get (or reasonably expect to get) £ x a week. It is within their power (barring illness) to secure that £ x. In contrast, benefit income often appears to be independent of an individual's own behaviour. Benefit may not be awarded, or may be withdrawn, for reasons entirely unconnected with (as well as reasons connected with) one's own behaviour. The result is that £ x from a certain source (earnings) is more than, or has a higher value than, £ x from an uncertain source (in-work benefits), and a source is more or less certain depending on the degree to which it is (thought to be) under one's control. Consequently, people do not treat all nominally equal sums of money as equivalent.

The importance of uncertainty and risk is increasingly being incorporated into economic theory (for example, in relation to consumer behaviour), though it has not yet featured substantially in that area of economics concerned with labour supply. Theoretically, there is no reason why econometric modelling of labour supply behaviour could not incorporate risk and uncertainty, and some work is indeed beginning to move in this direction (Jenkins and Millar 1989). However, simply incorporating variable amounts of risk and uncertainty into econometric models does not, and cannot, address *why* risk and uncertainty are important. To understand this requires a deeper analysis of the meaning of money, the significance of control over money sources, and through that, the integration of the economic and the social in people's lives, that is to say, in their motivations.

Beyond risk and uncertainty: the meaning of money

The framework of risk and uncertainty employed in the above analysis of unemployed people's labour supply attitudes and behaviour generates a major theoretical issue—that £ x is not necessarily equal to £ x because the value of a given amount of money is dependant on its source. This calls into question the way we think about and conceptualise money itself, and thus the assumptions made, not just in econometric work on incentives and disincentives to work, but in all economic decision-making, or, more broadly, all decision-making about the allocation of resources to different ends.

Social science theory and analysis has rarely questioned the nature of 'modern' money, tending to adopt uncritically the dominant view of money to which Western society is the collective heir. While there is an extensive anthropological literature dealing with 'primitive' currencies, modern money has been ignored 'as if it were not sociological enough' (Collins 1979: 190). As Zelizer (1989: 343–4) notes, in a rare sociological article questioning the meaning of money,

> To be sure Veblen (1899, 1953) alerted us to the social meaning of what money buys, and others have significantly furthered the social, cultural and historical analysis of consumerism . . . But the freedom of money itself is not directly challenged.

The supposed 'freedom' of modern money, and the corresponding investment of money with an inherent power, is an instance of technological determinism and of what Parry and Bloch (1989) term 'fetishism'—money becomes an agent in its own right rather than a phenomenon. A variety of perspectives on the meaning of money in Western thought have all attributed money with immense power deriving from the inherent capacity of money to create 'pure' (numerical) equivalencies—that is, one penny should always and everywhere equal one penny.

Simmel, for example, argued that the 'uncompromising objectivity' of modern money transformed the world into an 'arithmetic problem' (Simmel 1978: 412). Free from subjective restrictions, indifferent to 'particular interests, origins, or relations' (Simmel 1978: 373), money's liquidity and divisibility were, according to Simmel, infinite, making it 'absolutely interchangeable' (1978: 128). The very essence of money, claimed Simmel, was its 'unconditional interchangeability, the internal uniformity that makes each piece exchangeable for another' (1978: 441). This 'freedom' of money has been held to dissolve bonds between persons based on kinship and other ascriptive criteria; to effect that separation between people and things which, Mauss (1966) argued, was denied by many primitive and archaic societies; and, hence, money has been seen as an active agent in the movement from Gemeinschaft to Gesellschaft (Parry and Bloch 1989).

Not surprisingly, such a powerful agent has also been perceived as involving a morally dangerous alchemy. In his early essay 'The Power of Money in Bourgeois Society', Marx warned that the transformational realities of money

subverted reality 'confounding and compounding . . . all natural and human qualities . . . [money] serves to exchange every property for every other, even contradictory, property and object; it is the fraternisation of impossibilities' (Marx 1964:
169). Thus the impersonality and anonymity of money was argued by the major
social thinkers to lend itself to the impersonal and inconsequential relationships
characteristic of the market-place and even to a complete anonymity in exchange.
Money depersonalised social relations, reduced differences of quality to those of
quantity, denied the unique, and so its possession conferred an almost divine
power which thinkers from Aristotle to Aquinas to Simmel and Marx have all
identified as its dangerous yet exciting potential.

In the ideology of developed capitalism, money remains credited with a life-
like power and an inherently impersonal, amoral and calculating nature—hence
the questionable appropriateness of money as a gift where the gift is expressive of
relationships which are personal, enduring, moral and altruistic. Some spheres
(the 'non-economic') are therefore seen as in need of protection from the potentially 'evil' power of money, while in others (the 'economic'), avarice and self-
interest become the foundation of civilised society (Parry and Bloch 1989). In
contemporary Western society, considerable effort is invested in protecting one
sphere from the other because of the supposed ability of money to create moral
confusion. This, of course, is recognisable as the focus of New Right ideologies
of, and concern about, the respective roles of family obligations and the State in
social and economic life.

The presence of these traditions in Western thought and in social science
interpretation of money has led to the acceptance of a strict dichotomy between,
on the one hand, restricted currencies in non-western systems and 'modern'
Western all-purpose money, and, on the other, between the 'social' and the 'economic'. There have been, however, a number of important exceptions, such as
Simiand (1934), Sorokin (1943), Douglas (1967), to a lesser extent, Parsons (1967;
1971a; 1971b), and more recently Parry and Bloch (1989) and Zelizer (1989).

Simiand (1934), for instance, argued that the extra-economic, social basis of
money remains as powerful in modern economic systems as it was in 'primitive'
and ancient societies. Sorokin (1943) made the same argument in his brilliant
analysis of the persistence of qualitative distinctions in modern conceptions of
time and space. Parsons explicitly and forcefully called for a 'sociology of money'
which would treat money as one of the various generalised symbolic media of
social interchange, along with political power, influence, and value commitments
(Parsons 1971a: 241; 1971b: 26–7). However, Parsons still conceptually restricted
money to the 'economic sphere with money being the "symbolic" embodiment of
economic value, what economists in a technical sense call "utility"' (1967: 358).

Douglas (1967) suggested that modern money may not be so unrestricted and
'free' after all. Modern money, she argued (1967: 139), is controlled and rationed
in two situations: in international exchange and at the purely individual personal
level, where

many of us try to primitivize our money . . . by placing restrictions at the source, earmarking monetary instruments of certain kinds for certain purposes, by only allowing ourselves . . . certain limited freedoms in the disposal of money . . . Money from different sources is sometimes personalised and attracts distinctive feelings which dictate the character of its spending.

These restraints, Douglas noted, 'resemble strangely . . . restraints on the use of some primitive monies' (1967: 119–20). Douglas, however, suggested that these were individual 'quirks' or 'a clumsy attempt to control the all too liquid state of money' (1967: 138, 140). Thus Douglas, who has significantly advanced cultural theories of consumption, did not pursue the cultural analysis of money which her own reflections suggested.

Zelizer (1989) has argued that a purely utilitarian conception of 'market money' is inadequate, because it ignores the existence of 'special monies', such as 'domestic' money, which she saw as having extra-economic, social bases. Developing a sociological model of multiple monies, Zelizer argues, is part of a broader challenge to neo-classical economic theory. It offers an alternative approach not only to the study of money but to all other aspects of economic life, including the market:

> . . . economic processes of exchange and consumption are one special category of social relations, much as is kinship or religion. Thus, economic phenomena such as money, although partly autonomous, are interdependent with historically variable systems of meanings and structures of social relations (Zelizer 1989: 371).

In similar vein, Parry and Bloch (1989) use cross-cultural and historical evidence to show that there is no one world view to which the technology of money necessarily gives rise, and argue that the meanings of money are constructed from the interaction of money with pre-existing world views and especially existing long-term cycles of exchange. Money does not mean what money (technically) does. Not only does money mean different things in different cultures, but it may mean different things within the same culture.

Parry and Bloch conclude that we have to shift our focus from a consideration of the meanings of money to a consideration of the meanings of whole transactional systems. They argue that a significant regularity across many cultures can be identified—the existence of two separate but related transactional order, the first of which involves transactions concerned with the reproduction of the long-term social or cosmic order, and the second, transactions concerned with the short-term arena of individual competition and acquisition. Bloch and Parry (1989) document these two spheres, and the dynamic relations of conflict and continuity between them, for a number of societies, though not for contemporary Western society. In every case, a series of procedures could be identified through which goods derived from the short-term cycle were converted into the long-term transactional order. The meanings attributed to money in any particular instance then became a kind of epiphenomenon of regularities which existed at a deeper level (Parry and Bloch 1989: 28–9).

Through their analysis of 'what money means', Parry and Bloch thus come to a re-examination of the concept and nature of motivation. In a similar way, through from a different starting point, Parsons (1964: 53) suggested that there were two different 'orders' of motivation:

> the immediate goal of economic action in a market economy is the maximisation of net money advantages or more generally of the difference between utility and cost. Choices, so far as they are, in the immediate sense, 'economically motivated' are, in the first instance, oriented to this immediate goal. It is certainly not legitimate to assume that this immediate goal is a simple and direct expression of the ultimate motivational forces of human behaviour. On the contrary, to a large extent its pursuit is probably compatible with a considerable range of variation in more ultimate motivations. Indeed it [is my] principal thesis . . . that 'economic motivation' is not a category of motivation on the deeper level at all, but is rather a point at which many different motives may be brought to bear on a certain type of situation.

Further, and in a manner which might be seen to closely parallel Parry's and Bloch's notion of the existence of relations of both conflict and continuity between long-term and short-term transactional orders, Parsons (1964: 57) suggested that when and where 'self-interest' and moral sentiments conflict, *neither* will have automatic primacy:

> In situations of strain [moral sentiments] may well come to be in radical opposition to the self-interested impulses of the actor; he [sic] is the victim of difficult conflicts and problems of conscience . . . This is not in the least incompatible with the strict requirements of economic theory for that requires only that as between certain alternatives, choice will be made in such a way as to maximise net money advantages to the actor, or to the social unit on behalf of which he acts. Both in the ultimate goals to which the proceeds will be applied, and in the choice of means there is no reason why . . . moral sentiments should not be involved. But there is equally no reason why, on a comparable level, elements of self-interest should not be involved also. Indeed, the distinction is not one of classes of concrete motives, but of types of element in concrete motives. In the usual case these elements are intimately intertwined.

'The economic' and 'the social' in labour supply motivations

I noted earlier that while people were concerned about the overall level of their income, they were also concerned about how different forms of income could, and would, contribute to overarching objectives, strategies and values—most prominently the maintenance of a basic standard of living for the family unit, and through that the maintenance of the family itself. Thus, individuals and families were capable of, and were aware of, ways to maximise income which in the short-term might have resulted in a weekly income of £ x + y compared with £ x (that is, ways of thinking which fitted the short-term cycle identified by Parry and Bloch). But these strategies were subordinated to longer-term objectives (such as securing the family); that is, short-term advantage was measured in terms of the extent to which it could be 'converted', in Parry and Bloch's terms, into 'goods' belonging to the long-term reproduction of the social order.

What, though, were these longer-term objectives or strategies? As pointed out earlier, McLaughlin et al (1989) found that decision-making focused around 'basic household needs'. Exactly what these were (apart from the obvious negatives, such as not going hungry, not having no clothes, etc.) was not particularly clear from this research which began with a different focus. Yet these basic household needs formed the pivot around which men and women attempted to manipulate their labour supply, and formed the reference point against which potential opportunities in the labour market were judged. Similarly, Jordan et al (1992) found that, although one could not speak of a household work strategy, there was a household *expenditure* strategy. It is likely that 'basic household needs' and 'household expenditure strategy' describe much the same empirical phenomena. In both studies, people had a long-term commitment to, and motivation towards, some level and types of expenditure which were not negotiable. Although obviously some of this was to do with absolute physical survival, much of it was not, and derived from people's perceptions of what family life should be like, and the kinds of experiences which parents ought to be able to provide for their children.

The significance of the normative roles of fathers/husbands/men or mothers/wives/women in motivations to search for, apply for, accept or reject jobs has traditionally been described (and put to one side) as 'social' factors. For both men and women, in McLaughlin et al (1989), Smith (1990) and Jordan et al (1992), 'social' concerns were dominated first by the protection of children's welfare, and secondly by the welfare of the adults. In both cases, welfare was about physical survival but also, and more critically, it was about people's capacities to participate in relationships with other people outside the immediate household (including the ability of children to relate to other children on reasonably equitable terms). Various consumption imperatives followed from these meanings of welfare, imperatives which then set the parameters within which unemployed adults attempted to manipulate their labour supply. To put this in theoretical terms, consumption behaviour was constitutive of relations between people.

To the extent that consumption is constitutive of relations between people, rather than between people and things, household expenditure strategies and definitions of 'basic needs' may be regarded as the expression of, in Parry's and Bloch's terms, the longer-term transactional cycle, which in its broadest sense is about the place of the individual in the collective reproduction of society. Labour supply behaviour represented unemployed people's attempts to effect some kind of reconciliation between the two transactional 'orders' of short-term maximisation and long-term reproduction. A household income or expenditure strategy is not something that is fulfilled over the course of a few weeks—it represents much longer-term commitments to the relation between the individual and the society of which he or she is a part, with the individual's position within the household occupying a critical mediating role. In contrast, the focus of economists' concerns—the immediate relationship between income-in-work and income-out-of-work—belongs only to the shorter-term cycle of individual acquisition.

Clearly money is a means to certain ends rather than an end in itself and, despite the clichéd nature of such a statement, it remains important, because it highlights the importance of 'ends' in human activities. Such an approach to labour supply attitudes and behaviour is important in two respects: first, it can explain the level of responsiveness (or the lack of it) to local labour market conditions found empirically in many studies of unemployment; and second, it suggests that expenditure/consumption behaviours, in so far as these are constitutive of relations between people at all levels in society, are the engines of income/wealth generation activities, and through that 'economic development' generally.

As regards the first point, neo-classical economics argues that high levels of unemployment in some areas are perpetuated, if not caused, by a failure of local wage rates to drop to the point at which further labour demand would be generated. This failure is often attributed to the existence of social security benefits which provide a floor below which wage rates will not drop. In contrast, the kind of analysis developed in this chapter argues that expenditure needs form the floor below which income rates cannot fall. These apparently material needs differ somewhat between different localities within one society, but to the extent that localities are united in some way as a society, then these 'material' needs (which are in fact both material and non-material), cannot differ beyond a certain degree. Thus in McLaughlin et al (1989), for example, there was evidence that unemployed people in the Northern Irish labour market studied (Coleraine) were responsive to the very depressed conditions of their local labour market—the income per household member sought from employment was lower than that of their counterparts in West Yorkshire, but not by a large amount. There was a level below which people could not go without abandoning their stake in society. In other words, there were basic expenditure requirements common to unemployed households in all the four labour markets studied, around the margins of which there was some movement, dependent on the state of the local market.

As regards the second point—that expenditure and consumption behaviours are engines of income/wealth generation activities—Mingione (1985: 25) argues that the interrelationship of the social and the formal economy 'constitutes the reason for the connection between the reproductive cycle of the unit and the general process of accumulation or development'. It is, of course, generally accepted that what has been termed 'the social economy' plays a primary role in the production and reproduction of labour with its responsibility for the care of children, elderly, sick and disabled people. However, integration of cultural perspectives on consumption with economic perspectives on labour supply and wealth-generation activity, such as I have attempted in this chapter, supports Gershuny's theory (1978) that there is not merely an interrelation between the household sector and the 'formal' economy, but that the 'domestic' sector may well be the causal factor for economic development.

Conclusion

As Hollis and Nell argue (1975: 54), economic maximisation is not sufficient as a rationale for economic activity. Rational economic 'man' is obscure:

> We do not know what he [sic] wants. But we do know that whatever it is, he will maximise ruthlessly to get it . . . as consumer he maximises utility through the omniscient and improbable comparison of, for instance, marginal strawberries with marginal cement.

Whatever the limits of the kind of analysis I have pursued in this chapter, what is important is the need to challenge the standard dichotomy between the economic and the social; to develop analytical tools which are not dependant on this dichotomy; and thereby to bring a fresh approach to analysis of empirical material on people's motivations. My aim has not been to assert the priority of 'the social' over 'the economic'. The notion of a longer-term transactional cycle, for example, should not be taken to imply some kind of static overarching order to which people slavishly attempt to reconcile their individual money acquisition. Rather, the emphasis is on the *relationship* between the short-term and long-term cycle and hence on the engines of socio-economic change. There is no doubt that, in Northern Ireland and much of western Europe as we enter the twenty-first century, long-term unemployment and low levels of labour demand represent a disjunction between these two cycles and the partial, but often creative, resolutions sought by research 'subjects' in these circumstances should be examined seriously, rather than regarded as 'errors' in the predictability of econometric models.

References

Atkinson, A. 1981. Unemployment benefits and incentives. In J. Creedy (ed.), The Economics of Unemployment in Great Britain. London: Butterworths.

Bloch, M. and J. Parry (eds.) 1989. *Money and the Morality of Exchange.* Cambridge: Cambridge University Press.

Collins, R. 1979. Review of The Bankers by Martin Mayers. *American Journal of Sociology* 85, 190-94.

Dawes, L. 1993. *Long-term Unemployment and Labour Market Flexibility.* University of Leicester: Centre for Labour Market Studies.

Douglas, M. 1967. Primitive Rationing. In R. Firth (ed.), *Themes in Economic Anthropology.* London: Tavistock.

Gershuny, J. 1978. *After Industrial Society.* London: Macmillan.

Hollis, M. and E. Nell 1975. *Rational Economic Man.* Cambridge: Cambridge University Press.

Hutton, W. 1995. *The State We're In.* London: Jonathan Cape.

Jenkins, S. and J. Millar 1989. Income Risk and Income Maintenance: Implications for Incentives to Work. In A. Dilnot and I. Walker (eds.), *The Economics of Social Security.* Oxford: Oxford University Press.

Jordan, B., S. James, H. Kay and M. Redley 1992. *Trapped in Poverty? Labour-market Decisions in Low-income Households.* London: Routledge.

Lane, R. 1991. *The Market Experience.* Cambridge: Cambridge University Press.

Layard, R. and S. Nickell 1987. The Labour Market. In R. Dornbusch and R. Layard (eds.), *The Performance of the British Economy.* Oxford: Oxford University Press.

Lea, S., R. Tarpy and P. Webley 1987. *The Individual in the Economy.* Cambridge: Cambridge University Press.

Marx, K. 1964 [1844]. The Power of Money in Bourgeois Society. In *The Economic and Philosophic Manuscripts of 1844.* New York: International.

Mauss, M. 1966. *The Gift.* London: Routledge and Kegan Paul.

McLaughlin, E. 1991. Work and Welfare Benefits: Social Security, Employment and Unemployment in the 1990s. *Journal of Social Policy* 20 (4): 485–508.

____. 1992. *Understanding Unemployment: New Perspectives on Active Labour Market Policies.* London: Routledge.

____. J. Millar and K. Cooke. 1989. *Work and Welfare Benefits.* Aldershot: Avebury.

____. and P. Quirk (eds.) 1996. *Policy Aspects of Employment Equality in Northern Ireland.* Belfast: Standing Advisory Commission on Human Rights.

Millar, J., E. McLaughlin and K. Cooke 1989. The Employment Lottery: Risk and Social Security Benefits. *Policy and Politics* 17 (1), 75–81.

Mingione, E. 1985. Social Reproduction of the Surplus Labour Force. In N. Redclift and E. Mingione (eds.), *Beyond Employment: Gender, Employment and Subsistence.* Oxford: Blackwell.

Ormerod, P. 1994. *The Death of Economics.* London: Faber and Faber.

Ortiz, S. 1973. *Peasant Farmers in Colombia.* London: LSE Monographs No. 46.

Parry, J. and M. Bloch 1989. Introduction: Money and the Morality of Exchange. In M. Bloch and J. Parry (eds.), *Money and the Morality of Exchange.* Cambridge: Cambridge University Press.

Parsons, T. 1964 [1940]. The Motivation of Economic Activities. In T. Parsons *Essays in Sociological Theory.* New York: The Free Press.

____. 1967. On the Concept of Influence. In T. Parsons *Sociological Theory and Modern Society.* New York: The Free Press.

____. 1971a. Higher Education as a Theoretical Focus. In H. Turk and R. Simpson (eds.), *Institutions and Social Exchange.* New York: Bobbs-Merrill.

____. 1971b. Levels of Organisation and the Mediation of Social Interaction. In H. Turk and R. Simpson (eds.), *Institutions and Social Exchange.* New York: Bobbs-Merrill.

Simiand, F. 1934. La monnaie, réalité sociale. *Annales Sociologiques* ser. D, 1–86

Simmel, G. 1978 [1908]. *The Philosophy of Money.* London: Routledge and Kegan Paul.

Smith, L. with E. McLaughlin 1990. *Labour Supply Flexibility and the Long-term Unemployed.* Sheffield: The Employment Service.

Sorokin, P. 1943. *Sociocultural Causality, Space and Time.* Durham, NC: Duke University Press.

Zelizer, V. 1989. The Social Meaning of Money: 'Special Monies'. *American Journal of Sociology* 95 (2): 342–77.

12 Parading tradition, protesting triumphalism: utilising anthropology in public policy

Dominic Bryan and Neil Jarman

On Sunday 7 July 1996, members of Portadown District Loyal Orange Lodge paraded to Drumcree Church for their annual Boyne commemoration service. When the Royal Ulster Constabulary (RUC) banned them from parading past a Catholic housing estate on their return journey, the men insisted that they would stay put until allowed to walk their preferred route. Over the next three days supporters of the Orangemen blocked countless roads, hijacked vehicles, burnt properties and rioted throughout Northern Ireland. Finally, on 11 July, less than twenty-four hours before the anniversary of the battle of the Boyne—the most important day of the year for many Ulster Protestants—the police reversed their decision, forcing the Catholic residents of the Garvaghy Road off the street to allow the Orangemen to parade into Portadown. Catholics were outraged at the police decision and three days of extensive rioting followed in nationalist areas of the north. 'Drumcree week' is estimated to have increased expenditure on security by £10 million. The Northern Ireland Tourist Board claimed that the loss of tourism, resulting from these civil disturbances, could be as much as £50 million (*Belfast Telegraph*, 11 September 1996). Long-term losses of business investment will add still further to the bill.

The dispute in Portadown was but one of more than 50 disputes over parades in 1996, albeit the worst. In 1995, protests and disturbances had also occurred at the Drumcree Church parade and at more than 40 other parades across the province. The vast majority of these disputes involved challenges to the right of Protestant organisations—the Orange Institution, the Royal Black Institution and the Apprentice Boys of Derry, referred to collectively as 'the loyal orders'—to hold 'traditional' parades through, or near to, Catholic communities. Such parades are perceived by many Protestants to be a vital expression of their British, Protestant culture and identity, and their political aspiration as unionists to remain part of the United Kingdom.[1] Any attempt to stop or to re-route the parades is perceived as an attack upon the Protestant community and culture. In contrast, for many Catholics who live on these routes, the parades are perceived as a triumphalist reassertion of Protestant domination over Catholics, which had been established with the victory at the Boyne in 1690, and confirmed in the north of Ireland by partition in 1921. In short, the parades are a ritual expression of the ethnic differences which exist within Northern Ireland.

Anthropologists should take a particular interest in these events for two main reasons. First, the discipline of anthropology has built up a significant corpus of knowledge on ritual action and symbolic expression. Whilst much of this material originated in a Durkheimian investigation into the nature and function of religious practice, and has concentrated on non-industrial, non-western societies, there has been a more recent recognition of the importance played by symbols and rituals in industrial societies (Anderson 1983; Boissevain 1992; Cohen 1985; Kertzer 1988). Second, the character of the parades, and of the related disputes, is such that the ethnographic method of research, with its sensitivities to nuances of meaning and understanding, has distinct advantages over quantitative methodologies (Caplan 1995). These disputes are principally about perceptions, about what people feel is happening to them, rather than about what others say did, or will, happen. Participants at a parade perceive themselves to be doing one thing, while those protesting perceive something quite different. The parades and the protests take place within public space and are therefore highly visible, with the intensity of the disputes attracting considerable attention. However, at the same time many of the issues have been clouded by vague claims and counter-claims. Ethnographic research, conducted sensitively, makes possible an exploration and analysis of the micro-politics of ritual occasions to reveal a more complex political dynamic than might be revealed using other methodologies. By examining specific ritual occasions, such as specific parades, it is possible to identify those localised political pressures which influence the more general political climate. We can thereby examine the complex network of political interests, which anthropology suggests underlies all large ritual occasions, and ask how these interests impinge on community relations.

Researching parades

Given the importance of the Orange Institution in the political and social spheres of life in Northern Ireland, there has been surprisingly little research published that looks specifically at parades. The significance of parades as a social phenomenon has been recognised by a number of historians, sociologists and political scientists (Gibbon 1975; Farrell 1976; Patterson 1980; Hill 1984; Bew, Gibbon and Patterson 1995), but only Wright (1987; 1996) gives any detailed consideration to the historically situated social function of such events. Anthropologists have also recognised the part played in community life by parading organisations and their associated rituals (Harris 1972; Larsen 1982; McFarlane 1989; Cecil 1993; Buckley and Kenney 1995), but none has explored the scale and intensity of the practice, nor has any substantive study of the loyal orders been published. Only Bell (1990), in his study of the role of marching bands among young people in Londonderry, has provided significant ethnographic research on an aspect of parading.

The comparative lack of qualitative analyses of parading is matched by a paucity of quantitative data. The veracity of the statistical material that is available has been questioned, particularly by those supporting the loyal orders. The only quantitative material derives from police sources, with none of the parading bodies keeping data on their own parades. Since 1985, the RUC has published annual figures for the total number of parades, which they classify as 'Loyalist', and as 'Republican' or 'Nationalist'. In 1995, the RUC recorded 3,500 parades in Northern Ireland. Of these the vast majority, 2574, were 'Loyalist'; 285 were categorised as 'Nationalist', and 617 were 'Other'.[2] These figures, compiled from the notification that parade organisers give to the police, have shown a general and systematic increase in the number of both loyalist and nationalist parades since 1985, although the number of nationalist parades has rarely constituted more than 10 per cent of the total. Although the statistics derive from police sources, which one might suppose Protestants would trust, in the current climate of contention, dispute and distrust, the figures have been challenged from the unionist side. They feel that their parades, and their culture in general, are under threat and deny that there has been any real increase in loyalist parades. The lack of reliable information on data collection methods from the RUC means that it is not possible to verify the rise in the number of parades which RUC statistics report. As a result, we can only speculate on which types of parade have shown an increase, if there has been an increase at all. There is no information available on the number of parades which are held by each of the particular organisations, nor on the number of parades held annually in any particular area. The lack of detailed information has contributed to current disputes: nationalists claim that they are suffering more and more parades, while the loyal orders claim that their traditions are being eroded. The raw figures underline the continuing importance of parades in Northern Ireland, but the lack of any detailed analysis, qualitative or quantitative, has helped to consolidate (mis)perceptions about why people parade, what it means to them and why others object to such practices.

The original impetus for our research was academic,[3] and was unrelated to the contingency of political process. However, early in 1995 it became impossible to ignore the changing political context within which the parades were taking place. We began to focus specifically on parades which were being contested and on those likely to result in public disorder. We travelled to parades across Northern Ireland, watched what took place, talked to people involved both in the parades themselves and in the protests and, most importantly, made contacts which could be followed up later. The results of this research were published in a report entitled *Parade and Protest* (Jarman and Bryan 1996). One of the aims of the report was to promote a broader understanding of the culture of parading, of the disputes, and of the diverse perceptions on either side. This entailed trying to identify the significant political pressures which influence the nature of parades: for instance, we tried to show how the parades were influenced by the weak authority structure within the Orange Institution; and how tensions exist within the parades due to the fragmentation of the unionist political block. We also tried to show how participants in the parades have a strong sense of local identity, something which highlights the importance of many smaller local parades as opposed to the larger parades on the Twelfth of July. But another aim was to provide some basic information: to look at the different types of parades and the different organisations involved; to look closely at the events themselves in order to analyse their internal political dynamic; to examine the role of the marching bands at Orange parades; to examine how parades are controlled by police and stewards; and to look at the role of spectators, music and alcohol. While funding bodies had been unwilling to provide money for a long-term academic study driven by theoretical interests in the nature of ritual, the nature of collective memory and the importance of material culture in constructing a social identity, the potential policy and political interests of the research promptly resulted in funds being made available to produce the report. Paradoxically, this could be done within the deadline set only because extensive research had already been completed.

'Tradition' and power

There has been a long history to pseudo-military parades in the British Isles. In Ireland, annual parades to commemorate King William III's campaign were held by state authorities throughout the eighteenth century. In the same period, the Freemasons, Jacobite supporters, a variety of agrarian secret societies and the Volunteers, all utilised public parades to express their social and political ideals (Jarman 1997a). The use of parades as a form of political expression was also common in Britain, though what came to distinguish the situation in Ireland was the lack of agreement on the nature of the state. During the nineteenth century, the custom of holding anniversary parades became a focus for political mobilisation in Ireland, both for those espousing Irish nationalism and for those supporting the Union with Britain, and political aspirations became increasingly linked with Catholic and Protestant ethnic identities. The Orange Institution, formed in 1795, became particularly important after the 1870s, when it was patronised by growing numbers of senior Unionist politicians and the urban bourgeoisie. Orange parades became overt political events at which politicians would speak directly to their voters. Parades were also used extensively, and in a similar fashion, by a variety of Catholic, nationalist organisations such as the Ribbonmen, the Ancient Order of Hibernians, the Irish National Foresters and the Irish National League.

One crucial element in the development of a parading 'tradition' was the relationship which those parading had with the state. Early Orange parades were effectively encouraged by the state during the 1790s, when the threat of a nationalist rebellion was high. However, when constitutional nationalism was in the ascendancy, during O'Connell's campaigns from the 1820s to the 1840s, Orange parades resulted in frequent sectarian clashes, required extensive policing, were officially discouraged and even banned. It was only in the later part of the nineteenth century that Orange parades gained a respectability among the middle and upper classes which allowed them to flourish relatively unhindered. Yet Catholic parades remained problematic, and attempts by nationalist organisations to parade in any but the most strongly Catholic areas were quickly stopped. Put simply, in the north of Ireland, even prior to partition, the number of places in which Orangemen were able to parade was always higher than for nationalists (Jarman 1997a; Wright 1996).

With partition in 1921, both northern and southern states constructed a collective identity based upon a single dominant ethno-religious group. Commemorative events which reflected these political identities were enshrined by the state, while events which seemed to challenge the legitimacy of the state were opposed. Between 1920 and 1972 almost every Cabinet Minister in Northern Ireland was an Orangeman and the senior Unionist politicians, from the Prime Minister down, addressed Orangemen at 'the Field' demonstration which marks the mid-point of each Twelfth parade (Bryan 1997; Harbinson 1973). Orange parades effectively became rituals of state, while nationalist parades and displays of flags were regarded as a threat to the state and consequently were restricted and sometimes banned under the 1922 Special Powers Act. These distinctions were consolidated by the 1951 Public Order Act, which required that five days notice be given before a parade could take place, unless the parade was 'customarily held along a particular route'. This meant that nearly all parades organised by the loyal orders were exempt from the provisions of this Act (Bryson and McCartney 1994: 144–56). It gave the so-called 'traditional' parade a special status over and above new parades, or over parades that had been unable to maintain a 'tradition'. The relationship of the state to public expression, in the form of parades, has provided the environment in which loyalist parades could flourish, while nationalist or republican parades were restricted.

The issue of the 'right to parade' has continued to play a key role in community relations in Northern Ireland. In the late 1960s the Northern Ireland Civil Rights movement focused attention on the discrimination against Catholics in housing and employment, and on the gerrymandering which took place to maintain Unionist power in areas, such as Derry, which had a Catholic majority (McCann 1974; Purdie 1990). During 1968 and 1969, civil rights demonstrations extended this challenge by directly questioning the hegemony of the loyal orders on the streets. The violent reaction of the police challenged the very basis of the northern state, and the British Army was brought in to undertake policing duties.

In 1970, as violence and disorder became widespread, all parades were banned for a six-month period, the first time such an extensive ban had been imposed since parades were re-legalised in 1872. By 1972 civil unrest had become so serious that the British Government closed down the Parliament of Northern Ireland at Stormont and introduced direct rule from Westminster. This significantly reduced the direct influence of the Orange Institution on the affairs of the northern state.

In the 1980s, parades once again became the focus and expression of significant political changes. The rise of Sinn Féin as an electoral force, following the 1981 Hunger Strike, led to a determination by both British and Irish Governments to forge closer policies on Northern Ireland. This in turn led to the signing of the Anglo-Irish Agreement in November 1985 which created a permanent body through which the Irish Government might make its views on Northern Ireland known. Unionists considered the Anglo-Irish Agreement a threat to the constitutional position of the northern state. For many of them, this was symbolised by the apparently more aggressive policing of parades. On the 12 July 1985, the RUC stopped a group of Orange lodges from using their 'traditional' route to the centre of Portadown through a predominantly Catholic area known as 'the Tunnel'. Over the next thirteen months there were six major civil disturbances in Portadown which resulted in numerous injuries, and the death of one man, killed by an RUC plastic bullet. For many Orangemen, the significance of these events was that the predominantly Protestant police force was no longer prepared to protect Orange parades at all costs, as they would have done during the era of the Stormont Parliament. It is not surprising that the police brought into Portadown were often accused of being Catholics, or members of the Garda Síochána (the Republic of Ireland police service), or British soldiers dressed as policemen (Bryan, Fraser and Dunn 1995). For Unionists, the blocking or re-routing of parades showed a tangible loss of their power.

More recently, in March 1992, a campaign to stop 'Orange' parades walking along the nationalist, 'lower' Ormeau Road in south Belfast began partly in response to the killing of five people by the Ulster Freedom Fighters in an attack on a bookmakers' shop the previous month. In July 1992 a small number of the participants in an Orange mini-Twelfth parade—which take place in the days leading up to the Twelfth—danced and waved five fingers at protesters as they passed the shop. The Secretary of State, Patrick Mayhew, suggested their behaviour would have 'disgraced a tribe of cannibals' (*Irish News*, 11 July 1992). When, on 31 August and 13 October 1994, the IRA and the Combined Loyalist Military Command, announced their ceasefires, it gave the opportunity for some communities in Catholic areas to be more openly assertive in their opposition to 'Orange' marches. Protests on the Ormeau Road intensified in early 1995 with the formation of a residents' group, the Lower Ormeau Concerned Community (LOCC), whose aim was to stop the parades or, at least, to engage the loyal orders in dialogue over their objections. A similar residents' group was subsequently formed on the Garvaghy Road in Portadown, the road along which the Boyne anniversary church parade 'traditionally' returned from Drumcree Church.

Once it became known that the spokespersons of a number of the residents' groups were former republican prisoners, the groups were regarded by many in the loyal orders as little more than a Sinn Féin front, and as part of a political assault on their traditions. Attempts at mediation or compromise proved, in the main, fruitless, and the RUC was left to decide whether a particular parade should be allowed to proceed or not. In 1995, the RUC banned the Drumcree Church parade from the Garvaghy Road, but after a stand-off lasting three days, from 9–11 July, an agreement was reached allowing a parade, without the accompanying bands, to pass the Garvaghy housing estate. The local Ulster Unionist MP, David Trimble, and the leader of the Democratic Unionist Party, the Rev. Ian Paisley, treated the arrival of the parade in Portadown as a victory, and the Garvaghy Road Residents' Group became more determined than ever that no parade would take place the following year (Jarman and Bryan 1996). The police also stopped most of the parades along the lower Ormeau Road in both 1995 and 1996, although in each year they have allowed the Orangemen to parade into the city centre to join the main parade on the morning of the Twelfth. On both occasions this has required massive policing: in 1995, local residents were blocked into their streets for much of the day; while in 1996 residents were effectively 'curfewed' for 24 hours from 6pm on the 11th until 6pm the following evening. In spite of continued protests at the re-routing of parades, it was the decision to ban the return leg of the Church parade from Drumcree which provoked the angriest response. During the four days that the police blocked the route in 1996, there were protest demonstrations by Orangemen, road blocks and major disturbances all over Northern Ireland. A Catholic taxi-driver from the nearby town of Lurgan was shot dead, allegedly by loyalist paramilitaries. Eventually, on 11 July, the police reversed their decision and the parade was allowed down the Garvaghy Road. The residents were physically and violently removed from the road by the police. In response to this volte face three days of extensive rioting broke out in Catholic areas across Northern Ireland. At a time when the 'peace process' was supposed to be reconciling the communities (although the IRA ceasefire had formally ended on 9 February 1996, an uncertain truce prevailed), the parade disputes seriously ruptured fragile community relations. At the same time, the vacillating decisions of the RUC and, in particular, the growing perception that they gave in to threats of loyalist violence, alienated many from both communities from the police.

Throughout these disputes, two positions characterised the debate. Members of the loyal orders demanded the right to march because of 'tradition', while residents who wanted to stop the parades demanded that they should be 'asked their consent' before Orangemen were allowed to march through their area. Irrespective of the moral justifications for each position, these were both clearly strategies of power. Orangemen, Blackmen, and Apprentice Boys were appealing to the past for legitimisation, a past in which their right to parade has been maintained because of their access to the state, and its control of legitimate force. The residents' groups were appealing for the right of local communities to exert greater control over their own areas. After all, they maintained, Catholics had long been prevented from holding parades in areas with a significant Protestant population. It is not difficult to grasp how the parading disputes have come to be seen as a localised version of the broader Northern Ireland problem.

Parade and protest

As already mentioned, our anthropological training influenced our research strategy in a number of ways. First, in the ethnographic methods used to collect information on the parades and disputes. Second, in the attempt to provide a clear understanding of the issues, particularly through an awareness of micro-political dynamics, through a discussion of the nature of the parading orders, and through the development of a typology of parades. Third, in the application to our data of anthropological understandings of ritual and 'tradition'.

There is an obvious tension between the need for practical, policy-oriented, research projects to be undertaken using ethnographic methods and the length of time required to carry out good quality ethnographic research. The need for qualitative material on parading has, in our view, existed for some time, but only after the events surrounding Drumcree in 1995 did it become possible to persuade potential sponsors of research of this. An application by the Centre for the Study of Conflict at the University of Ulster at Coleraine for funding for a long-term project concerning the public order implications of parading was turned down as recently as 1994. However, after the disturbances of 1995, which added at least £2 million to police expenditure, the Central Community Relations Unit, part of the Northern Ireland Office, agreed to fund a three-month study of attitudes to parading. Given the time constraints, and given that we already possessed significant background information, the major task of the research was to talk to key individuals in particular areas as well as to police and mediators. One of the major disadvantages of not spending a large amount of time in a specific area is that it is not easy to build relationships of trust. In the absence of such long-established trust, there is understandably some suspicion about exactly what role 'researchers' might play. We found this suspicion to be most obvious amongst loyalists, who feel their case has not been well represented by the media or by academics in the past. We tried to address this by making contacts at parades over a number of years and by being seen at a wide range of parades, not only those which were under dispute, though ultimately trust was only established in the process of researching and writing the report.

One of the difficulties that arises when analysing and writing about issues which are highly contested in Northern Ireland is that the researcher is easily assumed to favour one side more than the other. The terminology or phrasing used, such as naming Northern Ireland's second city as Derry (as Catholics tend to term it) or Londonderry (as Protestants tend to term it), will lead to the report being seen as biased and therefore dismissed without due consideration. On the other hand, there is a danger in writing something so anodyne that it disturbs no-one's preconceptions. We tried to address the matter of trust and bias together by being open about to whom we had spoken, and about to whom we would be speaking in the future. We also ensured that we interviewed as wide a range of people, from as many of the areas that were under dispute, as possible. We used a system of feedback during the research whereby everyone interviewed received draft copies of the report, and their comments were, as far as possible, incorporated into the final version. They were also sent a copy of the final report prior to publication. Whilst the feedback process was time-consuming, it was essential in building trust and maintaining relationships. It had a further advantage in that when the report was eventually published, those who were likely to be asked about its contents had a reasonable idea of what it contained. One of the strengths of ethnographic, qual-itative, research lies in the close relationship established between researcher and individuals in the communities of study, and it is important in short-term studies such as that reported here that methods are used to strengthen those relationships. The extensive process of fieldwork—visits to parades, small-talk with Orangemen, bandsmen and protesters, interviews and feed-back—was important in creating the level of trust that made people willing to meet us, and has remained important in allowing us to continue to participate in the debate.

The report itself (Jarman and Bryan 1996) contains three main parts. The first part examines the historical background to the disputes, some of which we referred to above, considers the organisational structure of the loyal orders, and offers a typology of the different types of parades. The second part analyses the events of the 1995 marching season, while the third part presents perceptions of parades, the reasons for the disputes and possible ways to resolve the problem.

There is a perception within the Catholic community that all 'Orange' parades are the same, and each one is just the same men wearing different regalia, making another triumphalist display. In contrast, within the loyal orders there is a clear distinction between an Orange parade, a Black parade, an Apprentice Boys parade and a loyalist band parade; and there is a clear distinction between a church parade and a commemorative parade such as the Twelfth. Any understanding or mediation that might take place between a residents' group and parade organisers needs to be aware of these perceptions. Consequently, we tried to indicate the dif-ference between each of the main loyal orders, as well as looking at the role the marching bands play in the culture of parading.

Whilst all the loyal institutions have a hierarchical structure, there is a strong sense of fraternal equality within them. The Orange Institution, which is the largest and politically most important of the loyal orders, is based on a series of 'private' Lodges,[4] each of which send representatives to District Lodges, which in turn send representatives to the County Lodge and the Grand Lodge. Whilst the Grand Lodge acts as rule-maker and guardian for the Institution, the other levels are relatively autonomous and undue interference is frowned upon. For instance, Portadown No.1 District, which organises the Drumcree Church parade, has a strong sense of its own identity. After all, the Orange Order was founded just a few miles away, in Loughgall, and Orangemen in that area of County Armagh see themselves as the hub of Orangeism. Portadown is sometimes described as 'the Orange Citadel' (Jones et al 1996), and others have jokingly referred to it as the 'Orange Vatican'. Members of Portadown District Lodge do not expect to be told what to do by the Grand Lodge in Belfast, although the Grand Lodge might be invited to offer their assistance. Decisions concerning particular parades are not made by the Grand Lodge, but are made at a local level and in response to micro-politics both within the lodge and within the local community.[5] Such tensions have always existed within the Orange Institution, but have probably become particularly acute since the demise of Stormont reduced the power of senior Unionists and Orangemen, and since the Unionist political block fragmented.

Although the Orange Institution, Black Institution and the Apprentice Boys have fraternal links, they maintain a fierce independence of each other. A man might be a member of each of the three loyal orders, and yet unwilling to speak on their behalf. He might be an officer and spokesperson of one order and be involved in negotiations over a dispute, and yet be unwilling to participate at the same time on behalf of another order. Furthermore, officers have only a limited authority over fellow lodge members; they can negotiate but not agree to deals without gaining the approval of lodge or district. Such practices make negotiations slow, and when they take place against a fast approaching deadline, as is usually the case, lead to suspicions of stalling or prevarication among nationalist groups.

The development of 'blood and thunder' marching bands is also indicative of the changing power structure within the Protestant community. There has always been some form of musical accompaniment on Orange parades; drums and fifes were recorded at the first parade in 1796. However, the style of the bands has varied, as has the style of music. As sectarian tensions increased, in the late 1960s and 1970s, the power of Unionists and Orangeism decreased, the relationship between the police and working class Protestants deteriorated, and a more radical loyalism began to be expressed through paramilitary groups. At the same time, a new style of band emerged, independent of the loyal orders. These bands adopted a more aggressive, militaristic performance, played overtly sectarian music and displayed loyalist paramilitary symbols (Bell 1990; Jarman 1997a). The bands took names such as 'Volunteers' and 'Defenders', projecting themselves as 'defenders' of the Protestant community not only in the symbolic sense but also by their actions, at least in the case of those bands with connections to the paramilitary groups. If it was perceived, by some working class Protestants, that the police were no longer prepared to protect their interests and, in particular, were not capable of dealing with republican violence, then the community would have to defend itself. The appearance of blood and thunder bands within the parading sub-culture is part of this shift of power. As a result, the atmosphere of many parades, particularly those in Belfast and other urban centres, has changed since the 1960s (Bryan 1997). Although the Orange Institution has attempted to control these changes, by intro ducing a band contract which bands must sign when being hired by a lodge a by designating which types of flags are allowed on an Orange parade, such attempts have been relatively ineffectual, partly because of the decentralised sense of authority and partly because the blood and thunder bands are popular with the rank and file and with many spectators.

Just as many within the nationalist community have viewed all parades held by the various loyal orders as 'Orange' parades, so there has been a tendency to regard all parades as similar, i.e. triumphalist expressions of Protestant domination over Catholics. Members of the loyal orders, however, point to the diverse purpose, role, function and form of different types of parade. Failure to acknowledge this variety, and the diverse meanings of differing parades, is interpreted as a calculated political assault on Protestant culture. Although typologies are far from fashionable in anthropology, in trying to gain an understanding of the complex relationship between politics and parades we found it useful to distinguish between different types of parade. From one perspective, this proved valuable in indicating how a similar form of practice or of ritual, in this case parading, could have a variety of purposes and meanings. From another perspective, it offered an indication as to why some parades were considered more important to Orangemen than others, and why some protests were resisted with more vigour than others. This complex of parades, stretching from Easter until October, constitutes the loyalist 'marching season'. We identified nine relatively discrete types of parade.

1. *Main Commemorative Parades*: these include the July Twelfth parades at nineteen venues around Northern Ireland, the Black parades on the last Saturday in August and the Apprentice Boys parade in Londonderry on the Saturday nearest 12 August, commemorating the Relief of Derry in 1689. These parades attract members and bands from outside Northern Ireland— around 20 bands come from Scotland for the Belfast Twelfth each year.

2. *Local Parades*: these include the Mini-Twelfths, organised by many Districts in the weeks before the Twelfth; the Somme commemoration parades, held on 1 July; the Apprentice Boys parade on Easter Monday, and the Black parades held in Belfast in mid-August.

3. *Feeder Parades*: these are local parades that take place before and after the main commemorative parades. In the past, the Orangemen met at their local Orange hall and paraded to the railway station, where they took the train to the main venue. Nowadays, many lodges still parade locally before travelling elsewhere, although most use a bus rather than a train.

4. *Church Parades*: these are held by all the loyal orders on Sundays through-
    out 'the marching season'. Some are simply held for individual lodges, whilst
    others are held by a group of lodges or a District on specific anniversaries.
    There is always an annual Boyne commemorative church parade on the
    Sunday before the Twelfth and many lodges commemorate the Battle of the
    Somme on the last Sunday in June.

5. *Arch, Banner and Hall Parades*: these are occasional events held to mark the
    unfurling of a new banner, the opening of a new hall or the annual opening of
    an Orange arch. They usually involve a religious service and a speech from a
    local politician.

6. *Social Parades*: these include an increasing range of parades by the Junior
    Orange Order and Women's Orange Institution.

7. *Occasional Parades*: these are held for occasions such as the Tercentenary of
    the Battle of the Boyne (1990), and the Bicentenary of the formation of the
    Orange Order (1995).

8. *Competitive Band Parades*: these are social events, organised to raise money
    for a band. Many bands hold an annual parade on a Friday or Saturday dur-
    ing the marching season and offer prizes over which visiting bands compete.
    These competitions have developed since the mid-1970s, and may account
    for some of the apparent increase in the number of parades since the mid-
    1980s.

9. *Commemorative Band Parades*: these are organised by bands or supporters of
    loyalist paramilitary groups to mark the anniversaries of the Somme and
    Armistice Day; and for the anniversary of the death of members of paramili-
    tary groups who have been killed during 'the Troubles'.

The different types of parade reflect different elements of unionism, and of
Protestant identity, as well as changing political circumstances. Some of the
church parades have been held annually since early in the last century but many
of the commemorative and social parades are relatively recent 'traditions'. The
Easter parades, organised by the Apprentice Boys and the Junior Orange
Institution, were started in the 1930s, in opposition to republican commemora-
tions of the Easter Rising. The mini-Twelfths and band parades are products of the
Troubles, used to reinforce local territories and group solidarity, as well as
expressing new political groups and new political relationships (Jarman 1993).

Within this extensive culture of parading, some parades carry more symbolic
power than others. The main commemorative parades are rarely challenged in
substance, although some features may be contested, as was the 'walk' by the

Apprentice Boys around the walls of Derry—which is part of the annual com-memoration of the 1689 Relief of Derry—in 1995 and 1996. Most of the disputes occur at the smaller, local parades, but even here protests meet a varying response. Demanding the re-routing of the mini-Twelfth held by Ballynafeigh District along the Ormeau Road is a vastly different matter from demanding the re-routing of the Drumcree Church parade. Ballynafeigh is a small District, whose mini-Twelfth parade is not seen as very important, and there has been widespread disapproval of the behaviour of Orangemen at the 1992 event, even from within the Institution. Orangemen from country areas are also suspicious of city parades which they believe have become over-dominated by blood and thunder bands, and therefore influenced by loyalist paramilitaries, and at which there is more drinking than they might deem respectable. As a result, it has always proved difficult to mobilise much outside support for protests on the Ormeau Road. Similarly, it has proved relatively easy to get many of the feeder parades re-routed. Although challenges to 'rights' or to 'tradition' may provoke local anger, this is usually containable locally.

More resistance is offered to attempts to re-route church parades. Given the religious basis of the loyal orders, many members regard their church parades as the most important declaration of their faith and identity. Within this category the Drumcree Church parade is an exceptional event. It is a church parade that can be dated back to the early nineteenth century, and is held close to where the Institution was founded. As such, it attracts broad support within Orangeism and provides a symbol that can unite the disparate classes of the Protestant commu-nity, as well as those in both urban and rural areas. The re-routing of the Drumcree Church parade can be easily depicted as an attack on Protestantism itself, in a way that the re-routing of a mini-Twelfth cannot. There were also significant pressures in Portadown, which involve divisions among the local loyalist paramilitaries, which made a militant response to the situation more likely than might have been the case in Belfast. While the police re-routed a number of parades during 1995 and 1996, only the Drumcree parade was likely to provoke such a violent reaction.

Applying anthropology

Our approach to parades is anthropological, not only in the methodology utilised, the concern with particular micro-political processes, and the analysis of cate-gories, but also in a concern with ritual and 'tradition'. Our report (Bryan and Jarman 1996) suggested no explicit theoretical model, nor was it overtly compar-ative; nevertheless, we were able to draw upon a corpus of anthropological work that has examined the politics of ritual actions (cf. Binns 1979; 1980; Bloch 1986; Kertzer 1988; Cohen 1993). A key element of these approaches is that rituals are seen as dynamic events, which, although often giving the appearance of a lack of change and, therefore, of continuity, can actually be appropriated by different social groups. Moreover, they are themselves sites of political conflict. Just as Cohen (1993) has shown how the Notting Hill Carnival's role in creating a West Indian identity in London must be understood in terms of competing interests within the event, so parades in Northern Ireland can be viewed as arenas in which competing Protestant interests attempt to legitimise their political position. For example, the Belfast Twelfth may be a 'tradition' that can be traced back to the 1870s, but it is certainly not static in the way it expresses social relationships. At the turn of the century, many factory owners and businessmen were members of the Orange Order, and used the institution as a paternalistic organisation, providing funds for lodges to which their workers belonged. With the collapse of local industry during the 1960s and the reduction in power of the Institution, many middle and upper class members left the Order, which more readily reflected its working class base. As sectarian violence became common place in Belfast, the parades started to reflect the disenchantment that many working class members felt over the inability of the Orange Institution, the Ulster Unionist Party and the forces of the State to deal with the republican threat. Parades which, since the founding of Northern Ireland, had sustained calls to support the state of Northern Ireland, now began to express opposition to the way Northern Ireland was being governed. Some elements, particularly among the bands, were visibly hostile to the police. They, not the police, had become the real 'defenders' of the Protestant community. In examining such changes, it becomes clear that the sense of continuity and 'tradition' which underscores the legitimacy of these events does not necessarily indicate that the social relationships they express have remained static (Tonkin and Bryan 1997).

By viewing the marching season as a complex, dynamic element in the social and political relationships of Northern Ireland, it becomes possible to make a closer analysis of some of the recent disputes and the contrasting attitudes towards them. In the final part of our report, we reflected upon the attitudes and perceptions that people in both communities have of the parades. It is possible to draw some useful conclusions from an analysis of these attitudes. There is no doubt that in some senses the disagreements over the right to parade are understood in the same way by both those in the residents' groups and those in the loyal orders. Both sides acknowledge that there is a dispute over territory, and that the disputes are thereby symbolic of the wider political dispute. But on other issues the actions of opponents are misinterpreted, wilfully or otherwise. For example, in perceiving all parades as Orange parades, and in seeing all parades and parade organisers as basically the same, nationalist groups clearly misunderstand the more complex political differences in the Protestant community. The disparate nature of the loyal orders means that their representatives often find it very difficult to give firm commitments over events, and they certainly cannot give commitments over events held under the auspices of another Institution. This unease about giving commitments over future parades on the part of members of the loyal orders appears, to those with whom they are negotiating, to be evasive, but it also reflects real divisions and the disparate nature of authority that exists within the loyal orders.

Nationalists view the parades as triumphalist, as an expression of continued oppression within the northern state. Unionists see the parades as religious, and as 'traditional' and as part of their identity. Any attempt to oppose the parades is thus easily construed as part of a campaign to undermine the Protestant community. The political debate has focused around these two positions. Of course, if one looks at the historical development of the parades and sees them within the present political climate, it is possible to see both perceptions as 'true'. After all, the number of 'traditional' Orange parades does reflect the position of power which unionists have enjoyed in Northern Ireland, while the ability of the nationalist community to oppose, sometimes successfully, some of these parades reflects changes in those power relationships which have developed within a political environment often dominated by violent armed struggle.

While it was important to reflect upon people's varying perceptions of the parades, we also wanted to explore how they thought the issue could be resolved. Throughout the disputes of 1995, a range of suggestions had been put forward as to how the issue of contested parades might be addressed. In the course of our interviews, we asked what people thought of these suggestions and what alternatives they might have. The ideas increased both in number and in complexity over the course of the research. They ranged from processes and practices already being utilised, short-term changes in practices that might be implemented voluntarily, and longer-term options that would involve legislative change and enforcement. The main ideas which we discuss at length in the report are as follows (see Jarman and Bryan 1996: 114–36):

1. The options for a compromise through local negotiations, and role of mediation within this.
2. The possibility of adopting voluntary guidelines or principles for parades.
3. The benefits of voluntary codes of behaviour, with improvements in stewarding and self-imposed restraints on 'traditional' practice.
4. The value of an independent commission to address the parading issue more generally.
5. The role of the police in the disputes and problems with the current public order legislation.
6. The use of a parading tribunal, with powers to arbitrate on disputes, and made up either of members of the judiciary or of local people.
7. A more extensive system of 'planning permission' which might impose a range of constraints and conditions on parades and protesters.

Many of these ideas had been mooted before, but this was the first time that they had been brought together and discussed in any detail. We made no recommendations as to what we considered the best way forward, but we did consider some of the advantages and disadvantages of the varying ideas and options, and it was these possible strategies for resolving the dispute that were the focus of the press release and publicity accompanying publication of the report.

While the content of the study was obviously crucial to the critical acceptance of the report, and to its likelihood of being branded too 'pro' or too 'anti' one position or another, the timing of publication was also an important element in its reception. The 1996 marching season had begun in a blaze of publicity when rioting followed the re-routing of an Apprentice Boys parade on the Ormeau Road on Easter Monday. People began to take note of the problem once again, after ignoring it through the winter. A series of protests and re-routings kept the issue on the front pages of the local press throughout April and May, and it only temporarily disappeared in June when there is a lull in marching before preparations begin for the Twelfth. The report was published during this lull, in mid-June. Although many of the ideas for dealing with the issue had already been raised by politicians and commentators in the preceding weeks, they had not been elaborated nor analysed in great detail, and there was no firm consensus as to how to proceed. Our hope was that the report would contribute both through its content and its timely appearance. We feel that we were successful on both counts: *Parade and Protest* was widely publicised and discussed on television, radio and in the local press. It has since been utilised by a range of civil servants, politicians, religious leaders and many of those with whom we had conducted the fieldwork. To publicise the facts and ideas, we held public seminars, met with community groups, political parties, wrote articles for local newspapers and spoke to numerous journalists in the weeks and months that followed.

The immediate impact of the report was to add academic weight to the widespread calls being made for a serious review of the parading issue, and the need for some form of independent body to carry out this work. Such calls were reiterated throughout the early summer. In the aftermath of Drumcree, in mid-July, Sir Patrick Mayhew announced that he would set up an independent review into the problems over parades and demonstrations and the disturbances of 1996. While we hope that any recommendations eventually made by the review will begin to alleviate the problem of contested parades, there is still much work to be done.

Conclusion

Driven first by the interests and requirements of academia, our research initially addressed problems of the role of ritual in contemporary industrial societies and the use of material culture in political ideology. In its current phase, our research displays a greater concern with the pragmatic needs of social policy: how to avoid, control or reduce public order problems, and how to balance competing claims to civil rights. But in practice the gap between the two is not so great as it might seem. Anthropological theory and method continues to provide the bedrock of our working practice. Much of the public interest in our report was in the more pro-saic background information: on the loyal orders, on parade numbers and on the possible resolutions, rather than on the more anthropologically-informed analysis of perceptions and meanings. However, it was never possible to separate the two strands: the empirical data were as much a product of the painstaking fieldwork as an understanding of the competing perceptions of why someone acts in the way they do.

Academic anthropologists and those implementing public policy may appear to work to differing, and sometimes conflicting, rhythms. Anthropologists empha-sise the value of a long research programme, detailed data collection and a focus on subjective perceptions and meanings, while policy-makers often appear to want ready and generalizable solutions to difficult problems, and seem less will-ing to fund more abstract research proposals. But the gap can be bridged. Anthro-pologists can be responsive to changing socio-political circumstances, and can adapt their material to a variety of requirements beyond the confines of the acad-emy. Policy-makers can, and do, recognise the value of long-term research, of practical fieldwork methods which superficially might appear to involve little more than standing around and watching other people. But anthropologists also need to be able to persuade others of the value of their knowledge and experience: to maximise the impact of their research through the way it is publicised and to talk to as wide a range of interested parties as possible. Nevertheless, they also need some luck: to some extent we were in the right place at the right time, and we have been able to utilise and apply our material in unforeseen ways. Although the impetus for our research appears to have moved away from academia, we con-tinue to argue the case for anthropological methods and practice for future pro-jects.

Notes

1. By 'Protestant' and 'Catholic' communities we are referring to ethnic categories rather than to particular religious affiliations. There are individuals in both communities who identify themselves, and are identified by others, as coming from those communities but who hold no particular religious belief. We use the terms 'unionist' and 'loyalist' to denote belief in, and loyalty to, the United Kingdom and the Crown. Where these terms are capitalised—Unionism and Loyalism—they denote specific support for the Ulster Unionist Party and support for Loyalist paramilitary groups respectively.
2. These figures are taken from the *Chief Constable's Annual Report*. The category of 'Republican' was changed to 'Nationalist' in 1994; and the category of 'Other', which according to the RUC Central Statistics Unit contains events such as a Lord Mayor's Show, a Royal British Legion Remembrance Day parade, some St. Patrick's Day parades and parades by youth organisations, was introduced in 1995. Since some of the 'Other' events might well be perceived by some people as 'Loyalist' or 'Nationalist', this new category is somewhat problematic. See Jarman and Bryan (1996: 36) for a table of the figures from 1985–94.

3. Jarman has been studying nationalist and loyalist parades since 1990, with particular reference to material culture and social memory (Jarman 1992; 1993; 1997a; 1997b; in press). Bryan has been studying Orange parades in terms of anthropological theories of ritual since 1991 (Bryan 1994; 1995; 1997; in press; Bryan, Fraser and Dunn 1995; Tonkin and Bryan 1997). Both have utilised ethnographic and historical methodologies.
4. There are about 1400 private lodges in Ireland, each one in existence on the basis of having a 'warrant' which is issued and owned by the Grand Lodge of Ireland. Every Orangeman is in a private lodge.
5. It is interesting that just as some Protestants believe that the actions of Catholics are dictated by the Vatican in Rome, some Catholics view the Orange Institution in a similar conspiratorial way.

References

Anderson, B. 1983. *Imagined Communities: Reflections on the Origin and Spread of Nationalism.* London: Verso.

Bell, D. 1990. *Acts of Union: Youth Culture and Sectarianism in Northern Ireland.* London: Macmillan.

Bew, P., P. Gibbon and H. Patterson 1995. *Northern Ireland 1921–1994: Political Forces and Social Classes.* London: Serif.

____. and G. Gillespie 1996. *The Northern Ireland Peace Process 1993–1996: A Chronology.* London: Serif.

Binns, C. 1979. The Changing Face of Power: Revolution and Accommodation in the Soviet Ceremonial System, Part 1. *Man* 14: 585–606.

____. 1980. The Changing Face of Power: Revolution and Accommodation in the Soviet Ceremonial System, Part 2. *Man* 15: 170-87.

Bloch, M. 1986. *From Blessing To Violence: History and Ideology in the Circumcision Ritual of the Merina of Madagascar.* Cambridge: Cambridge University Press.

Boissevain, J. (ed.) 1992. *Revitalising European Rituals.* London: Routledge.

Bryan, D. 1994. Interpreting the Twelfth. *History Ireland* 2 (2): 37–41.

____. 1995. Orangutango. *Fortnight* 341: 14–15.

____. 1997. Ritual Tradition and Control: The Politics of Orange Parades in Northern Ireland. University of Ulster at Coleraine, unpublished PhD thesis.

____. in press. Ireland's Very Own Jurassic Park: The Mass Media and the Discourse of 'Tradition' on Orange Parades. In A. D. Buckley (ed.), *Symbols in Northern Ireland.* Belfast: Institute of Irish Studies.

____., T.G. Fraser and S. Dunn 1995. *Political Rituals: Loyalist Parades in Portadown.* Coleraine: Centre for the Study of Conflict.

Bryson, L. and C. McCartney 1994. *Clashing Symbols: A Report on the Use of Flags, Anthems and Other National Symbols in Northern Ireland.* Belfast: Institute for Irish Studies.

Buckley, A. D. and M. Kenney 1995. *Negotiating Identity: Rhetoric, Metaphor and Social Drama in Northern Ireland.* Washington: Smithsonian Institution.

Caplan, P. (ed.) 1995. *Understanding Disputes: The Politics of Argument.* Oxford: Berg.

Cecil, R. 1993. The Marching Season in Northern Ireland: An Expression of Politico-Religious Identity. In S. MacDonald (ed.), *Inside European Identities.* Oxford: Berg.

Cohen, A. 1993. *Masquerade Politics: Explorations in the Structure of Urban Popular Movements.* Oxford: Berg.

Cohen, A. P. 1985. *The Symbolic Construction of Community.* London: Tavistock.

Farrell, M. 1976. *Northern Ireland: The Orange State.* London: Pluto Press.

Gibbon, P. 1975. *The Origins of Ulster Unionism.* Manchester: Manchester University Press.

Harbinson, J. F. 1973. *The Ulster Unionist Party, 1882–1973: Its Development and Organisation.* Belfast: Blackstaff Press.

Harris, R. 1972. *Prejudice and Tolerance in Ulster: A Study of Neighbours and Strangers in a Border Community.* Manchester: Manchester University Press.

Hill, J. 1984. National Festivals, The State and 'Protestant Ascendancy' in Ireland 1790-1829. *Irish Historical Studies* XXIV (93): 30-51.

Jarman, N. 1992. Troubled Images: The Iconography of Loyalism. *Critique of Anthropology* 12 (2):133–65.

_____. 1993. Intersecting Belfast. In B. Bender (ed.), *Landscape, Politics and Perspectives.* Oxford: Berg.

_____. 1997a. *Material Conflicts: Parades and Visual Displays in Northern Ireland.* Oxford: Berg.

_____. 1997b. Material of Conflict, Fabric of Identity. In D. Miller (ed.), *Why Some Things Matter.* London: UCL Press.

_____. in press. Commemorating 1916, Remembering Difference: Parades and Painting in Belfast. In A. Forty and S. Kuechler (eds.), *Monuments and Memory: On Material Culture and Remembering.* Oxford: Berg.

_____. and D. Bryan 1996. *Parade and Protest: A Discussion of Parading Disputes in Northern Ireland.* Coleraine: Centre for the Study of Conflict.

Jones, D., J.S. Kane, R. Wallace, D. Sloan and B. Courtney 1996. *The Orange Citadel: A History of Orangeism in Portadown.* Armagh: Portadown Cultural Heritage Committee.

Kertzer, D. 1988. *Ritual, Politics, and Power.* London: Yale University Press.

Larsen, S. S. 1982. The Glorious Twelfth: A Ritual Expression of a Collective Identity. In A. P. Cohen (ed.), *Belonging: Identity and Social Organisation in British Rural Cultures.* Manchester: Manchester University Press.

McCann, E. 1974. *War and an Irish Town.* London: Penguin.

McFarlane, G. 1989. Dimensions of Protestantism: The Working of Protestant Identity in a Northern Irish Village. In C. Curtin and T. M. Wilson (eds.), *Ireland From Below: Social Change and Local Communities.* Galway: Galway University Press.

Patterson, H. 1980. *Class Conflict and Sectarianism.* Belfast: Blackstaff Press.

Purdie, B. 1990. *Politics in the Street: The Origins of the Civil Rights Movement in Northern Ireland.* Belfast: The Blackstaff Press.

Tonkin, E. and D. Bryan 1997. Political Ritual: Temporality and Tradition. In A. Boholm (ed.), *Political Ritual.* Gothenburg: Institute for Advanced Studies in Social Anthropology.

Wright, F. 1987. *Northern Ireland: A Comparative Analysis.* Dublin: Gill and Macmillan.

_____. 1996. *Two Lands One Soil: Ulster Politics before Home Rule.* Dublin: Gill and Macmillan.

Author Index

Subject Index